**SELF-TALK FOR
TEACHERS AND**

SELF-TALK FOR TEACHERS AND STUDENTS

Metacognitive Strategies for Personal and Classroom Use

Brenda H. Manning
Beverly D. Payne
The University of Georgia

Allyn and Bacon
Boston   London   Toronto   Sydney   Tokyo   Singapore

Copyright © 1996 by Allyn & Bacon
A Simon & Schuster Company
Needham Heights, Massachusetts 02194

Library of Congress Cataloging-in-Publication Data
Manning, Brenda H.
    Self-talk for teachers and students : metacognitive strategies for
personal and classroom use / Brenda H. Manning, Beverly D. Payne.
        p.   cm.
    Includes bibliographical references and index.
    ISBN 0-205-15948-6
    1. Teachers—Psychology.   2. Metacognition.   3. Self-talk.
I. Payne, Beverly D.   II. Title.
LB2840.M33   1995
371.1′001′9—dc20   95-32106
                                                           CIP

Printed in the United States of America
10 9 8 7 6 5 4 3 2 1   00 99 98 97 96

Dedicated with Supreme Love to Our
"Prematurely Gray" Husbands:

Walter Stewart Manning
and
David Allen Payne

Contents

Preface   xi

Acknowledgments   xv

Introduction   xvii

PART I: TEACHERS' PERSONAL USE OF METACOGNITION

Chapter 1   Reviewing Theories and Psychologies Related to Metacognition   1

Overview   1

Rational-Emotive Therapy   3

Transactional Analysis   6

Attribution Theory   12

Teacher Efficacy   13

Self-Regulated Learning   16

Self-Talk Levels   18

Self-Talk Components   19

Summary   22

Chapter 2   Fostering Positive Mental Growth of Teachers   23

Overview   23

Connecting Teachers' Personal Growth to Metacognition   23
Self-Awareness   25
Self-Acceptance   27
Self-Responsibility   40

Summary   44

Chapter 3 Eliminating Negative Thinking of Teachers 46

Overview 46

Teacher Stress 47

Teacher Anger 55

Teacher Anxiety 56

Teacher Frustration and Boredom 58

Summary 71

PART II: TEACHERS' PROFESSIONAL USE OF METACOGNITION

Chapter 4 Understanding Self-Regulated Learning and Teaching 72

Overview 72

Theory of Verbal Self-Regulation 72

Zone of Proximal Development 79

Concept of Mediation 80

Other-Regulation Models 80

Theories of Self-Regulated Learning 81

Vygotskian View of Self-Regulated Learning 82

Self-Regulated Teaching 84

Summary 85

Chapter 5 Applying the Cognitive Self-Direction Model to Teaching 86

Overview 86

Metacognitive Skills for Professional Development 86

Cognitive Self-Direction for Teaching: A Curriculum and Methodological Model 87

Results of the Implementation 92

Metacognitive Skills for Teacher Planning 93

Metacognitive Skills During Interactive Instruction 96

Metacognitive Skills During Classroom Management 99

Summary 102

Chapter 6   Using Other-Regulation Models for Teaching and Learning   103

Overview   103

Proleptic/Dyadic Instruction   105

Reciprocal Teaching   109

Cognitive Behavior Modification   112

Cognitive Self-Instruction   115

Modeling   116

Practicing   120

Cueing   127

Summary   132

PART III: METACOGNITIVE STRATEGIES FOR STUDENT LEARNING

Chapter 7   Researching Metacognitive Strategies for Classroom Use   133

Overview   133
Metacognitive Research on Self-Control   134
Metacognitive Research for Academic Uses   136

Student Use of Metacognitive Strategies   139

Summary   152

Chapter 8   Applying Metacognitive Strategies for Students' Learning   153

Overview   153

School Work Habits   154

Content Area Teaching   170

Summary   185

Chapter 9   Applying Metacognitive Strategies for Students' Personal Growth   186

Overview   186

Problem Solving, Decision Making, and Goal Setting   187

Learning to Use Healthy Self-Talk   194

Addressing Social Issues   199

Summary   210

Conclusions   211

References   213

Author Index   223

Subject Index   227

Preface

Based on our knowledge and past experiences as teacher educators, we believe that the best way for teachers to grow professionally is to assume responsibility for their own learning and teaching. A key to teachers taking charge of their own thinking is to become more metacognitive. The goal of this book is to link metacognition, which is a core component of teaching and learning, to the lives of teachers and students. This is the first book that puts together in one singular form the importance of metacognition for teachers. Included are specific and authentic examples of how teachers can use metacognition for themselves in a powerfully personal and professional way, with a transfer from the teacher to his or her students using concrete examples of actual and successful accounts from classroom teachers. These authentic activities and classroom ideas provide a concrete but not over-simplified version of teachers' mental constructions of metacognition for personal, professional, and classroom use. The teachers' overwhelming endorsements of metacognition have convinced us that this philosophy is worth the effort. Because of this endorsement, we believe this book can drastically improve the quality of teachers' lives.

Although there is no approach that yields 100 percent success, we have conducted over 10 years of evaluation of the metacognitive strategies that we write about in this book. We are confident that these strategies have changed lives for the better, for both teachers and students. In this book, we tell how. The evaluations have taken multiple forms, such as formal, controlled quantitative research studies (e.g., Manning & Payne, 1988, 1990, 1993, in press; Payne & Manning, 1988, 1990), case studies (e.g., Manning, 1988, 1990; Manning & Payne, in press), less formalized surveys of students, interviews with students, student teacher journals, self-talk logs, unsolicited letters, and notes, to name a few.

Over and over, year after year, students tell us that these strategies changed their lives. We felt very affirmed when one of the reviewers of this book decided to "trial teach" this book. This reviewer was not chosen by us, but by one of the editors at Allyn and Bacon. We did not know him, nor did he know us. Because he was so positive about this book, he released his name and affiliation to us. He teaches at a large and very prestigious teacher preparation college in northeastern United States. In short, he used this book with a class of teachers who were about midway in a master's degree program in curriculum and teaching. In his review of our book, he included the teachers' overall impressions and comments, as well as his own. We were very fortunate to have classroom teachers review our work. This does not happen often enough. Receiving strikingly similar comments to the ones we had been receiving for a decade from our own students was exciting and encouraging. A few unedited comments from the reviewer's students follow. These serve as much more objective assessments than our own students' comments would.

TEACHER A: *I had been reading for about an hour and my husband came over to see what I was reading because I usually can't keep with this kind of stuff longer than twenty minutes at a time. Here I was reading and rereading. I really began to see how people were thinking about how a person can learn to manage their own thinking.*

TEACHER B: *I sat down in the teachers' lounge and the conversation was going on about as usual when all of a sudden I realized the conversation was full of "stoppers." I hadn't realized before how negative we really were.*

Reviewer's General Comment

"The teachers are telling me that it is rare that they have coursework that has been so immediately change-producing."

The reviewer said he successfully used this book to help his teachers take charge of their own learning and teaching. *Self-Talk for Teachers and Students* provides creative and concrete ways to promote teacher empowerment and teacher reflection. It fills a gap in the literature because information about metacognitive strategies for promoting teacher empowerment, affective traits, mental coping skills, and reflection has been very limited.

As a result of reading this book, previous students have become more metacognitive, more reflective, more autonomous, and more proactive. These are important skills for teachers in a world where school reform is in desperate need of teachers to serve as change agents. Not only have these changes affected teachers themselves, both personally (Part I of the book) and professionally (Part II of the book), but there have also been benefits realized by the students of these teachers (Part III of the book). For example, one of our teachers told her story in this way:

TEACHER C: *I was 100 pounds overweight and in my seventeenth year of teaching first grade. Year after year I thought the administration was picking on me by giving me all the "bad kids." And I complained and grumbled to anyone who would listen for most of the year. After I took your class and learned how to verbally support and encourage myself, I lost 75 pounds and for some reason was assigned wonderful children that year and every year thereafter. I used to think it was the children's fault; now I know the poor atmosphere in my class was my own fault. I did not like myself and I didn't like my students either. Accepting students begins with teacher self-acceptance. I learned that from your class. When I assumed responsibility for myself, began to treat myself with respect, and supported myself verbally, my teaching and teacher-student and teacher-parent relationships improved. I thank you—but most of all, my students and their parents thank you.*

This book was written to showcase the teacher and student self-talk that serves as the vehicle for metacognition. It is through attention and monitoring of reflective self-talk that teachers and students become more metacognitive. As a result of becoming more metacognitive, personal and professional growth become highly probable.

There are many excellent books dealing with metacognition, but we do not know of one written specifically for teachers, beginning with the teacher as a person and emphasizing the affective as well as the cognitive aspects of metacognition. Each of the authors has fifteen years of experience in teaching and supervising prospective teachers, teaching future and current classroom teachers, and conducting hundreds of workshops for teachers. In addition, we have researched metacognition for teaching and learning with both young students and adult teachers for the past decade. We have learned a great deal from our students who were either past, present, or future teachers. Many have taught us that they have stressful jobs, with few resources directed at strategies to reduce teacher stress, anxiety, frustration, and anger. They have told us consistently that the most important topics, which they still remember years later, are the discussions about self-awareness, self-acceptance, and self-responsibility. For this reason, Part I of this book focuses on metacognition for the personal development of teachers. Part II deals with teachers' professional use of metacognition, such as teacher planning, interactive instruction, and classroom management (including teacher expectations) with a metacognitive focus. This information comes from our work with classroom teachers in their professional roles. Part III describes metacognition for classroom use, both teaching and learning strategies. In classrooms today, teachers and students both teach and learn together, sharing and serving reciprocally in these roles. Lampert (1984), in her research on teacher thinking, implied that researchers need to be more sensitive to the "real world" of teachers. Our students (teachers) have motivated us to write this book and to write it with teachers' needs in mind, using teachers' "real world" experiences as the foundation.

Included in this book are many examples, activities, cases, and suggestions for classroom practice. Examples and exercises in the book are set off in boxes. Each one of these is derived from our work with teachers. These are not made-up, imaginary suggestions; they were either experienced by teachers and shared orally or in writing with us, or developed by teachers for actual use in a classroom. The self-talk examples were selected from teacher research data whereby teachers recorded what they said to themselves during various teaching episodes. In addition, each chapter is organized so that learned metacognitive processes can be used to master the material. For example, self-questioning is a metacognitive strategy that aids comprehension; therefore, each chapter begins with a set of self-questions.

The classroom application of metacognitive processes is sequenced logically from teachers' personal and professional use, teacher modeling for the students, and examples of specific teaching strategies that have proven successful for academic learning and behavioral self-management of students. Our guiding philosophy is that teachers teach what they themselves know and have experienced (Goodlad, 1990). Therefore, one of the major goals of this book is to encourage the authentic use of metacognitive strategies and processes, both from a personal and a professional perspective. We have found that only when teachers have experienced the use of metacognitive strategies in their own personal lives and professional work are they likely to apply similar metacognitive strategies with their students. An overwhelming number of students we have taught are now better teachers because of the personal, professional, and classroom use of metacognition.

Acknowledgments

When we think of acknowledging support for writing this book, our first thoughts are of our husbands, Stewart Manning and David Payne. We are among the fortunate few who have wonderful marriages with beautiful, sensitive men of unfailing patience and good humor.

For everything that we have accomplished in our lives, we honor our parents: the late James Thomas Holcomb and Lucille Banister Holcomb, parents of Brenda Manning, and James Creighton Dean and LaWayne Chaplin Dean, parents of Beverly Payne. Our parents provided a stable, loving foundation for our lives and our work.

Next, we would like to thank our siblings for loving us, even though we often "mothered" them too much. We are both first-borns. Judy Alford and Kim Turner are Brenda's sisters. Pam Lynn is Beverly's only sister, and Jim, Jeffrey, and Jonathan are her brothers.

And our children—we have wonderful adult children. Brenda has two daughters, Jill and Ginger Floyd, and two stepchildren, Stephanie and Doug Manning. Beverly has three stepchildren, Mike, Jeffrey, and Karen Payne. Chelsea and Cheddar, Beverly's cocker spaniels, are like little children—somewhat unruly, but mostly playful, loving, and totally devoted. We have enjoyed our children and watched them develop into fine adults. Karen Payne is a doctoral student, studying geography at the Australian National University. Jeffrey Payne is a law enforcement officer in the town where we reside. Mike Payne is a doctoral student at the University of California at Davis studying veterinary pharmacology. Doug Manning is a junior at Georgia Tech in Atlanta, studying business management. Stephanie Manning is a production coordinator at a prepress company in Atlanta, Georgia. Ginger Floyd is a freshman at the University of Georgia, studying exercise science, and Jill Floyd is a public school kindergarten teacher at one of the local schools, Fowler Drive Elementary. These children have taught us much more than we have taught them.

We work alongside some great folks at the University of Georgia. We will not begin to single them out because we run the likely danger of omitting someone special. We do want to express appreciation to our friend and department chair, Dr. Denise Glynn. Thanks also to Beverly's sister, Pam Lynn, for providing us with photographs of children and their teachers from her school, Sandy Lane Elementary in Clearwater, Florida. We also extend our gratitude to Virginia Calder, art coordinator for the Center of Educational Technology at the University of Georgia, for many of the illustrations in the book.

Although the content of this book is ultimately our responsibility, many preservice and inservice students, graduate assistants, and classroom teachers have applied many of our ideas in a variety of challenging educational settings. Their work has inspired our own. We have been stimulated by their applications, refinements, and extensions of what they learned from us. Excerpts from some of their work are included in the book. Of course, the final draft would not have been possible without the outstanding efforts of the editorial and production staff at Allyn and Bacon and Lynda Griffiths of TKM Productions. We appreciate their support and expertise in making our vision a reality.

Without the help of our right hand, we would never have produced the manuscript for this book. We are referring to our own Stephanie Bales. She is outstanding, and we thank her for helping us with the technical side of presenting a professional document. Thanks to her with all our sincerity, respect, and appreciation.

We close by extending appreciation to each other. We have been friends for over a decade, realizing that it is rare for co-workers, in the same arena, to remain true friends. Too often, competition eventually erodes such relationships. Fortunately, we have placed friendship above the politics of the workplace. Without the contributions of collaboration, this book would have been less in explicit and subtle ways.

Introduction

Teachers are required to make diagnoses; develop and revise plans; implement lessons; provide meaningful experiences; nurture; communicate with learners, parents, and other teachers; involve all learners; and more. On average, teachers have 1,000 face-to-face interactions per day (Jackson, 1968), make critical decisions approximately every 2 minutes (Clark & Peterson, 1986), and lose 55 percent of their instructional time to disruption (Gottfredson, 1990, personal communication). Such statistics illustrate the complexity inherent in teaching. They also make essential the mental alertness, awareness, monitoring, and evaluation necessary to effective teaching and learning in the classroom. Such mental processes are what we mean by *metacognition*. The central aim of this book is to provide ways teachers can become more metacognitive, both personally and professionally.

In the Preface, we briefly mentioned the three parts of this book: Part I, Teachers' Personal Use of Metacognition; Part II, Teachers' Professional Use of Metacognition; and Part III, Metacognitive Strategies for Student Learning. We presented teachers' accounts and perspectives related to the many benefits of becoming more metacognitive. We addressed the question, Will this metacognition stuff make me a better teacher? Not only can metacognitive knowledge and experience improve teaching, but such knowledge and experiences can also improve the quality of teachers' lives in and out of the classroom. This teacher growth and development provide the fuel motivating the use of metacognitive strategies for these teachers' students. Teachers teach what they know and what they have experienced, first on a deep personal level, then on a professional level. These two levels lead naturally to classroom use of metacognition.

Because the word *metacognition* has come to have multiple meanings and multiple interpretations, we tried to substitute in this book an alternate word. Teachers are often turned off by the terminology until they experience benefits from using the "metacognitive" strategies. Then, they quickly generate their own revised definition of metacognition, followed by an affinity for anything metacognitive. But, because of this initial confusion, in a general sense, the word *metacognition* has become meaningless. Therefore, we must define specifically our meaning of metacognition for this book.

There are four guiding premises we have developed:

Premise One: Metacognitive strategies and processes must first be acknowledged and experienced in the personal and professional lives of teachers before they are inclined to use metacognitive strategies as a natural part of their own teaching.

Premise Two: Metacognition is a slippery and open-ended concept.

Premise Three: The definition(s) of metacognition for the teaching profession may necessarily deviate somewhat from the original definitions (mostly springing from laboratory research).

Premise Four: Metacognitive knowledge and regulation are core components of both teaching and learning.

Premise One: Teachers' Personal and Professional Knowledge and Use of Metacognition Are Prerequisites to Classroom Teaching and Learning of a Metacognitive Nature

Since "the processes that have recently earned the title metacognitive are central to learning and development" (Brown, 1987, p. 65), metacognition for teachers and students is critical. Becoming more metacognitive is not an optional skill for teachers and learners; it is a necessary skill. The growing ability to monitor and direct our own thinking—to keep track of how well we are comprehending and to select an effective strategy for solving a problem—is known as metacognition. It is difficult to consider being able to teach effectively without metacognitive skills. Not only do teachers need to be well versed in the knowledge, skills, and strategies we will call "metacognitive" but they must also connect with their own personal and professional metacognitive awareness and regulation. It is our basic contention that the high quality of teachers' metacognitive awareness and regulation is the foundation that determines the quality of instruction in classrooms. We believe that teachers who become familiar with the principles of metacognition, formulate their own philosophy using their personal metacognitive history, and develop their own professional goals related to metacognition will be the only teachers in a position to truly and realistically foster metacognition in the mental lives of school children.

Premise Two: Metacognition Is a Slippery and Open-Ended Concept

Metacognition has been called a fuzzy concept (Wellman, 1981, pp. 3–4), a mysterious apparatus (Marshall & Morton, 1978, p. 227), and a many-headed monster (Brown, 1987, p. 105).

Over the span of approximately three decades, the term *metacognition* has accumulated many definitions and interpretations. The term originally grew out of the research on metamemory conducted by Flavell and his colleagues (e.g., 1966, 1970). Due to the expansive and varied definitions of metacognition, it is possible for two metacognitive "experts" to engage in a conversation about metacognition and walk away believing that the other "expert" knows very little about metacognition. We do not claim to know all the faces of metacognition either. Definitionally, examples of metacognition range from identifying a main idea in a story (Baker & Brown, 1981) to error detection (Brown & DeLoache, 1978). To some, who speak from Flavell's original definition of metacognition—"knowledge and cognitions about cognitive, affective, perceptual, and motor human characteristics" (1987, p. 21)—metacognition means knowledge about thinking and mental experiences (usually ongoing ones) about thinking. It is thinking about one's own thinking, regardless of whether the subject matter of these cognitions is mainly cognitive, affective, perceptual, or motoric.

In this metacognitive camp, we hear people discussing knowledge of person, task, and strategy variables. Metacognitive *person* knowledge refers to knowledge about oneself as a thinker, comparisons between and among individuals related to cognitive variables, and universally held assumptions about cognitive matters. The metacognitive *task* variables encompass knowledge about the characteristics, demands, constraints, and parameters of a task. It is realizing whether a task is easy, average, or difficult. It is knowing the specificity of a particular academic or social task. The metacognitive *strategy* variables relate to a person's knowledge of how to proceed to focus, follow through, and finish a task (Manning, 1990).

Metacognitive strategy variables are sometimes referred to as *strategic knowledge.* The person, task, and strategy variables comprise and flesh out Flavell's definition of metacognition. Although these variables are discussed separately, in reality they are difficult to separate due to their interrelatedness. For example, it is very difficult to know strategies for beginning a geometry task (strategy variable) without simultaneously also interacting with your knowledge about how well you usually perform geometry tasks (person variable) and how difficult constructing a proof (task variable) is for you (person variable). The following table depicts Flavell's (1987) representation of this metacognitive domain.

Flavell's Representation Metacognitive Knowledge

Variables	Definition and Examples
Person	
Intraindividual	*Knowing yourself as a thinker* *Example:* Knowing you do better on objective test items versus essay test items
Interindividual	*Comparing cognitive enterprises between individuals* *Example:* Knowing your mother is better at mathematics than your father
Universal	*Knowing a commonly held belief about cognition* *Example:* Knowing the meaning of making a mistake on an academic task
Task	*Knowing the characteristics, constraints, parameters, and demands of a particular social and/or academic task* *Example:* Knowing that the science text is dense with new vocabulary words
Strategy	*Knowing how to proceed to perform a specific task* *Example:* Knowing that verbal rehearsal may aid retention of the science terms in the text

This "knowledge about cognition" phenomenon represents one distinct area of research (Brown, Bransford, Ferrara, & Campione, 1983). Flavell divides knowledge about cognition into metacognitive knowledge and metacognitive experiences, whereby this knowledge is activated. In the preceding discussion, we detailed what Flavell described as knowledge about cognition. These ongoing experiences, such as realizing when your comprehension is lacking or realizing that you do not remember something, serve to enlist metacognitive knowledge.

Certain conditions evoke metacognitive processes, such as performing a task that falls optimally somewhere between too familiar and too unfamiliar. If the task is too familiar, we may be operating at the automaticity level, which affords our minds to think about other things since we know this task inside and out. Therefore, metacognitive monitoring is not necessary to function well on this particular task. If the task is too unfamiliar, we may be so overwhelmed by the task that we cannot think about or monitor our own thinking because we are too busy thinking, or our hopeless attitude toward the task may shut down our thinking about this particular task, as we dwell more emotionally on our inability to perform the task. We are at a primary level of thought (cognition), which, in this case, precludes the secondary level of thought (thinking about cognition).

Other conditions that seem to stimulate metacognitive thinking are (1) very important tasks, such as taking our first drivers' test to get a driver's license, (2) challenging situations that put us in disequilibrium, such as lost keys, following a difficult recipe, mending a damaged relationship, or finding a new location; and (3) situations when physical or emotional pain do not overwhelm our thinking. It is more difficult for most of us to monitor our own thinking while in excruciating pain (e.g., kidney stone, migraine headache) or emotional dishevelment (e.g., unwanted divorce). To summarize, appropriate, important, and challenging tasks in school are important not only for all the usual educational reasons but also because they set the stage for metacognitive awareness.

In some researchers' minds, the metacognitive domain encompasses only this *"knowledge about cognition"* area. If metacognition is defined by this area exclusively, then such knowledge "refers to the stable, statable, often fallible, and often late-developing information that human thinkers have about their own cognitive processes" (Brown, 1987, pp. 67–68). In some cases, there is little or no acknowledgment of the importance of the second group of activities, referred to as metacognitive in the developmental literature. This second area is *regulation of cognition*. The two forms of metacognition (i.e., knowledge and regulation of cognition) are closely connected, and separating them is not really possible. However, they have been focused on separately in the literature; they are identifiable as two separate entities, and they do have different historical foundations. This fact causes confusion and sometimes a lack of progress in the field. Brown (1987) originally identified this source of confusion; however, it is repeated here for several reasons. First, it is a critical distinction to make in order to understand the epistemological and historical foundation of a particular researcher's work. Second, some individuals have obviously missed this earlier discussion, because we still confront this unidimensional view of metacognition in the literature and in our professional lives.

In the late 1970s, the term *metacognition* was enlarged to include regulatory functions, such as error detection (Brown & DeLoache, 1978) and problem defining, and self-guiding, self-coping, self-checking, and self-reinforcing while engaged in task performance (Meichenbaum, 1977). It is important to note that although knowing about cognition is stable and statable, regulating cognition may be relatively unstable and not necessarily statable. Indeed, self-regulation may occur below the level of awareness. In addition, regulation of thinking may be more dependent on the task and the situation rather than the age of the learner, as contrasted with knowledge of cognition. Self-regulatory cognition is critical to schooling. Teachers and students must be able to focus attention, define problems, detect errors, persist at tasks, monitor concentration, and bring tasks to completion.

In the literature, differentiations have also been made between the cognitive domain (cold cognition) and the affective domain (hot cognition). Brown (1987) emphasizes the importance of both and points out that the importance of hot cognition (e.g., mental attitudes about mathematics class) may have much more to do with school performance than we ever imagined. In this book, we focus more on hot cognition in Part I and Part III and focus more on cold cognition in Part II. However, our goal is to assist teachers in their understanding and application of metacognition; therefore, our primary responsibility is to their reality and the reality of classroom teaching and learning. When we consider the reality and complexity of the classroom, many of these arbitrary distinctions (e.g., hot from cold cognition, knowledge from regulation) seem to blur beyond recognition.

Premise Three: Traditional Definitions of Metacognition Must Be Modified to Fit the Complexities Inherent in the Teaching Profession

We believe that both knowledge and regulation of cognition are important; that both cold and hot cognition are important; and that laboratory research applied directly without adaptation to classroom settings is suspect. We certainly do not have all the answers about metacognition, but we believe that teachers need a book about metacognition written from teachers' perspectives. Teachers themselves have provided the definitions, examples, case history information, and activities in this text that deal with their own knowledge and experiences of a metacognitive nature. Using authentic teacher work in the area of metacognition we hope will help future teachers and current teachers become more comfortable emphasizing and fostering students' knowledge and regulation of their own thinking. The emergence of a teacher definition of metacognition is a legitimate and necessary function if we are to see teachers and students alike benefit from a heretofore psychologically obscured term.

An
Educational
Definition of
Metacognition

In a wonderful chapter written by Brown (1987), she emphasizes the diverse concepts that are encompassed by the term *metacognition*. She even questions if educators should continue to use such an expansive, elastic term. However, the term continues to be used especially in educational circles. Metacognition seems to be growing in popularity but not in clarity and precision. We agree with Brown; however, we find ourselves wishing to use the language that communicates best and interests our intended readers—teachers (both prospective teachers and current teachers) and perhaps administrators. Since there seems to be a growing interest among teachers in metacognition, we will attempt to define what teachers mean by this term and use it according to their definition. Overall, teachers have defined metacognition as awareness and regulation of their own mental and affective states of mind.

Premise Four: Metacognitive Knowledge and Regulation Are Core Components of Both Teaching and Learning

Part I:
Teachers' Personal
Use of
Metacognition

Metacognition for teachers' personal use is defined as the knowledge and regulation of teachers' thinking about their cognitive, social, emotional, and physical characteristics. This personal metacognition is considered a higher mental plane of functioning within oneself (intrapsychological). The knowledge and regulation relate to initiating facilitative and positive mental action to enhance teacher self-awareness, improve teacher self-acceptance, and reinforce self-guidance. In addition to motivating mental action to improve the personal dimensions of the teacher, metacognitive awareness and strategies for personal coping skills are addressed in order to decrease teacher stress, anger, anxiety, frustration, and boredom. It is hoped that such information will provide tools for change and enhancement.

It is a well-established fact that teachers with excellent personal strengths and mental coping strategies are better teachers, measured by a number of variables (e.g., higher self-esteem, Brookover, Beady, Flood, Schweitzer, & Wisenbaker, 1979; self-efficacy, Ashton, 1984). The intrapsychological state of the teacher has a direct effect on the interpsychological plane of teaching. Teachers are not in a position to model higher psychological and metacognitive levels for students if they have not experienced these levels first as a prerequisite to encouraging them in students.

Part II:
Teachers'
Professional Use of
Metacognition

Metacognition for teachers' professional use is defined as the awareness and regulation of teachers' thinking about their professional role in the teaching profession, such as planning, interactive teaching, and organizing the classroom. The backdrop of metacognition for the teaching professional is the notion of other-regulation (Vygotsky, 1978). Vygotsky hypothesized that everything is learned on two different planes. First, learning occurs on the interpsychological (between individuals) plane. The social context facilitates this level of learning. Then, as individuals process this information for their own use, learning occurs on an intrapsychological plane. This personal context of learning is qualitatively different from the social context of learning due to each teacher's unique history, interacting with the new information. Other-regulation in the teaching milieu relates to the teachers' metacognitive development, evolving from the teacher education scaffold (inter) to the prospective teachers' ownership and unique personalization (intra) of mental introspection and metacognitive skill for teaching. Brown describes other-regulation as one of the four roots of metacognition (1987).

The outcomes of metacognitive strategy use are to increase the awareness and monitoring of teacher introspection, to use this awareness to exercise proactive control over teaching situations, and to base this self-monitoring and metacognition on (1) the quality of teacher preparation, (2) unique internalization of this knowledge and skills via social constructivist principles, and (3) specific teacher-student interactions.

Part III: Metacognitive Strategies for Student Learning

After sufficient teacher modeling, teachers use informed training of metacognition to teach classroom literacy (Corno, 1991), or how to "read" a classroom. Theoretically, teachers move from the intrapschological plane (Vygotsky, 1978) of knowing to an interpsychological plane when teachers interact with and guide the learning of their students (Manning & Payne, 1993). Metacognitive strategies, that have appeared recently in the literature help teachers deliberate about how to teach children self-regulated learning skills and self-guidance, rather than shape their behavior from an external source (Meichenbaum, 1977; Zimmerman & Schunk, 1989). The regular classroom students who are experiencing concentration problems, academic learning problems, overly dependent problems, school work habit problems, or mild conduct problems receive metacognition instruction to help them improve in their ability to (1) concentrate, (2) comprehend and problem solve, (3) adapt, (4) cope with frustrating classroom tasks, and (5) reinforce helpful self-guiding metacognitive skills. The self-regulated learning literature (e.g., Rohrkemper & Corno, 1988) will inform this section.

In addition, teacher-developed and teacher-tested big books, games, and activities across the curriculum, and elementary and middle school grade span are included in this section. This final section also has great importance to the inclusion movement. Children with special learning needs especially benefit from the strategies presented in Part III.

In conclusion, teachers use their personal and professional histories of metacognitive knowledge and strategies in order to promote students' metacognitive knowledge and regulatory functions. Both knowledge and regulation of teachers and students are important and are introduced and discussed in this book. Once the realities of a classroom are viewed, it is easy to see that knowledge and regulation are intertwined and must be dealt with simultaneously. It may be possible to separate them for investigation in a laboratory setting, but this is not necessarily so in the classroom. We have learned a great deal about metacognition from the psychologists' laboratory. Now we welcome the opportunity and the challenge to report what happens when the complexity and unpredictability of the classroom meets metacognitive practice and research.

CHAPTER 1

Reviewing Theories and Psychologies Related to Metacognition

OVERVIEW

In this chapter an account of the learning processes, theories, approaches, and psychologies that overlap with or extend the concept of metacognition are presented. Rational-emotive thinking, transactional analysis, attribution theory, self-efficacy, self-regulated learning, self-talk levels, and the language of self-support are explained. The explicit and implicit connections between each one of these variables (e.g., attribution theory, self-talk levels) and metacognition are discussed within this chapter. No attempt is made to be all inconclusive or exhaustive. However, the choice to include a theory, or approach, or psychological idea was based on whether our previous work with teachers pointed to the importance of such a choice. Teachers have gathered a fuller, richer understanding of metacognition when impinging concepts, theories, etc., have also been explained. Metacognition as awareness and regulation of mental and affective states is interdependent upon a number of other variables, such as the ones addressed in this chapter.

Self-Questions

1. *Knowledge.* Name the three ego states of transactional analysis.

2. *Comprehension.* Define rational-emotive thinking.

3. *Application.* Explain how self-efficacy theory is related to metacognition.

4. *Analysis.* Discuss Butler's drivers, stoppers, and confusers that comprise maladaptive self-talk.

5. *Synthesis.* Combining Butler's steps for learning the language of self-affirmation, devise a plan for improving your own self-guiding speech-to-self.

6. *Evaluation.* Provide a list of benefits and drawbacks related to self-regulated learning.

Metacognition

Research on metacognition began in the late 1960s and the early 1970s when Flavell and his colleagues became interested in children's awareness of their own memory processes, termed *metamemory* (Corsini, Pick, & Flavell, 1968; Flavell, Beach, & Chinsky, 1966;

Flavell, Fredrichs, & Hoyt, 1970; Keeny, Cannizzo, & Flavell, 1967). According to Brown et al. (1983), a major contribution to the field of academic cognition during the 1970s was "the impressive body of knowledge generated on the subject of the development of active acquisition strategies of learning" (p. 77). Researchers were interested in children's knowledge and use of strategies, particularly those they used for purposeful remembering. This body of research formed the foundation for the metacognitive/learning strategy research of today.

Discussions appeared in the literature about the differences between cognition and metacognition. For example, Meichenbaum (1985) pointed out that cognition involves ongoing operations, such as memorizing; while metacognition includes mental overseeing, such as self-correcting. Similarly, "cognition refers to the actual processes and strategies . . . and metacognition is a construct that refers, first, to what individuals know about their cognitions and second, to the ability to control their cognitions" (Forrest-Pressley & Waller, 1984, p. 6, cited in Haller, Child, & Walberg, 1988, p. 5).

Some familiar examples highlighting this differentiation are provided in the chart below. An exercise that our students have found helpful is to develop several examples of cognition versus metacognition and discuss these examples in small or large groups. Refer to the chart and exercise below.

COGNITION VS. METACOGNITION
EXERCISE #1

Cognition	Metacognition
1. Calling the roll	1. Realizing that you left out someone's name
2. Having a conversation with your principal	2. Becoming aware that the principal is not happy with you
3. Writing an assignment on the board	3. Remembering that the students have already completed this assignment
4. _____	4. _____
5. _____	5. _____

The majority of the research on metacognition initially focused in the area of memory, followed by comprehension, problem solving, and self-control. An indepth look at these four major research areas by age level designations (i.e., preschool, early elementary, middle school, secondary/college, and adults) appears in Manning (1991). Classroom applications stemming from this research activity are included in Part III of this text, Chapters 7–9.

Metacognition, specifically for teacher education and teaching has not been as widely researched as metacognition for learning. A review of literature related to metacognition for teacher education and teaching is integrated throughout Part II of this text, Chapters 4–6.

The braiding of affective components of metacognition with the more cognitive concentrations has been evident in recent research activity related to metacognition. For example, when researchers study metacognition, they often also study affective variables such as motivation, attribution, and efficacy. All of the following sections of this chapter are examples of the more affective side of metacognition. Ann Brown (1987) refers to this side as "hot cognition." The first such theory that we will discuss is termed *rational-emotive therapy* or *rational-emotive thinking*. This theory is linked explicitly with metacognition because it involves mental realization of your beliefs that may lead to unhelpful self-talk that has the potential to be counterproductive to healthy living. Self-talk is a mirror of one's own thinking: one's own mental awareness of unhealthy beliefs. For example, believing that we have to be perfect, often leads directly to unhelpful self-talk (e.g., "I have to do everything just perfectly." "I can't make mistakes."). Then the unhelpful self-talk impacts on attitude, health, stress levels, behavior, and interpersonal relationships (e.g., negative attitude, high blood pressure, high levels of killer stress, poor choices, etc.). The metacognitive awareness is the important, initial step that fosters metacognitive regulation or modification of such unhealthy beliefs —> unhelpful self-talk —> poor attitudes, damaged health, poor relationships, etc. The Rational-Emotive Therapy is described in more depth next.

RATIONAL-EMOTIVE THERAPY

Rational-Emotive Therapy (RET) was originated by Albert Ellis around 1955. The major principle of RET is illustrated in the quotes of Epictetus (1 AD) in Enchiridion: "Men feel disturbed not by things, but by the views which they take of them," and William Shakespeare in Hamlet: "There exists nothing either good or bad but thinking makes it so." RET is based on a humanistic, educative model that offers a clear-cut theory of appropriate and inappropriate, rational and irrational, thoughts, feelings, and behaviors. The major premise is that people, even early in life, have many more choices than they acknowledge. Most conditioning in life is really self-conditioning. Teachers, counselors, therapists, and parents serve the role of clarifier: helping individuals to see more clearly that they have a range of alternative reactions for any given situation. A person's choice of reactions affects their mental health. RET attempts to show individuals how they behave in self-defeating ways and how they can change these ways.

The A-B-C framework is the cornerstone of RET. Behavioral or emotional responses are explained in this A-B-C framework: At point A (your Activating experience), we gather as much sensory information as we can. At point B (our Belief system), we process that information, weigh it, consider it, think it over. At point C (our emotional or behavioral Consequence), we react with our gut and tend to take some action about our Activating experience. Please refer to the chart below that may help you to visualize this process more completely.

RET FRAMEWORK FOR TEACHERS
(from the Teacher's Perspective)

A Activating Experience	**B** Belief System	**C** Emotional or Behavioral Consequence

EXAMPLES OF A—> B —> C

A Student Brings Knife to School	**B** This Behavior is Against School Rules; Students Are Not Supposed to be Armed	**C** Send Another Student for the Principal
	Accompanying Self-Talk: "She knows better than to bring a weapon. I need to send Joy for the principal. This is too serious for me to handle alone."	

At point B, we believe it is the self-talk of an individual that determines the subsequent response or consequence. For another example, an educational situation at point A could be that a student lies about something to a teacher. Point C is the teacher's emotional and/or behavioral response. Point B is the self-talk the teacher engages in which promotes the response at point C. The nature of the teacher's response C (e.g., rational, irrational, sane, crazy) is related to how he/she talks about this situation to self at point B. For example, the teacher who says to self at point B, "Well that little brat, I'll show Hugh who's the boss." will most likely react at point C in a recognizably different manner than the teacher who (at point B) says to self, "Why would Hugh not tell me the truth? I wonder if he is afraid of my reaction if he tells me the truth? I need to talk to him further."

The self-verbalization at point B mediates between situation A and response C. This is true in the clinical sense as described by Ellis, and it is also true for educational responses and other nonclinical populations. Rational-emotive therapy was originally developed as a cognitive behavior therapy for dealing with "mentally ill" or "emotionally disturbed" individuals. However, since its inception in 1955 the approach has been used successfully with many types of problems and individuals. For example, Howard Young (1984a, 1984b, 1984c) adapted RET to make it appropriate for adolescent, uneducated, poor, and highly religious individuals; Michael Bernard (1984) adapted RET for children and adolescents; Al Raitt (1988) applied RET to weight control; and Emmett Velton (1988) adapted RET for the treatment of heroine and methadone addictions.

According to RET (Ellis & Harper, 1975) there are a number of powerful, irrational, and illogical ideas that prohibit many people from leading an anxiety-free, unhostile life. The following irrational beliefs (Ellis & Harper, 1975) include:

IRRATIONAL BELIEFS

1. I must be loved and approved by all the people I find significant.

2. I must be thoroughly competent, adequate, and achieving.

3. When people act badly, I should blame them, and see them as bad, wicked, or rotten individuals.

4. I have to view things as terrible, awful, horrible, and catastrophic when things aren't going my way.

5. My happiness is caused by other events or people rather than by how I think, feel, and talk to myself.

6. If something seems unpleasant, dangerous, or fearsome, I should be preoccupied and continually upset over it.

7. I can more easily avoid facing many problems and self-responsibilities than undertake more rewarding forms of self-discipline.

8. Things that have happened in the past are all important, need to be continually worried about, and limit my possibilities for the future.

9. People and things should be different from what they are, and it is catastrophic if perfect solutions cannot be immediately found.

10. I can achieve maximum happiness by inaction or by passively and uncommitedly "enjoying myself."

Although individuals express their irrational beliefs in personally distinctive ways, these beliefs tend to be variations of three basic *musts*, *shoulds*, or *oughts*. These involve the following types of demands:

• *Demands about self*: "I must do well, and must turn into a horrible person if I don't." This belief causes a person to magnify the importance of never making a mistake. The self-talk accompanying such a belief goes something like this: "If I don't get this right, it will be horrible. I can't stand it if I don't do it perfectly!" The behavior that occurs as a result of such catastrophizing and awfulizing (as Ellis calls it), is most likely feelings of inadequacy, worthlessness, insecurity, anxiety, tension, depression, migraine headaches, nervous stomach, and other such unhealthy behaviors. The more rational belief is: "I will do my best. I don't want to make mistakes, but if I do I can stand it. It might be unfortunate, but it will not be awful." This is putting "mistake making" in its proper perspective. Other examples of rational self-talk may be "I am a human being which means I am prone to error. I'll do the best I can. If I make a mistake, I can handle it. It will not be the end of the world." Behaviors following such self-talk are much more likely to be relaxed and emotionally healthy.

• *Demands about others*: "You must treat me kindly, fairly, and considerately; and you rate as a rotten individual if you don't!" This leads to feelings of anger, resentment, hostility, and over-rebelliousness. The adaptive counterpart is "it is nice to have the approval of others. However, if I do not I will still be okay."

• *Demands about world/life conditions*: The universe must make things easy for me, give me what I want without too much trouble or annoyance; and I can't stand it when this terrible universe doesn't!" This belief leads to feelings of low frustration tolerance, avoidance, self-pity, and inertia. The adaptive/rational counterpart is "people are the way they are. I cannot change them but I can change the way I react to them." This third belief gave rise to Ellis' book entitled *How to Live with a Neurotic* (1975). These dogmatic and absolute beliefs lead to almost inevitable emotional distress and to self-defeating behavior. They all result in forms of acute and chronic whining about our own or others' failings.

These irrational ideas (Ellis & Harper, 1975, p. 197) are developed early in life from (1) our inability to think straight (e.g., childish need for immediate gratification rather than on future gains; inability to accurately distinguish real from imagined dangers); (2) our dependence as a child on the planning and thinking of others; (3) the superstitions and prejudices inculcated in us by our parents; and (4) the indoctrinations by the mass media of our culture.

Albert Ellis (1976) makes the important point that people often escalate their desires or wants into absolute *musts*. In fact, Ellis states that in most individuals, this pattern constitutes a biological tendency. However, Ellis points out that humans have a second basic biological tendency: the power of choice and the ability to identify, challenge, and change irrational thinking. RET holds that the best way to control our feelings is by using our willing-thinking processes—by reflecting, thinking, and telling ourself calming ideas.

We invariably talk to ourselves and the kinds of things we say to ourselves, as well as the form in which we say these things, significantly affect our emotions and behavior. Our moods significantly depend upon what we believe or tell ourselves. When we tell ourselves and believe in pessimistic, cynical, and hopeless ideas (irrational beliefs), we tend to feel sad, miserable, or depressed. On the other hand, when we tell ourselves and believe in optimistic, hopeful, cheerful ideas (rational beliefs) we tend to feel happy, elated, and joyful (Ellis, 1977).

Given that we have the power of choice and do not have to think irrationally, RET proposes change if we internalize three major insights:

THREE RET INSIGHTS

1. Past or present activating events do not "cause" disturbed emotional and behavioral consequences. Rather, our belief systems about these activating events largely create our disturbed feelings and behaviors.

2. Irrespective of how we have disturbed ourselves in the past, we now upset ourselves chiefly because we keep reindoctrinating ourselves with our irrational beliefs.

3. Because we are human and very easily (and to some degree naturally) tend to disturb ourselves and because we find it easy to cling to our self-defeating thoughts, feelings, and actions, we can overcome our disturbances in the long run mainly by working hard and repeatedly to dispute our irrational beliefs and the effect of those beliefs. (Dryden & DiGiuseppe, 1990, p. 10)

It is not a goal of RET to eliminate all negative feelings. Instead, the goal is to behave in ways that are not dysfunctional in the long run and enhance one's survival and happiness. If we accept reality and eliminate extreme, absolute evaluations of reality, we take a major step toward that goal.

How can we apply the ideas of RET to teaching and learning in regular education? We have found Ellis' ideas to be useful in dealing with mentally healthy individuals not just those diagnosed as "mentally ill." Even healthy individuals often catastrophize, awfulize, and talk to themselves irrationally. It is more a matter of degree of severity, which explains why a person becomes totally incapacitated (psychotic/mentally ill), or partially incapacitated (neurotic/emotionally disturbed), or occasionally incapacitated (bouts with tension headaches, occasional depression, stress, tension, anxiety). What Ellis has to say, we believe, is just as important to *prevent* irrational behavior, as it is to treat mental illness. We use his ideas frequently when dealing with troubled, anxious student teachers who are learning to teach for the first time. They often are operating from all three of what we term Ellis' *major irrational beliefs*: "I have to be a perfect teacher; everyone must think I'm doing a great job; and my pupils have to change and behave exactly the way I want." Such student teachers' beliefs cause difficult problems, as you might guess. If their belief system can become more rational (e.g., "No perfect teachers exist; that includes me! Everyone will not approve of everything I do; I'm learning; I'm supposed to receive some constructive criticism. These pupils are the way they are. They will only change when they see the need to do so. In the meantime, how can I react differently to them?") then these student teachers are much more likely to find student teaching a pleasant, more successful experience. Beyond analyzing our beliefs and self-talk for rationality, the next discussion is related to overseeing our thinking in view of three ego states: adult, parent, and child.

TRANSACTIONAL ANALYSIS

Transactional analysis (TA) is a helpful framework for looking at verbal intra-action within an individual, as well as verbal interactions between individuals. If you recall from the introduction, we mentioned that teachers have approximately 1000 face-to-face interactions per day. The majority of these interactions are verbal in nature. Teachers talk to students, parents, peer teachers, administrators, janitorial staff, paraprofessionals, clerical staff, bus drivers, and themselves. We know from Butler's (1992) clinical research that individuals make approximately 50,000 self-talk utterances per day — this includes teachers. Therefore, teachers spend a huge percentage of their time talking to others and to themselves. Since TA is based on verbal exchanges, teachers find this approach related to their daily lives. They also tell us how much TA improves understanding of themselves, as well as their students. This understanding has helped many of our prospective and inservice teachers improve their ability to communicate; and therefore, build stronger and more positive relationships with their students and with themselves. Included next is one example from a classroom teacher about TA.

Teacher A: When you first talked about TA in our class, I thought to myself, "What a bunch of bull." Then the more we talked, the more I got to thinking. I have a 30-minute commute to and from our class, and I thought all the way home about how Demetrious uses a great deal of *adapted* child. He often whines, plays the victim, and complains that someone is picking on him. I usually let him wear me down; and then, I end up whining something sarcastic back at him. I realize I am just perpetuating this negative characteristic. So today, when he started with the whining, I used my most calm, rational "adult" with him: "Demetrious, are you having a difficult time today? Can you tell me the problem in your regular voice so that I can understand better?" To my surprise Demetrious explained calmly, softly, and very maturely what was bothering him. He really had a legitimate concern. I had just tuned him out because his whiny voice was grating on my nerves. For the first time all year Demetrious felt understood; I stayed calm; and together we solved his problem. You can't ask for better. Tell your students that TA is not a bunch of bull. It is very relevant to communication, listening, and relationships in the classroom.

According to TA everyone has three parts or persons, within himself or herself: the Parent Ego State, the Adult Ego State, and the Child Ego State. The ego states of TA are closely tied to the three elements of the psychoanalytical theory of Sigmund Freud: (1) the id, instinctual drive (Child); (2) the superego, restrictive force over these egocentric drives or needs (Parent); and (3) the ego, which serves as the mediator balancing between hedonism and repression (Adult). Individuals are in a constant, dynamic state of interplay among these three constructs, as the ego referees between individual urges and restraint. Eric Berne (1964) in the book *Games People Play* and Thomas Harris (1969) in *I'm OK-You're OK: A Practical Guide to Transactional Analysis* have translated these abstract Freudian concepts into practical application for adults, teachers (Ernst, 1973), children (Freed, 1971), and teens (Freed, 1973).

Berne observed overt behavior as individuals played their internal tapes from these stored-up experiences. Stored experience is quite similar to Vygotsky's idea of internalization: that is, children are first regulated by significant others' verbalizations. Then the children internalize these parent verbalizations, which subsequently and strongly influence children's self-language and verbal self-regulation of their own actions. TA proponents arc saying the same thing when they talk about replaying the stored-up tapes from our past. This idea of repeating stored-up experiences is also at the heart of understanding why abused children frequently become abusive parents, why parents parent the way they were parented (Friday, 1977), and why teachers teach the way they were taught (Goodlad, 1984).

According to TA an ego state is a consistent pattern of feeling, directly related to a specific pattern of behavior. It is like we have three people inside of us, each of whom feels and behaves differently from the other. These ego states are a result of all the stored-up experiences and interactions that are recorded in the brain—like a tape recorder. The brain has recorded every experience we have ever had.

How do the three ego states or voices work? To explain, our *Parent* state contains attitudes and behaviors learned from our parents and other authority figures when we were children. The *Adult* state is the part of our personality that is most like a computer. It is rational, responsible, emotionless, and expert at processing data and solving problems. The *Child* state resembles what we were like when we were little. Our Child has the same feelings and ways of behaving we had when we were very young. Each of our three states has definite ways of feeling and behaving. To explicate, we will take a closer look at each of these states or voices.

Parent

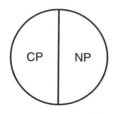

This state contains both the good and bad remembrances of our parents or whomever raised us. The Parent can be critical, or nurturing, or both. When we are critical, prejudiced, act authoritarian, and hurt or punish others, that's our "critical" Parent. If we have too much critical Parent we tend to play the role of prosecutor. However, sometimes our critical Parent can be very valuable, such as when we yell at a child in order to keep him or her from getting hurt. Verbal clues to this voice are "You must," "You should," "You should not," "You always," "You never," or "Don't." The "nurturing" Parent tends to play the role of rescuer and goes around "saving" people who don't really need to be "saved." It describes people who have a compulsion to help others with their problems even if they don't need the help. A positive side to the nurturing Parent would be a mother looking after her baby or assisting people when they really need comfort.

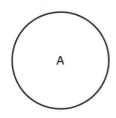

Adult

As children move from being toddlers, they begin to store rational information for use in later events. The Adult is the "intelligent," natural thinking part of the personality that is rational, emotionless, processes data objectively, and solves problems. Too much Adult can really bore people to tears because the Adult never laughs or expresses feelings. On the other hand, if we don't have enough Adult, we won't be able to take care of ourselves. Verbal clues include the "W" questions: who, what, when, where, and also how. Other examples are "In my opinion," "Let's take a closer look," and "Now I see the way this works."

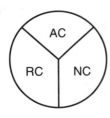

Child

This aspect comes from our recordings which deal with our feelings and sensory input throughout our lives. There are three parts to the Child Ego State. The "natural" Child is the part of us that spontaneously expresses our feelings of happiness, love, and joy—the giddy lighthearted kid in us. The "adapted" Child is the part of us that collects bad feelings such as anxiety and depression. This part often plays the role of the victim or persecuted. We are probably playing a victim role if others are always putting us down or trying to comfort us and we feel depressed and blame ourselves and others a lot. The "rebellious" Child part is the one that is defiant or stubborn toward others. However, there are some unfair situations when we need to stand up for our rights and challenge others.

When viewing the three ego states, it is important to note that no one ego state is constructive or destructive in itself—it depends on the appropriateness of the situation. In addition, it is important to keep a balance among the three. For example, too much Child can lead to irresponsibility; too little Child can lead to lack of creativity and spontaneity. Too much rebellious Child can cause us to lose friends, but too little can cause us to be passive wimps that people run over. Too much nurturing Parent causes "smothering," and too little causes "coldness." Too much Adult causes us to be boring and nonfeeling, and too little causes us not to know how to solve problems and look after ourselves. On the following pages are six examples of dialogue between a student and teacher.

While the primary focus of TA is on the social transaction of ego states between persons (interpersonal), hence *transactional* analysis, a secondary focus allows for the *structural* analysis of an individual's ego state (intrapersonal). Listen to the voices within you and you will "hear" your Parent (Critical/Nurturing), your Child (Rebellious/Natural/Adapted), and your Adult. We may not always hear the words, but we will get messages from the feelings within us. Remember, we are all three persons. Look inside yourself and try to determine which part of you, you allow to control your behavior and to "hear" what you are telling yourself, about yourself. Ask yourself some of the following questions: How do I treat myself? Does my Adult run my life so much that I rarely laugh and kick up my heels? Does my Parent really treat my Child with love? Do I have a scolding Parent inside me? Page 11 shows four examples of internal exchanges.

EXAMPLE 1

TEACHER: Do you know the answer to the problem?

STUDENT: Yes. It's 52.

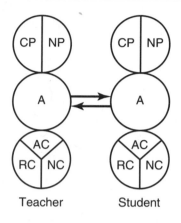

EXAMPLE 2

STUDENT: Oh no! I've lost my paper. What am I going to do?

TEACHER: There, there. Don't worry. Everything's going to be alright.

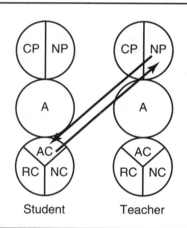

EXAMPLE 3

TEACHER: Aren't you finished yet?

STUDENT: I'm always the last one finished. I'm just stupid.

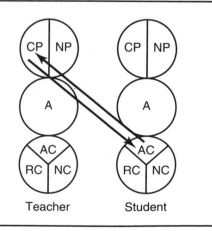

EXAMPLE 4

TEACHER: Can you tell me more about that?

STUDENT: Yes.

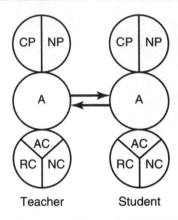

EXAMPLE 5

TEACHER: Shame on you. You should know better than that. Now don't let me catch you out of your seat again.

STUDENT: I'm sorry (sniff, sniff). Please sir, I'm sorry.

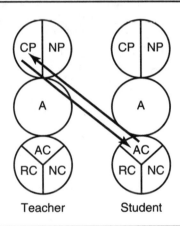

EXAMPLE 6

STUDENT: Mrs. Dean, do you want today's assignment by Friday?

TEACHER: Sit down!!

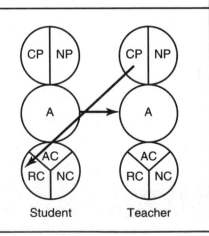

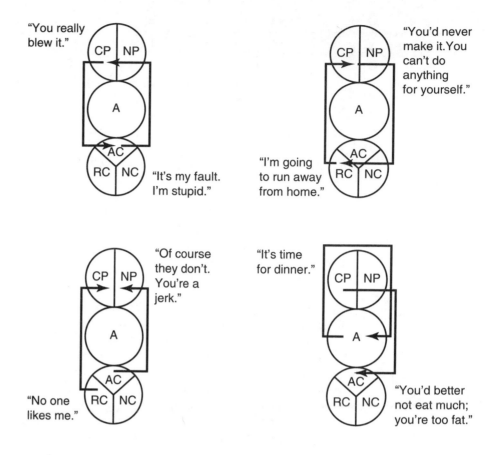

The premise of TA is that all individuals need to feel adequate. Our attitude towards our worth and the worth of others is called our life position (Harris, 1969). There are four basic life positions:

FOUR LIFE POSITIONS

1. I'M OK, YOU'RE OK. This is basically the only healthy position.

2. I'M OK, YOU'RE NOT OK. This person thinks he or she is faultless and is suspicious of others. This is a paranoid position.

3. I'M NOT OK, YOU'RE OK. This person thinks he or she is no good or worthless while others are good and worthwhile. This person has low self-esteem and really doesn't like him or herself.

4. I'M NOT OK, YOU'RE NOT OK. This person thinks he or she is worthless and so are others. This person has little hope and often nothing to live for.

For the most part, our interactions with our parents and significant others reinforce in us these life positions or attitudes toward ourselves and others. If the messages we received from our parents were supportive, encouraging, and positive then our life position is probably, "I'm ok, you're ok." If, however, the messages from our parents were unclear, negative, or harmful then we may have adopted one of the other three life positions. It is important to keep in mind that these messages are no longer coming from our mothers or fathers. They are now coming from inside of our own head—we control them or can learn to control them via metacognitive awareness and regulation. This mental monitoring and regulation of our adult, parent, and child messages are aspects of metacognition. Another theory that overlaps with metacognition is attribution theory, discussed next.

ATTRIBUTION THEORY

Attribution theory is one of the most popular theories for explaining classroom motivation. Our beliefs and attributions about why we succeed and why we fail affect motivation. Attribution theory seeks to understand the perceived causes (the "whys") or how a person's construction of excuses and justifications explain their past behavior and motivate their future behaviors.

Bernard Weiner (1979, 1980), an influential theorist in the area of attributions, suggests that most explanations for success or failure can be classified by three dimensions: locus (internal versus external), stability (stable or invariant versus unstable or variant), and controllability (controllable versus uncontrollable). The first dimension, locus of causality, corresponds to the perception of the cause of events as being internal to the individual or external to the individual. For example, causes within a person include such things as intelligence, effort, or physical attractiveness, while external factors include task difficulty and luck. Stability, on the other hand, refers to whether the cause is independent of time or is time-dependent. For example, ability is perceived as relatively lasting, as opposed to effort, which can vary considerably over a short period of time. The third dimension, controllability is strongly related to evaluative consequences of behavior. Controllability refers to how much control the person has over his or her behavior. For example, a person is assumed to have more control over effort than over ability.

Within this three-dimensional system, Weiner (1979, 1980) postulated that in achievement-related contexts, there are eight major causes to which successes and failures are attributed. These eight major aspects of attributions and the three major dimensions are presented in Table 1–1. Each of the eight causes can be classified along the three dimensions. For example, ability is regarded as being uncontrollable, internal, and stable. Luck is regarded as uncontrollable, external, and unstable.

It is easy to see from Table 1–1 how students might seek to explain success and failure differently. When students who are usually successful fail, they may make internal, controllable and unstable attributions such as "I didn't study enough this time." The usual result of this kind of thinking is a focus on strategies for succeeding the next time. On the other hand, students who believe their failures are due to lack of ability (stable, internal, uncontrollable attribute) are unlikely to expect to succeed in similar tasks and are unlikely to exert much effort in the future. These students often seem resigned to failure, are depressed, and may even develop "learned helplessness," the feeling that they are doomed to failure. Keep in mind that when individuals attribute failure to something they cannot control they have little motivation to try. Consequences of attribution have affected a person's expectancy for future performance (McMahan, 1973; Weiner, Nirenburg, & Goldstein, 1976), persistence (Rest, 1976), learned helplessness (Miller & Norman,

TABLE 1–1   Weiner's Attributions for Success and Failure

CONTROLL-ABILITY	INTERNAL		EXTERNAL	
	Stable	*Unstable*	*Stable*	*Unstable*
Uncontrollable	Ability "I'm smart" "I'm stupid"	Immediate/Temporary Mood; health	Task Difficulty "It was hard" "It was simple"	Luck "I was lucky" "My luck ran out"
Controllable	Typical Effort How hard I usually work	Effort "I didn't try hard" "I studied hard"	Teacher Bias Typical help from the teacher	Unusual Help from others

Source: Weiner, B. (1979). A theory of motivation for some classroom experiences. *Journal of Educational Psychology, 71,* 3–25. Copyright 1979 by the American Psychological Association. Adapted by permission.

1979), affective reactions (Sarason & Stoops, 1978), task choice (Nicholls, 1984), and study strategy use (Palmer & Goetz, 1988).

It is important to remember that all these aspects of attribution—ability, effort, luck, etc., are *perceived* by the individual. Our perceptions moderate between environmental stimuli and our responses. The picture or image we create of ourselves and the self-worth generated from this image will affect our approach and level of performance in solving life's problems.

Weiner's (1979) classification system has received attention in cognitive intervention studies, where a change in subjects' behavior has been a major goal. For example, Kurtz and Borkowski (1984) reported that learners who believe their efforts will reap success are more likely to use what they have learned in a different context. Borkowski, in Meichenbaum (1977), emphasized the importance of incorporating attention to attribution theory with metacognitive strategy training. A subject's attributions are instrumental in situations where a behavior change is sought. Changing behavior without changing unproductive attributions will not result in a lasting, cross-situational change. For example, if young elementary children believe that their teacher is responsible for their behavior at school (externality attribution), they are much less likely to respond to cognitive behavior modification (CBM) strategies. These children need to see themselves as responsible (internality attribution); therefore, a cognitive strategy aimed at teaching responsibility for their own behavior is very important. Borkowski has repeatedly urged the inclusion of attribution retraining in such cognitive strategy studies. Manning (1988) reported success in changing first-and third-graders' locus of control (similar to Weiner's locus and responsibility dimensions), while at the same time producing improved classroom conduct. These benefits were maintained after one and three months and transferred to another classroom context and to home. Manning's study documents the relatedness of attribution theory to cognitive strategy studies. They seem to go hand in hand. Other recent training efforts have combined an attribution training component within metacognitive strategy training packages (McCombs, 1988). A companion to attribution is another self-system term *self-efficacy*. Efficacy is an appropriate and important consideration when metacognitive awareness and regulation are important educational goals.

TEACHER EFFICACY

Teachers play a critical role in the classroom environment. Teacher beliefs and expectations of their effectiveness as teachers have been shown to affect student attitude and achievement. These teacher beliefs and expectations are sometimes referred to as teacher efficacy. Specifically, teachers' sense of efficacy refers to the degree to which teachers believe they have the ability to affect student performance (Ashton, 1984). Gibson and Dembo (1984) support the identification of teacher efficacy as the variable accountable for individual differences in the effectiveness of teachers.

Theory of Self-Efficacy

Much of the construct of teacher efficacy is based on Albert Bandura's (1977) conception of the cognitive social learning theory of self-efficacy. Bandura maintains that personal efficacy is concerned with the conviction that we can successfully execute the behavior required to produce outcomes. There are two components to this overall theory: response-outcome expectancies and efficacy expectations. Response-outcome expectancy is defined as "a person's estimate that a given behavior will lead to certain outcomes" (Bandura, 1977, p. 193), whereas efficacy expectation is defined as "the conviction that one can successfully execute the behavior required to produce the outcome"

(Bandura, 1977, p. 315). The difference between response-outcome expectancies and efficacy expectations is that even though we may believe that certain actions will produce certain outcomes, if we do not believe we have the capability to deliver the action, such knowledge will not encourage us to attempt the desired outcome (Bandura, 1977). For example, a teacher, Pam, might realize that singing a song will enhance a lesson, but will not do so because she believes she is unable to sing well enough. How much effort and perseverance we are willing to put forth for a desired outcome is a direct result of our efficacy expectations.

The dimensions of self-efficacy include strength, magnitude, and generality (Bandura, 1977). The stronger the perceived self-efficacy, the more likely we are to persist in the behavior. The tasks are generally ordered according to their level of difficulty, and we proceed from simple tasks, to more imposing performances. The magnitude of the task increases as we become more proficient. Generality refers to mastery for a specific situation being implemented in a similar situation.

Judgments of self-efficacy are based on performance attainments, vicarious experiences of observing others' performances, verbal persuasion, and/or physiological states (Bandura, 1977, 1982). These approaches to instruct an individual in self-efficacy beliefs become informative through cognitive appraisal by the individual (Bandura, 1980, 1981). The most influential source of efficacy information is attainment because it is based upon personal mastery experience. A successful outcome will continually reinforce self-efficacy and is not affected by an occasional failure.

Another source of information about our own capabilities is the influence of vicarious experience. To see others successfully performing in similar situations can raise efficacy expectations. For example, if a teacher is able to see a colleague discipline a student without adverse consequences, the observer can be persuaded that he or she also has the capability to master comparable endeavors. We persuade ourselves that if others can do it, we can accomplish or at least improve our performances.

Verbal persuasion is often used to influence behavior because of its ease and availability. Through verbal persuasion we are led to believe that we can overcome our difficulties and that we do possess certain capabilities to successfully perform. However, the reality of our actions can easily repudiate any enduring effects from verbal persuasion. If successful, the mastery reinforces self-efficacy; if unsuccessful, the failed execution of the behavior takes precedent over the verbal persuasion. The value of verbal persuasion is in convincing others, particularly children, to attempt performances that they might not have tried on their own.

Last, emotional arousal is another source of efficacy information. Our physiological state is reflective of our judgment of self-capabilities and sensitivity to stress, especially when faced with aversive events. Unusually high emotional arousal debilitates performance and the resulting perception of unsuccessful performance only increases the thoughts of failure, thus compounding the level of distress and further impairment.

These sources of information that we use in evaluating our capabilities are integrated into self-efficacy judgments on an individual basis (Bandura, 1981). The impact of these perceptions depends upon how each experience is cognitively appraised. The perceptions are addressed with self-referenced thoughts which become the mediation for the relationship between knowledge and action. The determination of which activities are chosen and the rate at which the skill is acquired is partly determined by the judgments of our own capabilities. The more we perceive a success rate for a certain behavior, the more the behavior is reinforced and mastered, thus leading to a higher degree of self-efficacy.

Construct of Teacher Efficacy

Teachers' sense of efficacy is the construct hypothesized to mediate between many variables that contribute to the teacher's perception of self-performance as well as to actual performance and student achievement (Denham & Michael, 1981). In other words, it is teachers' beliefs that they can help students learn or the extent to which teachers believe that they have the capacity to affect student performance. Teacher efficacy has been shown to be related to student achievement (Armour et al., 1976), teachers' classroom management strategies (Ashton & Webb, 1986), teachers' adaptations of innovations (Berman, McLaughlin, Bass, Pauly, & Zellman, 1977), teacher competence (Trentham, Silvern, & Brogden, 1985), and student performance (Midgley, 1989).

While many researchers have treated teacher efficacy as a unidimensional trait (Barfield & Burlingame, 1974; Hoover-Dempsey, Bassler, & Brissie, 1987; Trentham et al., 1985), others have distinguished two-dimensions, following Bandura's (1977) theory of self-efficacy (Ashton & Webb, 1986; Denham & Michael, 1981; Gibson & Dembo, 1984). The work of Gibson and Dembo (1984) resulted in a reliable measure of two constructs of teacher efficacy. Ashton and Webb (1986) refer to these two dimensions as personal teaching efficacy and general teaching efficacy. Sense of personal teaching efficacy refers to "individuals' assessment of their own teaching competence" (p. 4). Sense of teacher efficacy refers to "teachers expectation that teaching can influence student learning" (p. 4). In other words, teaching efficacy is the extent of belief that teaching can have an influence on student learning, regardless of obstacles such as the students' family background and students' ability; while, personal teaching efficacy is the teachers' perception of their own teaching abilities to influence student learning. For teachers to positively impact students' self-concept and performance they need to integrate these two dimensions into a single course of action. In order to understand the construct of teachers' sense of efficacy and its relationship to teachers' classroom performance and to student achievement, a few examples of related research are discussed next.

Ashton and Webb (1986) in their studies with middle school and high school teachers found a positive relationship between teacher efficacy and student achievement. The evidence here suggests that teacher efficacy attitudes are situation specific and can be expected to vary depending on the subject matter being taught.

In a recent study of the socialization of student teachers, Hoy and Woolfolk (1990) found that at the conclusion of the student teaching experience, personal sense of efficacy had increased while general teaching efficacy had decreased. Hoy and Woolfolk attributed the increase in personal teaching efficacy of student teachers to be a result of increased confidence in their ability to manage and control a classroom. The decrease in general teaching efficacy as a belief developed during the student teaching experience because of the varied home backgrounds and experiences of the children. Another conclusion is that in schools where teachers and administrators have high expectations for students and where teachers receive assistance from their principals in solving instructional and management problems, teachers sense of personal efficacy is higher.

Guskey (1988) found that teachers who had high levels of self-efficacy were the most receptive to the implementation of new instructional practices. A longitudinal study conducted by Midgley, Feldlaufer, and Eccles (1989) of middle grades teachers and their students examined the relationship between students' beliefs in mathematics and their teachers' sense of efficacy. Results demonstrated that students who had mathematics teachers with high levels of efficacy experienced greater success and had more positive feelings about the content of mathematics.

While the studies presented here do not represent an exhaustive accounting, the available literature relating efficacy to teacher beliefs and behaviors is limited. However, the majority of studies indicated a positive relationship.

What does all this mean for you as a prospective teacher? "Self-limitation of career development arises more from perceived self-inefficacy than from actual inability" (Bandura, 1989, p. 1179). In other words, the extent to which a person is successful or unsuccessful in his or her chosen profession is dependent more on the *belief* about their capabilities to perform adequately than from lack of ability. Belief or efficacy expectations do affect the way learners perform on tasks. Because teachers are expected to manage a wide range of social and academic processes each day, their beliefs concerning the efficacy of their efforts may be important determinants of their persistence, motivation, metacognition, and the quality of their efforts. Self-efficacy theory predicts that teachers with a high sense of efficacy work harder and persist longer, even when students are difficult to teach, in part because these teachers believe in themselves and in their students (Woolfolk, 1993). This positive mental stance most likely affects the quality of our metacognitive awareness and regulation. As we will see in the next discussion, high efficacy affects our tendencies toward greater self-regulated learning.

SELF-REGULATED LEARNING

Most of the definitions of self-regulated learning include components of metacognition, motivation, and proaction. For example, self-regulated learning by students describes "the degree to which they are metacognitively, motivationally, and behaviorally active participants in their own learning processes" (Zimmerman & Schunk, 1989, p. 4). Pintrich and Degroot (1990, p. 33) detail the three components of self-regulated learning as (a) students' metacognitive strategies for planning, monitoring, and modifying their cognition, (b) students' self-management and control of their effort on classroom academic tasks (e.g., task persistence, blocking distractors), and (c) cognitive strategies that students use to learn, remember, and understand (e.g., rehearsal, elaboration, and organizational strategies).

Another researcher, Lyn Corno (1987, pp. 249) characterizes self-regulated learners as "(a) enactive, (b) facilitators of their own learning that sustain self-motivation, (c) self-starters, and (d) students who seem to make learning easier for themselves." The unique characteristics of classrooms often necessitate students' coping skills. Even in the master teacher's classroom, students will occasionally experience some degree of frustration and/or boredom (Rohrkemper & Corno, 1988). Students who are able to adapt by modifying the task, themselves, or the situation are exercising self-regulated learning. Self-regulated learning characteristics are dependent upon personal and environmental conditions. Even students who use a great deal of self-regulation do not always use the strategies. For example, for a particular classroom task, students who often use self-regulated learning may slip in and out of this use during the task and across tasks. Therefore, even students who use self-regulation often can improve in their use when they learn appropriate points of application. In addition, students who do not use self-regulated learning techniques can be taught to do so. It is important to keep in mind that the use of self-regulated learning strategies does not mean that a person is a self-regulated learner. No one is self-regulated all the time, during every classroom task. For example, a student may employ self-regulated learning strategies for mathematics, but not for language arts; before lunch, but not as much after lunch; at school, but not at home.

Self-regulated learning for classroom functions includes such habits as starting assignments on time, asking relevant questions, persisting with tasks, self-guiding to facilitate learning, and completing work promptly and accurately. Focusing attention, following through, and finishing a school task promptly and correctly are also considered skills of self-regulated learning (Manning, 1990). Three conditions that foster or hinder self-regulated learning are motivation, self-discipline, and cognitive competency (Corno, 1987).

Motivation theory promotes the idea that engagement in academic tasks depends partly on an individual's incentives. What we value varies among individuals and across time within an individual. Therefore, one's motivation to pursue a task is specific and personal. Another dimension of motivation is perception of task assignments. These perceptions include beliefs that a task is easy, difficult, boring, overwhelming, or totally irrelevant to one's life. A person's motivation to learn does or does not set up a condition for self-regulated learning.

A second determiner is what Corno calls *volition* or self-discipline. Volition is distinct from motivation in that it manages motivational processes such as self-percepts and attributions (Corno, personal communication, June 1990). According to theories of volition, motivated individuals may not possess enough self-discipline to selectively avoid unproductive intentions or distractors (Kuhl & Beckmann, 1985). These individuals do not have enough self-management skill to control their own learning. These distractors may come in the form of (1) competing, off-task thoughts, (2) irrelevant distractions such as someone moving about, (3) anxiety about the task at hand, (4) physical conditions such as anemia or other energy-draining ailments, or (5) combinations of above. Students may be capable, motivated, and still lack self-regulatory skills, due to inadequate self-discipline. Such students do not seem to have the adequate, powerful self-management skills required to overcome environmental distraction or competing emotional or physical needs.

The third condition required for self-regulation is *cognitive competency*. When students do not possess productive learning strategies, deficits in cognitive competencies are blamed. Students may be motivated to learn, have volitional skills required to focus, maintain attention, and finish tasks; but lack the cognitive skills required for awareness of effective learning strategies and how and when to use them. Indeed, as Corno points out some psychologists (e.g., Sternberg, 1982) believe that knowing when and how to use cognitive self-instructional strategies is a major aspect of intelligence (p. 252).

Deficits of this sort cause many students to view school as beyond their capabilities. Destructive thoughts such as these often cause students to experience lowered expectations for success and a lack of confidence in their own efforts to compensate for their failures in school. Seligman (1975) terms this self-limiting belief "learned helplessness." Often students who hold this belief will refuse to try in school. They give up. They drop out. Corno (1987) states that the most powerful and reliable motivator for school tasks is to teach students how to become self-motivated, by teaching them how to manage and control their own learning (p. 253).

Corno talks about how teachers are most often told to plan exciting, attention-grabbing lessons that eventually wear the teacher out and really do not help children overcome self-regulation/self-management learning deficits. Research studies such as those of Corno and Mandinach (1983), Corno and Rohrkemper (1985), Novak and Gowin (1984), Palincsar and Brown (1984), and Manning (1988) have documented that teaching self-regulation of learning is possible and "leads to the kinds of success experiences in school that in turn relate to positive feelings about oneself as a learner and a competent person" (Corno, 1987, p. 252).

Schunk (1986) discusses the verbal substrate of self-regulated learning. He defined self-regulated learning as a "process whereby students' cognitions (i.e. speech to self) manifest themselves in planful behaviors oriented toward learning" (p. 347). He based this assumption upon research evidence that self-verbalization is a key process that can help develop self-regulated learning among students. For example, as a type of rehearsal, verbalization may improve coding, storage, and retention of material; and thereby facilitate subsequent use and retrieval (Denny, 1975). Verbalization can help students maintain a positive task outlook and cope with task difficulties by including coping statements (Meichenbaum & Asarnow, 1979). In general, most of the research evidence suggests beneficial results, specifically that facilitative self-guiding speech promotes students' appropriate learning habits and metacognition. Recently, the links between strategy knowledge and the emergence of the two self-systems—attributional beliefs and motivation, and their role in energizing self-regulatory processes have become the most important aspects of the current version of metacognitive theory (Borkowski, Day, Saenz, Dietmeyer, Estrada, & Groteluschen, 1992). Since verbalization is considered a key process that aids the development of metacognition and self-regulated learning habits, it is important to understand how to develop supportive self-talk. The next two sections address facilitative internal dialogue (self-talk) and how to develop a language of self-support.

SELF-TALK LEVELS

Shad Helmstetter is a behavioral psychologist in the field of self-management. He believes that what we say to ourselves (our self-talk) determines our success at everything we attempt. Our past history and social interactions with the significant others in our lives contribute greatly to the content and form of this self-talk.

Counterproductive self-talk comprises 77% of everything we say to ourselves, according to the research of Helmstetter and other behavioral researchers. This maladaptive self-talk originates from our past negative programming contributed by social interactions. If we grew up in a fairly average, reasonably positive home, by the time we were eighteen we were told "No" or what we could not do, more than 148,000 times (Helmstetter, 1986, p. 8). This negative programming comes from well-intentioned parents and significant others who are attempting to protect us. As they guide us they often evaluate our every performance and our subconscious records these opinions (e.g., "don't do that, you can't do this, etc.''). Not nearly as often are we told what we can do or accomplish in life. This disproportionately high negative programming from others leads to negative internal dialogue. This is the same concept as Vygotsky's internalization, the three inner constructs of transactional analysis, and the three judges described by Butler (discussed in the next section of this chapter).

The brain does what it was designed to do: it simply records everything it receives. Helmstetter (1986, 1987) uses the analogy of the human brain as a personal computer's three basic parts: a "video" screen, a keyboard, and a program disk. The human body including our brain has similar parts. In humans, our appearance and our actions, the things we "display" to the world is comparable to the computer's video screen. The computer keyboard is similar to our five senses. Anything we see, hear, touch, smell, taste, or anything we say to ourselves is programmed or recorded into our brain through our keyboard. The floppy disk is our subconscious mind—where everything we experience is programmed or recorded. It is important to remember that whatever is programmed into your subconscious mind is *permanently* programmed.

Helmstetter is strong in this message that the brain creates whatever we tell it because he believes that the subconscious portion of the brain (floppy disk) has no choice, no evaluation, and makes no counterarguments. This portion of the brain accepts without evaluation whatever it is told. Then the mind regulates health, personal relationships, careers, and futures according to these messages. Helmstetter's perspective reminds one of information-processing theory, in the sense that whatever is put into the mind (input) will affect output: garbage in, garbage out.

Helmstetter (1986) defines self-talk in the following way: "self-talk is a way to override our past negative programming by erasing or replacing it with conscious, positive new-directions" (p. 59). Helmstetter names five levels of self-talk starting with the least beneficial and moving up to the most beneficial:

Level I Self-Talk	Negative Acceptance "I can't" "If only I could"
Level II Self-Talk	Recognition of the need to change "I need to" "I should"
Level III Self-Talk	Decision to change "I never" "I no longer"
Level IV Self-Talk	The Better You "I am"

Level V Self-Talk   Universal Affirmation
                       "It is"

Self-Talk Levels I and II have not worked to help anyone grow, change, or get better. Replace Levels I and II with Levels III and IV self-talk. On the surface, Level II self-talk may appear helpful, "I need to lose some weight." However, Helmstetter says the unspoken, but still-programmed remainder of such statements is "but I won't" or "but I just can't right now," etc. Level II self-talk does not promote accomplishment, instead it promotes excuses, then "guilt, disappointment, and an acceptance of our own self-imagined inadequacies" (p. 62). To remove frustrating roadblocks, Level III, IV, and V are the ones to use for helpful self-talk. Application of some of Helmstetter's ideas for teachers are found in Chapter 3.

SELF-TALK COMPONENTS

Pamela Butler (1992) discusses the kinds of self-talk we use. She mentions that we often use overbearing Judges rather than realistic Guides. She has developed a procedure for changing these Judges into a language of support. One of the first steps involves learning to recognize our unhealthy self-talk. A definitional section related to the three judges is provided below in order to facilitate such recognition:

DRIVERS: The unrealistic, relentless internal push to "get busy," "do it right," etc. Not to be confused with motivation or drive which can be healthy.

DRIVERS

Be Perfect	Pushes us constantly to perform at unreasonable levels. Limits us to 100 percent or nothing, with nothing in between, all or nothing attitude: "If I can't teach this lesson perfectly, I won't try at all."
Hurry Up	Pushes us to do everything quickly. One of the major contributors to the Type A behavior, associated with heart disease: "I better hurry because all the other teachers are ahead of me in this book."
Be Strong	Regards any need as a weakness to be overcome. Feelings of loneliness, sadness, or hurt are intolerable. Prevents us from asking for needed help: "I'm a new teacher. If I ask too many questions, they'll think I'm dumb."
Please Others	Involves an intense fear of rejection, even when the disapproving person is unimportant to us. We lose sight of our own feelings: "These students may not like me if I am too demanding. They have to like me or it will be awful."
Try Hard	Impervious to the setting of appropriate limits for ourselves. Taking on more and more responsibility without considering our own limitations. The inability to say No: "Why do I keep saying I'll be on another committee? I don't have a single free night during the week. I'm exhausted."

Next is a list of permitter self-talk statements that are suggested as a verbal way to combat the unrealistic Driver self-talk. Teachers who have begun to fight back with these verbal combatives report self-satisfaction that carries over into a more relaxed classroom.

DRIVERS AND PERMITTERS

Driver	Permitter Self-Talk
Be Perfect	There are no perfect human beings. Why do I keep trying to be a perfect teacher? Being my best and accepting mistakes is a healthier way to teach.
Hurry Up	It's okay to take the time these students and I need. We will learn well what we are learning instead of trying to finish the book first.
Be Strong	It's okay to have feelings and okay to express them. It is okay if I feel sad about where some of my students have to sleep at night.
Please Others	Pleasing others is rewarding, but it becomes maladaptive when we lose sight of our own feelings, in exchange. It's okay to please myself, too. I will lose who I am if I do not acknowledge my needs.
Try Hard	It's okay to recognize my own limits; it's okay to give my responsibilities enough time, backing, and energy to succeed.

The second group comprising Butler's judges is called Stoppers.

STOPPERS: Interfere with our spontaneous self-expression and therefore limit us. These are the internal messages that tell us "no," "don't," "only if," etc. The stoppers keep us from asserting ourselves.

STOPPERS

Catastrophizing	Verbally rehearsing horrible events that might occur if we were to engage in certain behaviors. We exaggerate the risk of engaging in that behavior so much, that we decide to do nothing: "If we go on field trips, the bus may break down, or the students may be more unruly, or we may get too far behind in our other work, etc."
Negative Self-Labeling	Attaching arbitrary judgments to natural, healthy impulses: "I'd really like to tell my principal how much I appreciate all that she does, but she might think I'm trying to get a raise or something extra, so I won't."
Rigid Requirements	Imposing a set of conditions that must occur before an action can take place. Usually begins with the word "If": "If everyone will approve of my suggestion, then I'll speak out at our next faculty meeting."
Witch Messages	Restraining ourselves with the word "Don't." Some examples are "don't change," "don't be yourself," "don't grow up," "don't be different." "Don't be so strict about this—just because we aren't told ahead of time about afternoon faculty meetings—don't be fussy about this."

Again there is a set of permitter self-talk statements to counteract the stoppers in our running day-to-day dialogue. These are important to remember when we notice that we are squelching our healthy, natural impulses to express our feelings and behaviors.

STOPPERS AND PERMITTERS

Stopper	Permitter Self-Talk
Catastrophizing	So what if? So what if the bus breaks down. They'll just send another one to carry us. It might not be so pleasant but it won't be catastrophic, or even awful.

Negative Self-Labeling	Many good acts of mine are squelched because I call myself or my behavior bad names. When I start this again, I'll just ignore it!
Rigid Requirements	These "Ifs" keep limiting my alternatives and block my feelings and behaviors. Next time I hear a rigid "If," I'll just go beyond it!
Witch Messages	Assert my right to listen and honor all aspects of myself.

The final group comprising Butler's Judges is called Confusers.

CONFUSERS: Using confuser self-talk distorts our own reality. This kind of self-talk, like the other two, is a maladaptive way of talking to ourselves. Some people have referred to the confuser self-talk as defective thinking, or irrational thinking.

CONFUSERS

Arbitrary Inference	Conclusion that is drawn without careful consideration of all the facts involved: "The student is not looking at me so she must not be listening to me."
Misattribution	The direction of blame or responsibility is moved away from the real causative agent onto something or someone else (similar to external locus of control mentioned earlier in this chapter): "That student makes me furious."
Cognitive Deficiency	The failure to be aware of the complete picture; tunnel vision: "The reason Stewart is failing is because he does not concentrate."
Over-generalization	To recognize only the similarities between people or between events and to ignore differences. Racial, cultural, and gender prejudices are based on this confuser: "I'll carry to class some of my *Sports Illustrated* magazines for my boys to read."
Either/Or Thinking	Seeing everything as black or white, agree or disagree; no consideration is given for degrees, continuum, or in-between ground. Dichotomous thinking is a synonym: "Since I am a teacher, I keep being asked if I am authoritarian or permissive. I'm really not either one, but I feel forced to choose one."
Vague Language	The use of words that have not been defined clearly by ourselves (e.g., success, happiness, wealth): "I just want to be a success in my teaching."
Magnification	Overestimation of the importance of an event or a situation; blowing something out of reasonable proportions: "I am a terrible teacher."

And again, we can distort our reality less if we are alert to the confuser self-talk utterances such as arbitrary inferences, either-or thinking, and magnification. A list of ways to combat this confusion is presented below.

CONFUSERS AND PERMITTERS

Confuser	Permitter Self-Talk
Arbitrary Thinking	Be specific here. When I say "I'm a failure as a teacher" what I really mean and should say is that half of my class failed their midterm examination.

Misattribution	Students don't really make me furious. I choose to react in a negative way to their classroom behavior. What steps can I take to react in a more positive way? I am in control of my emotions; my students are not.
Cognitive Deficiency	What's the whole picture? A school problem is rarely so simple that it can be explained by one factor. What are other contributing factors to this problem?
Over-generalization	Oops, watch it! Ginger is the best basketball player in my class. Why did I assume that only the boys would want to read *Sports Illustrated*? Come to think of it, Sam would rather read poetry than play sports at recess.
Either/Or Thinking	I can think in degrees, and in between ends of continua. I will stop allowing others to categorize me so easily as either this or that. It often is not that simple and depends a great deal on the specific situation.
Vague Language	Success is in the eye of the beholder, just as beauty is. I must be sure I know how someone is defining their success, their happiness, etc.
Magnification	Bring it down to size by dating and indexing. Dating means to tell precisely at what particular time something occurred (e.g., I was a terrible teacher last Friday when I was having PMS). Indexing means being specific about the uniqueness of each person or event (e.g., Ms. X is a stricter teacher during academic learning time and Ms. Y is a stricter teacher during free time).

Metacognition as awareness and regulation of thinking involves processes such as becoming aware of our own inner speech, how we are driving, stopping, and confusing ourselves. The five steps needed to foster a language of self-support include (1) Awareness; Listen to what you are saying to yourself; (2) Evaluation; Ask if your self-talk is helpful; (3) Identification; Determine what Driver, Stopper, or Confuser is maintaining your inner speech; (4) Support of yourself; Replace unhelpful Judges with Permitters; and (5) Develop a guide; Decide what action will fit with your more helpful way of talking to yourself. In addition, the steps to learn a language of support necessitates self-questioning, self-correcting, and self-reinforcing. These are also subskills of metacognitive self-regulation. Therefore, metacognition is an integral part of learning to talk to ourselves in a healthy, facilitative manner.

SUMMARY

Beginning this chapter is a glimpse at the historical development of metacognitive processes and a differentiation between the constructs of cognition and metacognition. Then a collection of theories, concepts, and approaches is presented that overlaps with the definitions of metacognition. These theories, concepts, and approaches also are intended to provide a deeper and richer understanding of the motivational, affective components of metacognition. Theories and/or approaches that are discussed include rational emotive thinking, transactional analysis, attribution theory, self-efficacy theory, self-regulated learning, self-talk levels, and the self-talk components.

CHAPTER 2

Fostering Positive Mental Growth of Teachers

OVERVIEW

Metacognitive knowledge and monitoring to enhance positive mental states in teachers (i.e., self-awareness, self-acceptance, and self-responsibility) are addressed in this chapter. This discussion will first center around the direct link between the internal (intrapersonal) state of teachers and their resultant social (interpersonal) skills with students. The reciprocal relationship, when the social experiences of the teacher impact upon the mental well-being of the teacher, is also described. Finally, metacognitive strategies are outlined that foster the development of greater teacher self-awareness, self-acceptance, and self-responsibility which in turn promotes greater awareness of students' strengths, acceptance of students, and responsibility for the classroom environment. The chapter begins with a rationale concerned with why personal dimensions of the teacher should be approached through metacognitive lens.

Self-Questions

1. *Knowledge.* What is psychocybernetics?

2. *Comprehension.* Compare and contrast teacher self-awareness with teacher self-acceptance.

3. *Application.* Describe the connections between metacognition and teacher self-awareness, self-acceptance, and self-responsibility.

4. *Analysis.* Explain the components of I-messages and why each one is important.

5. *Synthesis.* Outline several ideas for ways to teach self-awareness, self-acceptance, and self-responsibility to your class of students, modifying some of the suggestions in this chapter.

6. *Evaluation.* What are the cautions and encouragements for addressing the personal dimension as a component of metacognition for teachers and students.

CONNECTING TEACHERS' PERSONAL GROWTH TO METACOGNITION

In the classroom, the degree to which teachers are able to identify their own strengths and limitations will determine the degree to which they are able to identify their students' strengths and limitations. Teacher self-awareness is crucial because it predicts keen awareness of students' characteristics. *Intra* determines *inter*. Therefore, teacher self-awareness, which is a metacognitive skill, is a means to an end. The end is the educational goal of identification of students' strengths and limitations. The means is teachers' own mental self-awareness of their own strengths and weaknesses. Know yourself in order to know others.

The same kind of philosophy is applied to teacher self-acceptance and self-responsibility. Again the *intra*psychological functioning (e.g., self-acceptance and self-responsibility) determines the teacher's ability to accept students and regulate classroom functioning. Often when we teach this concept, students will respond with: "If you don't like yourself, others won't like you." This may sometimes be true, but it is not the point we are trying to make. Instead, if they understand the real message here, it has nothing to do with students accepting the teacher; it has to do with the teacher accepting the students based on the teacher's self-acceptance. Self-acceptance becomes a means, enabling the acceptance of others. When a college student responds with: "If I accept myself, then I am more likely to accept my students," this undergraduate receives an "A." Seriously, this prospective teacher has accurately assessed the intended message (i.e., It is very important for teachers to possess self-acceptance, not as a selfish preoccupation with self; but because this kind of acceptance fosters the acceptance of others, which is absolutely essential in the classroom). The single most important factor in motivating students is encouragement. By focusing on students' strengths, their feelings of confidence and self-worth are enhanced.

The same "*intra* to *inter*" thinking can be applied to self-responsibility. Self-responsibility is a prerequisite to responsibility for others. The teacher who loses his/her temper (e.g., shouts, goes crazy) is modeling out-of-control behavior. The first ingredient in a well-managed classroom is a responsible teacher. This is not to say that self-regulated teachers never have classroom management problems. It is to say, however, that the other-controlled teacher will more likely have students who are incapable of exhibiting self-guidance. Students often learn responsibility from a responsible teacher model. Said another way, teachers who are unable to manage themselves, frequently have great difficulties managing the complexity of a classroom. *Inter* follows *intra*.

It is important to note that *intra*psychological functioning is also affected by *inter*psychological situations. There exists between the two an element of reciprocity. In Eastern thought, this concept is called "karma" which means that "for every social transaction, there is an emotional reaction" within us. For example, if we, as teachers, mistreat a student, that social transaction or mistreatment will come back and reside within us, affecting us adversely. We live in a closed system, according to the concept of karma. If on the other hand, we treat a student kindly, this act of kindness returns to us and we are positively affected. We feel good about ourselves and our abilities to treat others in a caring manner. Therefore, teachers affect and are affected, with each decision they make and exercise. Therefore, teacher decision making should be mentally monitored and regulated by the teacher.

To sum, the self-awareness, self-acceptance, and self-responsibility (intrapsychological functioning) of the teacher should be fostered because the *intra*psychological relationship of teachers within themselves will directly affect the teachers' ability to know, accept, and guide their students. It is vital to our educational future for teachers to build strong relationships and interactions with students. In addition, it is also important that teachers become aware of the effect that their social interactions have upon their mental attitude. Teachers can never mistreat or treat children kindly without experiencing corresponding negative or positive feelings within their own psyche. This is due to the reciprocal characteristic between *intra* — *inter* functioning.

The remainder of the chapter provides activities, exercises, and further explanation of the personal dimensions of self-awareness, self-acceptance, and self-responsibility. We realize that some of our ideas may require intense introspection and mental deliberation.

We ask that you approach this material with an open mind and more than likely it will be an enriching personal and professional experience for you.

Self-Awareness

Many, or possibly most of us, do not see ourselves clearly. We often magnify our weaknesses and minimize our strengths. The result is seeing a distorted view of ourselves. We know that how we view ourselves in large part is the result of how we were reared and our interactions with significant others (Chapter 1). Our goal is to help you create a clearer and more accurate description of yourself.

SELF-AWARENESS EXERCISE #1

Take a few minutes and think about your own genuine strengths and limitations. Use the categories of cognitive, social, emotional, and physical to guide your thinking. You may either divide your paper in half and write *strengths* at the top of the page and *weaknesses* at the bottom or place a plus (+) next to assets and a minus (-) next to your limitations. To assist you we have provided definitions and a strength example from each of the four areas. *Cognitive*: knowing, intellectual functioning, characteristics of the mind. A cognitive strength is the ability to reason well. *Social*: one's relationship between self and others. A social strength is friendliness. *Emotional*: one's relationship with oneself. An emotional strength is positive self-esteem. *Physical*: pertaining to the body. A physical strength is stamina.

Now look back over your list to see what you have learned about yourself? Have you listed more strengths? More weaknesses? Do you have a majority of items in one or more categories? What can you say about this picture of yourself? If you have listed many more weaknesses than strengths you are being too hard and expecting too much of yourself. In addition, if you are the kind of person who dwells on your weaknesses this may cause you to become overly judgmental and critical of others. Certainly, there is nothing wrong with having faults. We all have them. Everyone is a unique combination of strengths and weaknesses. The problem lies not in recognizing our weaknesses or limitations but in our "overindulgence" of these weaknesses so that they have a disproportionate influence on how we view ourselves and our subsequent behavior with others.

Look back over your list of weaknesses. Examples of weaknesses many students often see in themselves are: fat, shy, uncoordinated, or dumb. These words have negative connotations and should be eliminated from your list, if not your vocabulary. Try instead, changing the item to be purely descriptive. For example, rather than saying "shy" try "When I am with people I do not know, I do not like to initiate a conversation." Try to revise the item so that it is limited to a particular situation where the trait occurs. Now take some time and revise each of the weaknesses keeping the following suggestions in mind: (1) eliminate overly general pejorative language, (2) be accurate and factual, and (3) relate the weakness to a specific situation.

The next step in self-awareness is to become aware of, acknowledge, and share your strengths with others. Look back over your list of strengths and try to think of any you have overlooked. Think of kind words your family or friends have said to you and include these. This list should now provide a starting point at which you may reflect about what a unique person you really are. We would like for you to go a step further and take these isolated words and write complete sentences creating a more accurate description of yourself. For example, one of our students, Denise, used the word "musical" to initially describe herself. In her revision she changed it to, "I have a beautiful voice and love to sing." In Chapter 1 we talked about how a majority of our thoughts about ourselves and our self-talk is negative. We have spent a lifetime listening to other people say negative things to us, and then internalizing these statements and repeating them over and over until we believe we really do possess all these negative qualities. This is the first step in creating a new and positive picture of yourself.

SELF-AWARENESS EXERCISE #2

Now it is time to share your strengths orally with a fellow student. An initial response is often to moan and groan and say, "Do we have to?" After you get past your initial reticence you will enjoy this activity. Really you will. While sharing your strengths it is very important that you maintain eye contact and that you "objectively" and "non-comparatively" report your strengths to your partner. When you have finished describing your strengths, reverse roles and you become the listener while your partner becomes the discussant.

How did orally sharing your strengths with another person make you feel? Students often describe themselves as "anxious" or "embarrassed." Most of us are not accustomed to thinking about our strengths and even less comfortable talking about our positive attributes with someone else. The American culture endorses being modest about our accomplishments and strengths. We have all heard the phrase, "Actions speak louder than words." Often, our parents raised us with the admonition, "Do not brag, it is conceited." This kind of thinking is counterproductive. It is time for you to acknowledge your strengths, capitalize on them, and share them with others. We are all unique combinations of strengths and weaknesses, with no two individuals identical in every respect. Successful, happy people dwell on their strengths, not their weaknesses and this is what you should begin doing. As you become more adept at recognizing and expressing your own strengths, you will in turn, be more likely to recognize and acknowledge the strengths of others, particularly the children in your class. We want teachers to dwell on their strengths so they will be more likely to dwell on the strengths, not the weaknesses, of their students.

SELF-AWARENESS EXERCISE #3

In order to continue thinking about and internalizing your strengths, we suggest that you write a cognitive, social, emotional and physical strength each time you come to class. If your college teacher agrees, these should be given to your college teacher and he or she will make comments about how a particular strength will be helpful in teaching. By the end of the term, students usually report an increased self-awareness and appreciation of themselves. Using all four areas (i.e., cognitive, social, emotional, physical) helps them to see a total person and transfer this holistic view to finding strengths in their students.

Later in this book we will discuss other ways of helping you to remember your strengths. For example, in Chapter 3 we will describe the steps involved in making a self-talk tape where affirmations are recorded and listened to throughout the day. Cue cards containing brief affirmations are described in several subsequent chapters.

Self-Acceptance

We would like to propose for your consideration the idea of "range of tolerance level" concerning your own imperfections and mistakes. In our past classes, we have had our students write what they say to themselves when they spill something, forget something, or mispronounce a word. Everyone spills. Everyone forgets. Everyone mispronounces words. Everyone makes mistakes. Young children will certainly spill, forget, mispronounce words, and make other human errors. The point is that the manner in which you treat yourself during or after mistake-making will be similar to the reaction you will have when someone else makes that same mistake. When we broaden our range of tolerance for ourselves when mistakes are made, we simultaneously broaden our range of tolerance for other people's mistakes. For example, if we can turn over a glass of orange juice without verbally flagellating and condemning ourselves (e.g., "I'm so stupid! What a klutz!") then we are much more likely to stop verbally beating up others when they make similar human errors. This is not to promote acceptance of slovenly behavior and a lowering of standards. It is an acceptance of humanness, in ourselves first, followed by an acceptance of others. We don't have to love the spilled orange juice mistake, but we can respond in a more caring way to ourselves (e.g., "What a mess! I need to clean this up now."). The focus is on the mistake itself, not on the condemnation of the person making the mistake. Once we become more accepting of ourselves, even in the face of mistake-making, then we are more accepting of others and tolerant of their mistakes. Individuals who are overly critical and judgmental of themselves tend to be critical and judgmental of others.

Laughter, Joy, and Happiness

Some of educator Leo Buscaglia's ideas about the celebration of each person's uniqueness have particular application to our discussion of both self-awareness and self-acceptance. In his books *Personhood* (1978), *Living, Loving, and Learning* (1982), and *Loving Each Other* (1984), Buscaglia's message is always the same: we are all human beings, with strengths and weaknesses, but we are all unique, wonderful, important people. We must let people know that we make mistakes, do not have all the answers, and that we experience the gamete of human emotions. The emotions that Buscaglia believes are particularly beneficial for humans to experience are joy and happiness. The physical manifestation that expresses these emotions is laughter. All too often humor and laughter are absent from our schools and classrooms. We are so busy writing objectives, staying on task, meeting standards, managing students, and the like that we often forget that schools are places where "human beings" live, work, and play. John Dewey once said, "Education is life itself, not just the preparation for life." We must allow and even encourage the expression of all human emotions (channeled constructively, of course) in our classrooms, but particularly laughter. As a teacher, you need to value humor as a way to make teaching and learning more fully human. Take every opportunity to laugh at yourself and share your mistakes with your students. This way, children understand that incorrect answers, making mistakes, and being foolish are not the end of the world. They see that after all, everyone of us is "human" and making mistakes a natural part of life. We shouldn't take ourselves too seriously. Laughter enhances our level of self-acceptance.

Laughter has a number of distinct advantages, particularly within our schools and classrooms. First, it helps us cope better with psychological and physical adversity. Our brains release over 2,000 chemicals that produce changes in our bodies. One of these biochemicals, endorphins, serves as a natural pain-killer, helps to strengthen our immune system, and encourages a sense of well-being.

Norman Cousins, long-time editor of *The Saturday Review*, wrote a book in 1981 called *Anatomy of an Illness* in which he related his personal conquest over a debilitating disease. Essentially his spine was disintegrating and he was experiencing excruciating pain that kept him from sleeping. He implemented a program of laughter therapy including Marx Brothers and Candid Camera episodes as well as excerpts from funny books such as E. B. White's *Subtreasury of American Humor* (1941). He found that ten minutes of genuine belly laughter provided him with at least two hours of pain-free sleep. Cousins credited his recovery to his laughter therapy. However, he does not say that all diseases can be cured through laughter but that humor, laughter, and a positive outlook will help your body to mobilize itself to fight disease.

Laughter is also a physical and social relaxant. Laughter and muscle tension are incompatible. If you are performing a task that requires concentration, such as hitting a softball, dunking a basketball, threading a needle, or carrying something heavy and someone says something funny, what happens? You have to stop the activity; you find it impossible to keep your muscles tensed while laughing. Similarly, laughter eases social tension. If a person is nervous, anxious, frustrated, or uncomfortable, humor breaks the ice and makes the situation more bearable by relieving the emotional pressure.

Laughter is also a good workout; it aids circulation, enhances respiration, and massages the abdominal muscles. And finally, laughter is pleasurable for its own sake—it is nice to listen to! It is difficult to hear people laughing without catching the laughing bug yourself. Join in, it's healthy!

Buscaglia advocates, some would say even preaches, the value of positive thoughts, words, and actions. He discusses the importance of finding our strengths, our uniqueness, developing them and sharing them with others. What do you share of yourself with others? Are you a model of fear, incompetence, and disillusion, or are you a model of spontaneity, laughter, joy, sensitivity, and maturity. Obviously, if you are going to be a teacher you need to be a person who radiates these latter characteristics. The teacher who possesses these sorts of "human" characteristics fosters them in children.

One of our graduate students who was married with two children was particularly affected by Buscaglia's words. She discussed with her husband and children Buscaglia's advice to examine your words and see if they are joyful or hurtful. Unbeknown to her, the ten-year-old daughter, Valerie, began recording instances of "joyful" and "hurtful" words uttered by the mother, father, brother, and herself. Following is an excerpt from the daughter's record.

	RYAN	VALERIE	MOM	DAD
Joyful Words	Wow! I love you. You are a sweetie. I'll encourage you.	You are the sweetest mom. Would you like anything? You are my precious. You're the best. I love you Dad.	You have a kind heart. I love you too. That's great. You are a good thing. Thank you for being kind to Ryan. Thank you for flushing, ha, ha.	Way to go! You are a sweetie. I like how you ate your salad. I love you. That is super!
Hurtful Words	Get it now! You're mean. Give me that control. Your stomach looks like a beachball. If you make me walk I'll scream.	Go away! I don't want you in here. Stay away. You are aggravating me to death.	Brush your teeth with toothpaste. You yelled that. Clean up this pit.	Don't be a baby. Calm down and hush up. You are not doing that now. You said the *d* word at Stone Mountain.

Take the time to examine your own words to others. Are they joyful or hurtful? If your words contain a lot of negative, hurtful messages, then self-acceptance is poor. On the other hand, if your messages are mainly positive and joyful, self-acceptance is high.

The environment we grow up in plays a large part in determining how we feel about ourselves. Unquestionably, the parental care you received in the early years played an enormous role in defining your image of yourself. All through childhood, parents and significant others, including relatives, teachers, and friends, told us with their words and actions which of our behaviors were acceptable and which were unacceptable. The words and actions of the parent or significant others range from harmful and negative (i.e., criticizing, discouraging, yelling, creating obstacles, blaming, shaming, sarcasm, physical punishment) to helpful and positive (i.e., smiling, touching, kissing, cuddling, holding, hugging, complimenting, encouraging, listening, answering). How we feel about ourselves, to a large extent, is dependent upon and interconnected with the judgments of the significant others in our lives. A positive, supportive environment will enhance the development of a sense of self-worth. The opposite environment will more than likely contribute to the development of children and ultimately adults who have low self-worth.

The following story is adapted from an activity in Canfield and Wells's book (1976) entitled *100 Ways to Enhancing Self Concept in the Classroom*. This story will help to illustrate how a person's self-worth can be adversely affected, even destroyed by the words of others.

> This is the story of Josh. Notice what a healthy and happy child he is. Josh possesses characteristics and traits such as "smart," "kind," "neat," "friendly," and "athletic" to name a few. As you read his story we want you to tear off a piece of Josh each time you read something negative or detrimental to his self-concept.

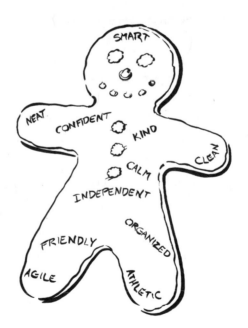

Joshua got up one morning feeling pretty good about himself. He had a good nights sleep and was ready for the day. His mother called from downstairs, "Get up Joshua, you're always running late. What do you want to do, miss the buss? Hurry!

He tried to hurry, but got his shoes on the wrong feet, then he forgot his belt and buttoned his shirt crooked. When he got downstairs, his brother laughed at him and his mother said, "Just look at you, do you want to look silly going to school? Let's get you straightened out. I always have to do everything for you. And another thing, did you make your bed? Don't know why I'm asking, of course you didn't— you never do anything without being told. Now eat your breakfast, and hurry."

Joshua got on the bus feeling a little rough, but not completed destroyed. As he started to sit down in one seat, the person there said, "Yuk, I don't want to sit with a silly old boy." So he went and sat by himself.

At school he went to his class where he put his things in his desk, then began looking for his pencil. Where was that pencil? Oh yes, it was in his room at home—how stupid—it sure couldn't help him there. "I can't remember anything at all."

His teacher, Mrs. Filibuster, came in and looked especially stern to him today. "Oh well, here goes: good morning, Mrs. Filibuster, how are you?" "Joshua, whatever are you doing here? It's too early for you to be in class, you should be in the cafeteria with your group—can't you remember anything?" "Sorry, Mrs. Filibuster—I forgot." Off Joshua trudged to the cafeteria to wait 2 minutes until the first bell rang to come to classes.

I sure do wish I could do a better job remembering and being a person people would be proud of, thought Josh.

When class finally started, Josh remembered he didn't have a pencil, so he raised his hand and said, "Mrs. Filibuster I don't have a pencil, may I borrow one?" "Josh, you had plenty of time to get a pencil this morning when you were in the room. I can't believe you came with no pencil. How do you expect to do anything? You'll just have to stay in at recess to do the work with a borrowed pencil while other children are out playing—good grief what are we going to do with you?"

Josh's day seemed to be going downhill, so he was very glad when it was over. He just must have gotten up on the wrong side of the bed because he (1) had to redo his math paper because it was messy; (2) wasn't called on when he really knew the answer, but was when he didn't; (3) dropped his milk at lunch; (4) had to go to the bathroom, but wasn't allowed, so he wet his pants.

How glad he would be to get home! When he finally did, his brother said, "Josh, don't forget you can't go out to play until your room is completely clean!"

What is left of Josh? You are most likely left holding only a small part of what once was a very healthy child. Keep this small remembrance of Josh as a reminder of the impact your words have on others.

After hearing these negative and demeaning comments long enough the child internalizes them, begins to talk to self in a similar way, and finally comes to believe them. An impressive body of research documents how teachers' words and actions affect how children feel about themselves. This process is commonly referred to as teacher expectations.

Teacher Expectations   When children enter school they soon are confronted with the fact that teachers have different expectations for different students (Good, 1986). According to Good (1987), early in the school year a teacher forms expectations based on students' achievement and behavior. However, a variety of other factors, such as how students present themselves or are labeled, also influence teacher expectations (Dusek & Joseph, 1983; Fredricks, 1974; Spencer-Hall, 1981). Teacher expectations can be defined as inferences that teachers make about the future academic achievement and general classroom behavior of students, based on what they know about these students right now (Good, 1987).

Are the expectations that teachers have for their students a problem? Certainly, accurate expectations are extremely important because they allow teachers to set realistic academic goals and to plan appropriate instruction. However, teacher expectations become harmful when they are based on inaccurate information, are rigid and unbending, and result in inappropriate treatment of students (Patriarca & Kragt, 1986).

Unfortunately, considerable research evidence, based on observation studies, has documented differences in teacher behavior toward high and low expectation and high and low achievement students. This teacher treatment tells students how they are to behave and perform. If the treatment remains consistent, a student's self-concept, conduct, levels of aspiration and motivation, and interactions with the teacher are affected. In turn, these student variables reaffirm the teacher's initial beliefs as accurate. If teacher expectations are unaltered, student overall achievement as well as other outcomes are modified. Those students receiving high expectation treatment perform near potential, while those considered "lows" do not gain as much academically as they would have if they had been taught differently. This pattern has become known as the "self-fulfilling prophecy" (Brophy & Good, 1974).

The "self-fulfilling prophecy" was initially described in a well-known study by Robert Rosenthal and Lenore Jacobson. In 1968, they collaborated in writing *Pygmalian in the Classroom* where they reported results of a study on the impact of teacher expectations. In the study, teachers at Oak Grove Elementary School were told that, based on an intelligence test, students in their classes were "late bloomers" and were "likely to show unusual intellectual gains in the year ahead." In actuality, the students had been chosen at random, and were of the same ability as their classmates. Eight months later, when the students were tested again, those who had been identified as "late bloomers" showed greater gains in IQ than their classmates. Rosenthal and Jacobson cited that the reason for these gains was the fact that the teachers held artificially high expectations for them. The authors referred to this phenomenon as the Pygmalian effect or a self-fulfilling prophecy.

Publication of *Pygmalian* was surrounded in controversy (see Elashoff & Snow, 1971). Replications of the study have failed to produce the same results. However, a great deal of research has continued by many different investigators and generally supports the idea that teachers' expectations can and do affect classroom behavior and student achievement (Brophy, 1987; Cooper & Good, 1983; Dusek, 1985), particularly in the earlier grades.

Brophy and Good (1974) developed a model to describe how teachers' expectations can become self-fulfilling prophecies:

1. The teacher expects specific behavior and achievement from particular students.

2. Because of these expectations, the teacher behaves differently toward different students.

3. This treatment by the teacher tells each student what behavior and achievement the teacher expects, and it affects the student's self-concept, achievement motivation, and level of aspiration.

4. If this teacher treatment is consistent over time, and if the student does not actively resist or change it in some way, it will shape the student's achievement and behavior. High-expectation students will be led to achieve at high levels, but the achievement of low-expectation students will decline.

5. With time, the student's achievement and behavior will conform more and more closely to that expected by the teacher.

Results from classroom interaction studies indicate that teachers generally respond less favorably to students they perceive as low achievers and more favorably to those they perceive as high achievers. After reviewing the research on behavior associated with teacher expectation effects, Rosenthal (1974) identified four general factors: socioemotional climate, verbal input, verbal output, and feedback. His convenient scheme for summarizing teachers' differential treatment of high and low achieving students is presented in Figure 2.1.

At this time we would like to make several points about the differential treatment of students by teachers. First, Brophy (1983) indicates that even though student achievement is affected by teacher expectations, these effects probably make only 5 to 10 percent difference. Second, differential student treatment does not occur in all classrooms. Third, some forms of differential treatment may be appropriate at times. As teachers we should

---

Socioemotional Climate of Classroom

Low expectation students receive *less*

1. smiles
2. head nods
3. forward body lean
4. eye contact
5. support and friendliness
6. friendly interaction and are seated further away from the teacher

than high expectation students.

Verbal Inputs

Low expectation students receive *less*

1. opportunities to learn new material
2. difficult material
3. benefit of doubt in borderline cases in the grading of tests
4. use of effective instructional methods when time is limited

than high expectation students.

Verbal Outputs

Low expectation students

1. receive less wait time for answering a question
2. receive less clue giving
3. receive less repetition of questions
4. receive less rephrasing of questions
5. are called on less often to respond to questions

than high expectation students.

Affective Feedback

Low expectation students receive

1. more criticism for failure or inappropriate response
2. less praise following an appropriate response
3. less attention and interaction from teacher
4. more interaction with teacher privately than publicly
5. briefer and less informative feedback to their questions

FIGURE 2–1
Communication of
Low Expectations

than high expectation students.

---

hold high, positive, and realistic expectations for all students, but that does not mean that we should provide identical treatment for all students. Based on careful assessment of individual students' needs, teachers might provide differential treatment.

Research shows that undesirable differentiation of treatment for students can be avoided or eliminated. The guidelines provided in Figure 2.2 can help teachers to minimize the negative effects of teacher expectations.

FIGURE 2–2 Guidelines for Avoiding the Negative Effects of Teacher Expectations

Use information about students from tests, cumulative folders, and other teachers very carefully.

Examples

1. Some teachers avoid reading cumulative folders at the beginning of the year.
2. Be critical and objective about the reports you hear from other teachers.

Be flexible in your use of grouping strategies.

Examples

1. Review work of students in different groups often and experiment with new groupings.
2. Use different groups for different subjects.
3. Use mixed-ability groups in cooperative exercises.

Make sure all the students are challenged.

Examples

1. Don't say, "This is easy, I know you can do it."
2. Offer a wide range of problems, and encourage all students to try a few of the harder ones for extra credit. Try to find something positive about these attempts.

Be especially careful about how you respond to low-achieving students during class discussions.

Examples

1. Give them prompts, cues, and time to answer.
2. Give ample praise for good answers.
3. Call on low achievers as often as high achievers.

Use materials that show a wide range of ethnic groups.

Examples

1. Check readers and library books. Is there ethnic diversity?
2. If few materials are available, ask students to research and create their own, based on community or family sources.

Make sure that your teaching does not reflect racial, ethnic, or sexual stereotypes or prejudice.

Examples

1. Use a checking system to be sure that you call on and include all students.

2. Monitor the content of the tasks you assign. Do boys get the "hard" math problems to work at the board? Do you avoid having students with limited English give oral presentations?

Be fair in evaluation and disciplinary procedures.

Examples

1. Make sure equal offenses receive equal punishment. Find out from students in an anonymous questionnaire whether you seem to be favoring certain individuals.
2. Try to grade student work without knowing the identity of the student. Ask another teacher to give you a "second opinion" from time to time.

Communicate to all students that you believe they can learn—and mean it.

Examples

1. Return papers that do not meet standards with specific suggestions for improvements.
2. If students do not have the answers immediately, wait, probe, and then help them think through an answer.

Involve all students in learning tasks and in privileges.

Examples

1. Use some system to make sure you give each student practice in reading, speaking, and answering questions.
2. Keep track of who gets to do what job. Are some students always on the list while others seldom make it?

Monitor your nonverbal behavior.

Examples

1. Do you lean away or stand farther away from some students? Do some students get smiles when they approach your desk while others get only frowns?
2. Does your tone of voice vary with different students?
3. Do you avoid touching some students in your class?

Source: Woolfolk, A. *Educational Psychology*, 5/E. Copyright © 1993 by Allyn and Bacon. Reprinted by permission.

Rational Thinking   An important aspect of self-acceptance concerns the internal messages we give to ourselves. In Chapter 1 we discussed Ellis's rational-emotive therapy (1962, 1969, 1977) and Butler's (1981, 1992) and Helmstetter's (1986, 1987, 1991) ideas of self-talk and internal dialogue. The ideas put forth by these individuals have consistently documented the link between what we say to ourselves, and what we feel and how we behave.

If you remember from our discussion of Ellis's rational-emotive therapy; a stimulus or activating event (Point A) does not exclusively cause an emotional response or behavior (Point C). But rather, it is a person's beliefs (mediations that include self-statements and thoughts) that affect emotions and behaviors (Point C). The self-verbalizations at Point B mediate between the situation/stimulus A and response C. If this self-talk is negative, irrational, critical, and self-defeating it contributes to maladaptive intrapsychological functioning. If a majority of our self-talk is negative (Helmstetter, 1986), it certainly will have a disproportionately negative influence on how we view ourselves. What we learn to accept is a less than positive picture or image of ourselves. If on the other hand, our self-talk is positive, rational, uncritical and supportive, it promotes healthy intrapsychological functioning.

A great deal of research in the field of education and psychology supports the assumption that when teachers better understand, accept, and like themselves they have a much greater capacity to understand, accept, and like students. *Intra* to *inter*! For example, previous research has found that "above average" levels of self-esteem are positively associated with greater acceptance of others (Swinn & Geiger, 1965), better adjustment (Williams & Cole, 1969), greater social effectiveness (Shrauger & Rosenberg, 1970), and positively related to school environment (Purkey, 1970). Significant relationships have also been found between teacher self-regard and such factors as how effective they tend to be as teachers (Noad, 1979; Usher & Hanke, 1971), how well students see themselves (Landry, 1974), and how well students achieve (Aspy & Buhler, 1975).

If we have a positive, realistic, accepting view of ourselves, we tend to respond to people and situations in similar positive and accepting ways. The following example will also illustrate the A-B-C framework of Ellis's rational emotional therapy. Look at a third grade teacher in response to the following classroom situation. The students have been asked by the teacher to work independently on a creative writing assignment. During this assignment, two students carry on a private conversation, ignoring the teacher's directions. The students' behavior (Point A) can elicit two different types of self-talk or internal dialogue (Point B). The teacher may think or say to self, "What's wrong with Jared and Josh? I told them to do this assignment by themselves, and those two did not listen. They never listen. What do I have to do, stand on my head to get them to pay attention? Fine, I will give them a zero." A second way of responding is more positive and realistic. "Jared and Josh are whispering. I wonder if they misunderstood the directions. I will go over and ask them quietly if they have any questions about the assignment and remind them that they are to work by themselves."

Clearly, in the first example, the teacher's perception and self-talk are self-defeating. The teacher exaggerates the meaning of the students' behavior and overgeneralizes the situation by assuming personal inadequacy. This teacher's self-talk is self-defeating, negative, anxiety-provoking and reflects low self-worth. The second example reflects a more positive and realistic appraisal of the situation and certainly forms a more positive and constructive pattern of internal self-statements. In other words, if teachers have a positive and realistic view of themselves they also tend to perceive students as valuable, able, and responsible.

This classroom example also can be explained through the Ellis A-B-C framework. Point A is the students' talking. Point C is the teacher's behavioral response. Point B is the the teacher's self-talk that promotes the response at Point C. The nature of the teacher's response C (e.g., rational, irrational, sane, crazy) is related to how he/she talks about the situation to self at point B. The verbal self-regulation comes into play at point

---

RATIONAL THINKING EXERCISE #4

Listen for the demands that people make, including yourself. Listen further for the meaning or evaluations they attach for not getting their demands fulfilled. Check to see whether you can recognize an activating event (A), a rational or irrational belief (B), and an emotional consequence (C). Try this one:

A student tells you that he thinks he failed his test and is very depressed. He says: "I think I failed the test. It's awful. I'm so stupid, I'm never going to pass anything." A _____, B _____, C _____.

Discussion: The emotional consequence (C) is what he feels—depressed. The activating event (A) is his thinking that he failed the test. (A) is a statement about reality as the child perceives it; it is a fact. There is no rational belief stated here. Several irrational beliefs may be found: "It's awful. I'm so stupid. I'm never going to pass anything." All of the irrational belief self-statements are evaluative, exaggerated distortions of reality and depression inducing.

B and affects responses at point C. In the present example, if the teacher engaged in the first sample of self-talk (Point B), the resulting teacher behavior at Point C would more than likely be very negative. The second set of self-talk dialogue would probably result in a more rational and sensible teacher response. Please complete Exercise #4.

Self-Image Another important aspect of self-acceptance is a favorable self-image, or the positive visualization of ourselves as worthwhile individuals, capable of accomplishing the goals we set for ourselves. Maltz (1960) describes how we can achieve goals via facilitative self-imaging.

Maxwell Maltz, a plastic surgeon, became interested in the personality effects of facial plastic surgery. There were dramatic and sudden changes in most individuals' personality when their faces were changed. However, what intrigued Maltz the most were the cases in which patients continued to feel inadequate and experienced feelings of inferiority even though the "ugly" facial feature had been corrected. For these people the reconstruction of the physical appearance itself was not the reason for improvements in personality variables, such as self-esteem or self-confidence. Maltz began referring to the "face of personality." If this mental image of oneself did not change along with the physical improvements of the face, then the individual continued to behave in a scarred, distorted, or inferior manner. In his further investigations, he found that if "old emotional scars" (Maltz, 1960, p. vii) could be removed, then the individual improved, even when reconstructive surgery had *not* taken place. The individual's mental "picture" of self was a key to personality and behavior. This image of self, if favorable, is an important contribution to unconditional self-acceptance.

Many questions remain about exactly how this self-image influences thought, feelings, and behavior of people. It is assumed that a positive self-image creates a more positive disposition, more adaptive thinking, feelings, and behavior. Negative self-images evoke just the opposite; more negative thoughts, feelings, and behavior. How does this link occur between self-image and internal/external events? To answer this question Maltz proposed that Cybernetics, which is a science that grew out of the work of physicists and mathematicians, provided some very important insight. Cybernetics relates to teleology or the goal-striving, goal-oriented behavior of mechanical systems. Cybernetics explains the purposeful behavior of machines.

Obviously, people are not machines; but, their brains may function in ways similar to machines. Cybernetics' proponents claim that individuals possess a "goal-striving, servomechanism consisting of the brain and nervous system, which is used by, and directed by the mind" (p. 12). This "Creative Mechanism" (p. 12) within us is nonevaluative and works systematically toward goals: both positive and negative ones, depending upon what thoughts, beliefs, and interpretations we describe to ourselves. Accordingly positive internal or mental activity begets positive external or behavioral activity in our lives. If we want to achieve positive goals we must furnish a positive program for our Creative Mechanism to process. Combining a healthy capable self-image with purposeful goal seeking resulted in the principles of Psychocybernetics (Maltz, 1960). Two of the methods of psychocybernetics are "creative mental picturing" and "creatively experiencing through imagery."

Visualization of the goals desired in life is an example of "creative mental picturing," while seeing ourselves actively accomplishing and experiencing these goals, through mental reflection is an example of "creatively experiencing through imagery." Both methods aid the nonevaluative servomechanism of our brains to work more efficiently for us. A clear, distinct, and specific picture has been played out in our minds which facilitates accomplishment of individual goals. This type of visualization has been used in a variety of settings. For example, Siegel (1986, 1989) uses visualization in the treatment of cancer patients. Gallwey writes about combining facilitative self-talk with imagery to improve the game of tennis (1974, 1976). This mental imaging and verbalization of various sports techniques help the player to automatically perform these methods in a more relaxed and efficient manner. If these mental methods "work" in medicine and sports, then teachers may find that visualization and verbalization of a personal and professional goal are very helpful additions to teacher thought processes. There is compelling reason to believe that the principles of psychocybernetics are transportable across the professions. The fundamental point to remember is that the quality of visualization and verbalization may be directly affected by the self-image or said another way, the visual representation we see when we think of ourselves. The unconditional acceptance of ourselves as a worthwhile, important person shapes the way we see ourselves, and this image in turn sets the boundaries for individual accomplishment.

An important part of teaching is setting goals for class, small group, and individual student accomplishments. The teachers' self-acceptance as they visualize these classroom goals may be an important consideration. If self-acceptance is poor, then teachers may be setting up themselves for failure without even realizing it. On the other hand, if teachers are positive about themselves, then they may see their goals as obtainable because, at another level, they believe in their own capabilities to make these goals a reality. They set in motion this goal-directed servomechanism of the brain, to which Maltz refers, and the mind starts immediately to work toward goal achievement (according to Maltz, 1960).

An example of such an experience that comes to mind is of a nontraditional college student who commuted two hours every weekday to attend the university. She left behind a working husband and four sons, ages 2 to 11. She had a great deal of self-acceptance and believed that she would be successful in obtaining her goal of becoming a teacher. Toward the end of her four-year program when she had to be in a school, student teaching at 7:45am in the university town, an hour away from home, she almost dropped out of the university. She had to get up each morning at 4:00am in order to complete all of her other responsibilities at home. However, she managed to graduate with honors. Later when she was enrolled in one of our graduate courses she said, "You know the only way I made it was that I kept seeing myself walking across the stage in my black graduation cap and gown with my four sons screaming, 'Yay, Mom! Way to go, Mom!' That picture in my head kept me going." A follow-up exercise is suggested next.

VISUALIZATION/VERBALIZATION EXERCISE #5

Take a few moments to think about what you see when you see yourself in your mind's eye. Write down some words that describe who you are. In pairs talk about this description and try to determine if your self-image is mostly positive or mostly negative.

Think about a goal you have for your personal and/or professional life. Mentally visualize this goal and then see yourself obtaining this goal. Experience what emotions you feel when you reach your goal. Talk to your partner about this goal and your reaction to obtaining it.

A-B-C Framework and Futurizing

Some of the ideas and concepts set forth by Wayne Dyer (1978, 1980) can also be used to increase a person's self-acceptance. We first introduce Dyer's A-B-C framework. Please refer to Figure 2.3.

The reason that Dyer's ideas lend themselves to metacognition and self-acceptance is because they act as stimuli to mental awareness and regulation of mental states that lead to a well-adjusted, self-accepting human being.

If we refer to Figure 2.3, start at point B. Most individuals remain in a physical state of wellness and a mental state of "mediocre okayness" for the majority of their lives. When we become physically or mentally ill at point A, we usually seek medical intervention to become better, so we can get back to point B, where we are satisfied to remain. There is another alternative, however, and that is the path from point B to point C. This path is taken by the teacher who is not satisfied with just being physically well or mentally okay. This teacher desires to be as healthy as he/she can be. Just how physically and mentally healthy can a person become? Teachers, who accept only the best healthy practices for themselves, care about their bodies and their minds. Certainly we would rather have self-respecting teachers like this teaching our children than ones who are satisfied with less than the best for themselves. Self-accepting teachers transfer this intra-concern to others (inter-concern). For example, a 15-year veteran teacher (overweight, complaining much of the time) did not like herself or anyone else. She listened intently to the discussion of the A-B-C idea. Two years later she came back to the university for a visit and was a different person. She talked about how this A-B-C concept began her thinking about herself. She lost 100 pounds and changed her attitude. She said, "I am not the same person and I am not the same teacher. My students are grateful. I thought it was the students' fault that my classes were always the worst ones, year after year, but it was my fault. I did not like myself and I did not like them either. When I felt better about me (intra), I began to feel better about my students (inter)." (Intra to Inter)

A-B-C FRAMEWORK

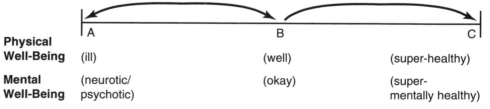

FIGURE 2–3
Dyer's Concepts for Teacher Self-Acceptance

	A	B	C
Physical Well-Being	(ill)	(well)	(super-healthy)
Mental Well-Being	(neurotic/ psychotic)	(okay)	(super- mentally healthy)

Source: The Sky's the Limit. Copyright © 1980 by Wayne W. Dyer. Reprinted by permission of Simon & Schuster, Inc.

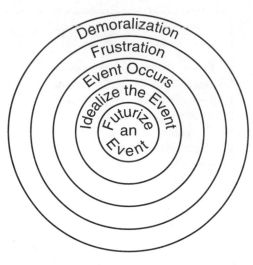

FIGURE 2–4
Futurizing Cycle

Source: The Sky's the Limit. Copyright © 1980 by Wayne W. Dyer. Reprinted by permission of Simon & Schuster, Inc.

The futurizing cycle (Figure 2.4) illustrates the self-defeating habit of postponing happiness to a later date. Happiness always stays one step out in front of the individual; therefore, the individual always plans to be happy—at a later date. Because of this, some individuals have never spent a solitary happy moment. The opposite of futurizing is goal-setting, whereby plans are made for the future; but, the individual is happy in the present moment, on the way to the goal.

Futurizing begins when a certain upcoming event in life (e.g., the weekend, a prom, graduation, marriage) preoccupies an unrealistic proportion of a person's thoughts. For example, some people routinely idealize the weekend, and waste hundreds of Mondays, Tuesdays, Wednesdays, and Thursdays. Each Monday they feel frustrated because the previous event (the weekend) could not possibly have matched the idealization, images, and thoughts of the weekend, which were unrealistic. As the frustration continues, the person begins to become demoralized: "Oh well, what's the use—I'll live for graduation." And the idealization begins anew with self-talk such as "I can't wait until I graduate. Life begins after graduation." In reality, life after graduation will have its pluses, but each life event comes with its own set of difficulties. Other typical events that people often idealize beyond realistic proportions are holidays, marriages, new jobs, graduate degrees, and the final futurizing event—retirement.

As each event brings with it, new problems, frustration followed by demoralization sets in and the cycle starts again—a new event is futurized. Perhaps this partially explains the high rate of depression and suicide at holiday times, and the frequent early deaths, shortly after retirement. Teachers who are constantly in a state of futurizing are not accepting themselves in the present. They are not making the most of each school day—they are living only for some future event. Beyond their frequent state of frustration and demoralization over "life," futurizers are also poor role models for children. Children begin futurizing early on (e.g., I can't wait for summer—who cares about these school days? I'm living for summer.). If children have futurizing teachers, they are much more likely to be unhappy, complaining frequently about the present. Teachers should point out this self-defeating cycle to students. Teach it. One example is to have young children create a "big book" together on the topic of "What's Wonderful About (The Grade They Are Presently In)." A suggested exercise for college students is presented next.

SELF-ACCEPTANCE EXERCISE #6

In small groups of three or four, brainstorm events that you futurize. Share examples of how you talk to yourself about these future events. As a group, choose one of your examples, write it on chart paper with the accompanying self-talk. Next, write how you might turn the futurizing into healthy goal-setting. Write suggestions for healthy, goal-setting self-talk that allows you to enjoy the present while you plan for the future.

How many babies have been born because marriages were "supposed" to be ideal; they realistically were not; so "I'll have a baby and then my life will be complete." Wrong! "Complete lives" include realism, whereby people accept that life events (e.g., births, retirements) will not produce perfect lives. In addition, all of us have our imperfections; but, happiness and self-acceptance can be chosen deliberately in spite of these shortcomings and challenges. In the words of William James: "The greatest revolution of our generation is the discovery that human beings, by changing the inner attitudes of their minds can change the outer aspects of their lives" (Weaver, Cotrell, & Churchman, 1988, p. 239). *Intra* to *inter*! It is important to recognize and use "goal-setting self-talk" and to recognize and stop using "futurizing self-talk." Examples of both are provided below.

Goal-Setting Self-Talk

What a great day! I need to study for my SAT for 2 hours before Saturday. But right now, I'm enjoying my walk.

I'm looking forward to a pleasant holiday. I want to see about two more gifts.

I will be married next summer. Right now, I'm enjoying my independence, being responsible for just me. It's a good time in my life.

Futurizing Self-Talk

When the SAT is over, I can smile again.

When Christmas comes, it will be the best time ever! I just can't wait! Everything will be perfect!

When next summer comes, if it EVER does, my life will be so much better. I'll be marrying the most wonderful guy in the whole world. I wish the days would go by.

SELF-ACCEPTANCE EXERCISE #7

As an out-of-class assignment keep a record of some of your self-talk (i.e., the things that you say aloud or silently to yourself) in response to at least three separate potentially stressful situations (e.g., when you are driving and someone cuts you off, you are waiting in a line at the grocery story and the person in front of you leaves to get an item he/she forgot, you trip and fall, someone breaks a date with you, or you give an incorrect answer to a question). Keep a small notebook handy and write down the actual words you use.

On the following day, take the next step and change any negative self-talk statements to positive ones. For example, instead of saying, "I don't have time to wait while that person goes to find a forgotten grocery item," try "I'll use this extra time to check my list and go through my coupons." Changing the statements to reflect positive thoughts should help you to cope with the situation more constructively. Remember, you may have a long history of flagellating yourself; it will take a lot of concerted effort to change the ways in which you talk to yourself.

Self-Responsibility

Effective teachers must be more than purveyors of information; they must be people who know something about themselves and how their own beliefs and feelings affect their work with students (Aspy & Roebuck, 1982). Feelings of personal responsibility are considered to be indicators of a healthy self-concept. Self-responsibility as defined here is explained as an aspect of the concept of locus of control. Before reading any further please complete the following exercise:

SELF-RESPONSIBILITY EXERCISE #8

INTERNAL-EXTERNAL LOCUS OF CONTROL SAMPLE EXERCISES

Julian B. Rotter developed a 29-item forced-choice scale for measuring an individual's degree of internal and external control. The Internal-External Locus of Control Scale is widely used. The following are sample items taken from an earlier version of the test, but are not contained in the final version. You can readily determine for yourself whether you are inclined toward internal or external control, simply by adding up the coices you make on each side.

I More Strongly Believe That:	**Or I More Strongly Believe That:**
Promotions are earned through hard work and persistance.	Making a lot of money is largely a matter of getting the right breaks.
In my experience I have noticed that there is usually a direct connection between how hard I study and the grades I get.	Many times the reactions of teachers seem haphazard to me.
The number of divorces indicates that more and more people are not trying to make their marriages work.	Marriage is largely a gamble.
When I am right I can convince others.	It is silly to think that one can really change another person's basic attitudes.
In our society a man's future earning power is dependent upon his ability.	Getting promoted is really a matter of being a little luckier than the next guy.
If one knows how to deal with people they are really quite easily led.	I have little influence over the way other people behave.
In my case the grades I make are the results of my own efforts; luck has little or nothing to do with it.	Sometimes I feel that I have little to do with the grades I get.

Source: Adapted by permission of Julian B. Rotter, *Psychology Today.*

Rotter (1966) explains locus of control orientation as the belief in one's personal control over successes and failures in one's life. People classified as *internals* believe that they have the power to change their world; that their successes or lack of successes are a direct result of personal efforts. Their rewards are a direct result of their efforts. *Internals* feel in control of life. On the other hand, individuals classified as *externals* believe circumstances are beyond personal control, and that successes and failures are determined by luck, fate, chance, or powerful others (Hill, 1978).

Research on locus of control indicates that *internals* have higher self-esteem, greater life satisfaction, personal competence, and overall well-being and that *externals*, on the other hand, have depressed affect, as well as elevated anxiety, hostility, embitterment, and strain (Campbell, Converse, & Rogers, 1976; Coleman, Hobson, McPortland, Mood, Weinfield, & York, 1966; Perlin & Radabaugh, 1976).

Research in the area of locus of control and teaching has resulted in major findings for the teaching profession and for the field of teacher education (Kremer & Kurtz, 1983; Sadowski, & Blackwell, & Willard, 1985). Teachers' locus of control has been found to relate to student achievement (Murray & Staebler, 1974; Rose & Medway, 1981) and to students' perceptions of classroom climate (Sadowski & Woodward, 1983). Rose and Medway (1981) found that students of teachers with a more internal locus of control orientation had higher achievement on a basic skills test. Likewise, Murray and Staebler (1974) found that students taught by *internals* gained more on an achievement test than those students taught by *externals*. Sadowski and Woodward (1983) examined teachers' locus of control and students' perceptions of climate of the classroom. Thirteen middle school teachers and 78 students were involved in the study. Twice during the school year the teachers completed a locus of control scale and the students completed a questionnaire concerning the classroom climate. The results suggest that teachers' locus of control orientations have a "moderate causal impact upon the students' perceptions of classroom climate" (p. 508). The authors concluded that internally controlled teachers are more likely to utilize activities that promote student motivation.

In classroom studies, teacher locus of control has also been found to relate to teacher effectiveness. Teachers with an external locus of control orientation feel a greater need to control their students; *internals* are willing to allow democratic processes to influence classroom activities (Barfield & Burlingame, 1974). In addition, investigations of preservice teachers' locus of control orientation have revealed relationships between both the student teachers' orientation and their perceptions of teaching situations (Kremer & Kurtz, 1983) and between their orientations and teaching performance (Sadowski, Blackwell, & Willard, 1985). In the Sadowski et al. study a locus of control scale was administered to preservice teachers prior to their field experience. Then, their teaching performance was rated six weeks later. Preservice teachers classified as *internals* were significantly more effective for five of the eight performance indicators as well as in their overall teaching performance.

An internal locus of control orientation is certainly a desirable trait for teachers. The research suggests a positive relationship between a teacher's internal orientation and (1) student achievement and (2) student perception of classroom climate.

Likewise, an internal locus of control orientation is a desirable trait for students. Studies reveal that students who are more internally controlled perform better on achievement tests (Gordon, 1977; Nowicki & Walker, 1973b), receive better grades, have higher self-concepts (Johnson & Kanoy, 1980), and perform better in problem-solving activities. On the other hand, an external locus of control orientation is associated with undesirable traits for students. Research suggests that students with an external orientation have lower self-concepts (Johnson & Kanoy, 1980), lower achievement, and lower grades (Gordon, 1977). Externality of locus of control orientation typifies the at-risk student. The typical dropout feels a lack of control over the world.

As you can see from the research findings, it is very important that as teachers we take responsibility for choosing productive emotions for ourselves—so that we are behaving responsibly. Teachers who feel that they are responsible are stronger than those who are controlled by others. If we give students the power "to make us angry" we are allowing them to exercise unhealthy control over us. Some students feel very powerful knowing they have the ability to set the teacher off in a tirade—"Watch the teacher go! I can make her crazy!"

The words and phrases we use either detract from or help us to become aware of our thinking and behavior, and able to take the necessary steps to reach our goals. In order to be fully-functioning, self-directed individuals, we have to take responsibility for our internal and external experiences. How often do we blame others for how we feel and what happens to us? This behavior encourages us to look outside of ourselves for answers. A much more productive mode of behavior is to look inside ourselves because we are in charge of how we feel.

Following are examples of assuming responsibility for oneself versus relinquishing this responsibility to others. We want to move from not taking responsibility for our thoughts, feelings, emotions, and behaviors to feeling empowered.

Other	Self
1. "He made me so mad."	1. "When I heard him say that, I felt sad."
2. "The traffic gave me a headache."	2. "I will take this opportunity to relax and meditate."
3. "It's your fault that I'm depressed."	3. "I realize I'm responsible for my own happiness."

It is not what people say to us that "makes" us feel things. People can't make us feel anything. In truth, we make ourselves feel certain ways by what we say to ourselves about other people, events, and ourselves. It is our self-talk that determines how we feel. Don't blame other people for how you feel and for what happens to you.

For example, in our college classes we often have several projects that require a great deal of planning, persistence, and hard work. Different students respond differently. One person sets a goal, develops a timeline, works diligently, and turns the project in on time. Another student in the same class procrastinates and waits until the last minute to complete the project and turns in work that is not acceptable. We often hear this type of behavior expressed in words such as: "If only you had given us more time," "You give us too much work to do." The truth is people, events, and circumstances are rarely the way we want them to be. The key is for us to change our own behavior through our own words. The choice is always ours. It is more facilitative to focus on our thoughts, visual images, self-talk and actions and stop blaming luck, fate, chance, other people, and circumstances for the things that happen to us.

So it is very important for teachers, for their own benefit, as well as for the larger picture, to be models of responsibility. Students need to see teachers who can exhibit self-guidance and take responsibility for their own behavior. Students often learn responsibility from a responsible teacher.

I-Messages   We have found that learning to use I-messages (Gordon, 1974) encourages us to speak from our own (internal) perspectives rather than blaming others (external) and using whiny, complaining you-messages (e.g., you make me so angry). I-messages have three components: (1) a nonjudgmental description of the inappropriate behavior, "When you . . . ," (2) the feeling this behavior evokes, "I feel . . . ," (3) the tangible effect the behavior causes "because . . . ." The parts of the I-message do not have to be stated in the above order. For example, "When paper is left all over the floor (description of inappropriate behavior), I feel very frustrated (feeling) when I have to pick it up after school (tangible effect)." An I-message is an honest message delivered to communicate an internal state. An effective I-message must focus on *myself*, rather than on the student and does not place blame on anyone. An example of a you-message is: "You always forget this trash. You drive me crazy." This teacher is not assuming responsibility for his/her own true feelings and is allowing someone else to manipulate his/her feelings. Sometimes teachers are discouraged about having to remember to use all three parts of the I-message. With practice, however, it becomes a very natural, honest, and self-controlled way to communicate. The tangible effect is sometimes hard to express, or it doesn't seem to be logical for some communications. Therefore, we simply say: "It is better to use I-messages, even if you omit one or two parts than to use you-messages." Some examples of both I-and you-messages are presented below:

You-Messages	I-Messages
You shouldn't laugh at my drawing.	I feel hurt when you laugh at my drawing
You people didn't put ELI 300 in your book.	I can't find the course listed in this book.
You are always coming in here late, interrupting everybody.	When you come in late, I have to wait to begin the lesson and I get irritated.

Speaking from one's own perspective, using I-messages promotes the teacher's feeling of responsibility. It also serves as a healthy communication model for students. Teachers who use I-messages report that students start using them also, and the climate in the classroom improves. You-messages bring out defensiveness and combativeness while I-messages foster cooperativeness. I-messages meet three important criteria that make them preferable over you-messages: (1) they promote a willingness to change, (2) they contain minimal negative evaluation of the student, and (3) they do not jeopardize the teacher-student relationship. A suggested "I-message" exercise is presented next.

SENDING "I-MESSAGES" EXERCISE # 7

The following chart lists potential conflict situations between students and a teacher. In Column II, write a typical you-message that a teacher might send. In Column III, write an I-message for each situation. Try to include all three parts. When you have finished, compare your "I-messages" with those in the key.

Situation	You-Message	I-Message
Example: A student keeps whispering loudly to a friend while you are trying to lead an important classroom discussion.	"*You* should know better than to talk when I'm talking. Don't *you* have any manners!"	"When you talk while I'm talking to the class, *I* feel frustrated, because I get distracted from what *I* want to say."
1. A student enters your class 10 minutes late for the third time that week.		
2. While you are writing on the chalkboard, one of your students throws a paper dart across the room.		
3. Your boyfriend/girlfriend is 20 minutes late for a date.		
4. A teacher is upset with a student who is dawdling rather than doing the assignment.		
5. Student has been sulking, withdrawn and acting sad all day. Teacher doesn't know the reason.		

KEY	
You-Message	*I-Message*
1. "Can't *you* be more considerate of the class. *You* are always late and interrupting us after we have begun the day."	"Pam, when you come in late *I* get frustrated because *I*'m distracted and have to stop what *I*'m doing."
2. *You* all should be ashamed. *You* know better than to throw darts.	"*I* feel like *I*'m being taken advantage of when one of you throws darts behind my back and *I* have to stop what *I*'m doing."
3. *"You*'re always late! You'll probably be late to your own funeral."	"When you're late, *I* always get worried because *I*'m afraid something has happened to you."
4. *"You*'d better stop dawdling and get busy on your work or you'll have to stay in at recess again."	"*I* get upset when you don't do your work because then *I* have to keep disciplining you rather than teaching you."
5. "Stop sulking *you*'re a big girl. Either brighten up or *you* can go outside and sulk. *You*'re taking something too seriously."	"*I*'m sorry to see you so unhappy but *I* don't know how to help you because *I* don't know why you're feeling so sad."

In addition to these "I-message exercises," self-control can be promoted via the use of self-talk statements that are modeled, practiced, and role played. Below is a sample classroom management problem with the corresponding helpful teacher self-talk. The self-talk is used as coping therapy to learn self-control for classroom use. These situations may be role played if your context allows for role play.

Teaching Situation: Shawn has not listened to you, the teacher, for the last hour. He has wandered around the room, disturbing the other students. When you ask him to sit down and get to work he responds: "You make me, you witch!"

Helpful Self-Talk: "Oh how I would like to spank him but that will not help anything. I'll just get more upset and it will not help Shawn either. Calm down first. It will be okay. Show the other children how to stay in control when Shawn lashes out like this. Be a calm, controlled role model." The teacher says calmly to Shawn: "When you speak to me that way, I am embarrassed, insulted, but most of all, I am hurt. I would like for you to write a plan to help improve your behavior. I will walk with you to the "Opportunity Time-Out Room." Prospective teachers often find it very helpful to develop their own scripts of helpful self-talk in response to various management discipline problem scenarios, such as this one.

In summary, when teachers become more aware, accepting, and responsible (*intra*) they are better able to *inter*act positively with their students. There seems to be a direct link between the intra-and the inter-psychological functioning of teachers. The essential need for teachers who know and accept students and who can organize and manage the classroom complexity is apparent.

SUMMARY

Teachers set the emotional climate in the classroom and serve as role models for students' coping skills. However, attention to teachers' affective strengths, such as self-awareness, self-acceptance, and self-responsibility is not likely to be sufficient for teacher growth, unless teachers are taught metacognitive awareness, monitoring, and regulation of their thinking related to these affective strengths. It is via this mental alertness and regulation that teachers use their strengths to full advantage in the classroom. For example, if a teacher is aware that she can calm herself down by counting from 10 to 1, quietly to herself; then, she is much more likely to use this skill to keep harmony during an angry student's outburst, instead of escalating the problem with a quickly spoken, angry counterattack.

In order to be an exemplary role model, teachers need a heightened sense of emotional well-being. Teachers possessing such strengths are in a position to create learning environments in which students feel physically and psychologically safe (Maslow, 1970) and learn optimally. Beyond developing optimum learning environments, Brookover's research evidence (1979) indicates that the self-esteem of the teacher is related to student success more than any other variable.

Metacognitive awareness, monitoring, and regulation of personal dimensions was addressed by exercises focusing on awareness of cognitive, social, emotional, and physical strengths and weaknesses. In addition, teacher self-awareness, teacher self-acceptance and teacher self-responsibility are considered prerequisites to awareness and acceptance of students and also to the guidance of students toward responsibility and autonomy. Self-acceptance is improved through human visualization, rational-emotive therapy, and breaking out of the futurizing cycle. Attention to self-responsibility includes learning to give I-messages, rather than angry you-messages, and awareness of locus of control orientations (i.e., more internal orientation versus more external).

CHAPTER 3

Eliminating Negative Thinking of Teachers

OVERVIEW

In this chapter, metacognitive strategies are discussed for the purpose of reducing unhelpful/excessive teacher stress, anger, anxiety, frustration, and boredom. A teacher's guide for the use of coping skills is included. Often this affective side of metacognition is not addressed; however, it is vital and most likely a prerequisite to the use of metacognition for teachers' cognitive skills. Perhaps in reality, it is the mastery of metacognitive/affective skills that determines if teachers will be sufficiently autonomous to implement the metacognitive skills for classroom use. In other words the teachers' mastery of the personal use of metacognitive coping skills may be a prerequisite to the mastery of the professional use of metacognition. It is highly probable that teachers must come through the affective/personal use of metacognition before teachers will realize the benefits and become empowered to also apply metacognition for their more cognitive/professional responsibilities, such as teacher planning, implementation, and classroom management addressed in Chapter 5. Therefore, this chapter includes an indepth look at how to use metacognitive strategies for personal coping skills to eliminate negative thinking of teachers.

Self-Questions

1. *Knowledge.* Define metacognitive/affective skills.

2. *Comprehension.* Provide examples of maladaptive teacher self-talk. Connect these examples with their accompanying irrational beliefs that lead to teacher stress.

3. *Application.* Explain the way teachers can change irrational self-talk by changing irrational beliefs first.

4. *Analysis.* Designate the components of Meichenbaum's self-statements to control teacher anger.

5. *Synthesis.* If teachers begin to use metacognitive coping skills what would be some possible benefits to our educational system?

6. *Evaluation.* Judge the strengths and limitations of metacognitive/coping skills for reducing teacher stress, anger, anxiety, frustration, and boredom.

TEACHER STRESS

In this chapter, metacognition techniques to regulate emotional reactions (i.e., stress, anger, anxiety, frustration, and boredom) for teachers are described. The purpose is three-fold: first, teachers acquire some viable techniques to reduce undesirable reactions; second, teachers are more likely to relate positively to students; and third, teachers who use and benefit from these techniques are much more likely to apply them for similar student needs, such as test anxiety in their students.

It is commonly known that teaching is perceived by many to be a stressful profession for a variety of reasons (e.g., *in loco parentis* role with no parent authority; accountability; complexity and unpredictability inherent in teaching). It is very difficult to find information related to diminishing teacher stress via metacognitive strategies. Meichenbaum (1977) provides information about stress-inoculation for a non-teaching population which can be adapted to use with teachers. To our knowledge, there are very few, if any studies, on the use of metacognition or self-talk to diminish teacher stress. Therefore, this section will be a synthesis, creatively developed, drawing on teacher education research, Edson's (1986) paper entitled "Communicating Intrapersonally about Stress: The Dynamics of Self," Anderson's (1981) booklet entitled *Thinking, Changing, and Rearranging*, and Meichenbaum's (1977) book entitled *Cognitive Behavior Modification*.

Medically speaking, stress is defined as a physiological reaction to an external force that is interpreted by the individual as causing conflict. The psychological definition implies that by using communication with self, individuals can change the stress level in their lives. Albert Ellis defines this self-talk as a mediator that intervenes between any situation and our response to that situation. (See Chapter 1, page 3 and Chapter 2, page 34 for an indepth discussion of this). Therefore, situations are viewed as neutral and what we say to ourselves about the situations causes the positive or negative reaction, correspondingly. In other words, our language creates reality. Since teachers can choose what they say to themselves, or at least they can be taught to modify self-talk, teachers can then regulate the amount of stress in their lives by choosing a language that is not in line with stress (e.g., "I can handle this—nothing is so important that I should stress myself like this and shorten my life").

It is usually not easy to begin thinking that emotions are chosen. Our social language indicates that we believe otherwise (e.g., I fell in love, I got a headache, I was struck by a feeling). Technically speaking, all of these statements are inaccurate. Depression is being treated very successfully in some clinics by teaching people to change their self-talk, using a language of self-affirmation (see Butler, 1992). In addition, Glasser (1984) believes that much of what we do, think, and feel comes from inside of us and is not a response to our environment and the people in it. Glasser says that we should say that we are "headaching" ourselves when we have tension headaches, not physiologically induced headaches (e.g., sinus). Instead we often talk as if the headache landed on our heads (e.g., I got a headache). Glasser says nouns such as "headache" and "depression" should be verbs (i.e., "headaching" and "depressing" ourselves). Meichenbaum (1977) states that when schizophrenics were taught to stop talking to themselves in crazy ways they stopped acting in crazy ways. The documentation of successes with clinical populations motivates hope that nonclinical groups, like teachers, can also benefit from "self-talk therapy." Caution is indicated here because we need to refrain from "blaming the victim." Teachers can choose and regulate many of their emotional reactions and their accompanying physical side effects (e.g., nervous stomach). However, physiological causes (e.g., ruptured disc) are beyond human choice and control. Distinctions between emotional and physical maladies should be remembered. In addition, the reciprocal relationship of thought and feelings must also be contemplated.

Changing irrational, unhelpful teacher self-talk is the basic mechanism of change needed to improve emotional reactions, such as stress levels. A procedure for doing this is provided by Butler (1992) and described next.

The Language of Self-Support: Self-Talk

According to cognitive semanticists and clinical psychologists such as David Burns (1980), Pamela Butler (1992), and Shad Helmstetter (1991), the daily running dialogue or commentary inside our heads has the potential to impact either positively or negatively on our feelings, level of stress, self-esteem, health, behavior, and interpersonal relationships. If we become aware of what we are telling ourselves: "What am I saying to scare myself? panic myself? worry myself?," then we have taken the first metacognitive step to a positive impact, rather than a negative impact. Once we become cognizant of the fact that the unhelpful things we are saying to ourselves are hurting us; then, we can make a conscious choice to talk to ourselves in more helpful ways. However it takes concerted effort, patience, and persistence. Unfortunately, we do not focus upon emotional health in our society as much as we might. For example, there is an increase in the number of people hiring their own personal trainers to teach them better nutrition and exercise. However, we haven't heard of emotional trainers being hired to improve emotional health. For just a while now, let us imagine that each of us has an emotional trainer to help us become aware of and to regulate the approximately 55,000 self-talk utterances spoken to ourselves per day. The quality of these utterances directly affects the quality of our lives. The emotional trainer might begin by asking us to take the following steps:

SELF-TALK EXERCISE #1

1. Examine the quality of day-to-day self-talk.

   a. First describe a brief, real-life episode you recently experienced. Then list statements and questions you said to yourself during or after this episode. Do this three times per day for one week.
   b. Carry a hand-held tape recorder and talk into it as you are talking to yourself during the day. Do this as often as you can for one week. Then transcribe the self-talk word for word.
   c. Keep a long-term self-talk journal for a month to six weeks for the same daily episode (e.g., preparing a meal).

After getting in touch with the way we usually talk to ourselves on a more personal level, these same three steps mentioned above can be applied to classroom episodes to examine the quality of teacher self-talk. Individually or in small groups, it is helpful to change any negative self-talk utterances to more positive ones. An example from one of our student teacher's experiences is given below and a corresponding blank worksheet that may be enlarged and copied is provided next for your use.

CHANGING UNHELPFUL SELF-TALK TO HELPFUL SELF-TALK

Situation: *Alonzo has done it again. He will not listen when I am trying to give directions for work. Instead he just wanders around the room.*

Unhelpful Self-Talk: *Who does he think he is anyway? I get so sick of his attitude! He won't even look at me. I think he hates me and sometimes I just want to give it all up!*

Helpful Self-Talk: *Alonzo is really having a problem with listening. I wonder if he even is aware of it? I'll continue with my directions because everyone else is listening. After I get the other students started, I'll have an individual talk with Alonzo and see if he and I can work out a plan to help him.*

CHANGING UNHELPFUL SELF-TALK TO HELPFUL SELF-TALK EXERCISE #2

Describe Situation/Context _____
_____
_____

Accompanying Unhelpful Self-Talk _____
_____
_____

Alternative Helpful Self-Talk _____
_____
_____

Please note that helpful and unhelpful classifications are value-laden. In some cases, it may be rather obvious what is helpful and what is not. However, it is also context-dependent. Something said in one situation may be helpful, and said in a different setting or at a different time may be unhelpful. The point worth remembering is that the *speaker* of the self-talk determines the helpfulness, not the listener. If the speaker determines that what she has just said to herself facilitates goal accomplishment and for her this is a helpful thing to say, then this opinion is considered the important and valid one. Another person might view the same self-talk statement, if spoken by him or herself, as an unhelpful statement. The classification of helpful and unhelpful self-talk is speaker-dependent.

Recall Helmstetter's estimate that 77% of our self-talk is negative. Similarly, if 77% of everything we ate was counterproductive to good health, then eventually we would most likely take steps to eat healthier foods or suffer the consequence of becoming ill. Then why is it that more of us do not take the steps needed to feed ourselves a higher quality of emotional self-talk? Our emotional trainer has helped us take Step 1: Become aware. Examine the quality of our day-to-day self-talk. Step 2 is to evaluate our samples of self-talk. We ask ourselves this critical question: Is my self-talk helping me? If not, then how can I change it so that it is healthier for me and for those around me? Step 3 is to specifically identify the Drivers, Stoppers, and Confusers (Butler, 1992) that are maintaining our inner dialogue. A list of these Judges that comprise the majority of our unhelpful self-talk was presented in Chapter 1, pages 19–22. Please review these carefully because an awareness of them is needed to develop a language of self-support.

Once we have become familiar with Butler's Judges, we start to notice and catch ourselves when we are driving, stopping, and confusing ourselves with these types of internal dialogues. If we call our emotional trainer back and say, "Well we've become familiar with all these judges, now what?" The trainer's response might include that we review a method for learning the language of self-support. We are most likely familiar with the tirades of self-criticism we deliver to ourselves each day. Learning a healthier way to verbally support ourselves is like learning a new language. For teachers who have tried it and been successful, the great effort is worth it. A few authentic examples are provided below.

TEACHER A: I was 100 pounds overweight and in my 17th year of teaching first grade. Year after year I thought I was being given all the "bad kids." And I complained and grumbled most of the year. After I took your class and learned how to verbally support and encourage myself, I lost 75 pounds and for some reason started to be assigned wonderful children. I used to think it was the children's fault; now I know the poor atmosphere in my class was my own fault. When I became responsible for myself, began to treat myself with respect, and support myself verbally; my teaching, and teacher-student, and teacher-parent relationships improved. Thank you.

TEACHER B: I teach all week and have a church where I am the minister. I teach 7th grade social studies. Once I had the tools to become more positive in my self-guiding speech, I allowed myself a nap and some leisure for the first time in my life. I had been hospitalized several times for nervous stomach and operated on once for ulcerated stomach; however, I really began to feel better when I stopped driving myself with all those Drivers we talked about in class.

TEACHER C: I had never taken a college examination without carrying along my bottle of Maalox. I learned a new way to talk to myself about tests, to calm myself down, and to view tests in a more realistic manner. For the first time ever, and now even five years later I take tests without nausea and vomiting.

To review the steps in learning a language of self-support, please see the chart below. Then each step will be elaborated in text:

LEARNING THE LANGUAGE OF SELF-SUPPORT

Step 1.   Be aware: Listen to what you and others around you are saying to themselves. *Self-Question*: What am I telling myself?

Step 2.   Evaluate: Decide if your inner dialogue is supportive or destructive. *Self-Question*: Is my self-talk helping me?

Step 3.   Identify: Determine what Driver, Stopper, or Confuser is maintaining your inner speech. *Self-Question*: What Driver, Stopper, or Confuser is maintaining my inner speech?

Step 4.   Support yourself: Replace your unhelpful self-talk with permission and self-support. *Self-Question*: What Permission and Self-Support will I give myself?

Step 5.   Develop a guide: Decide what action to take consonant with your new supportive position. *Self-Question*: What action will I take given my supportive position?

Awareness is the first step to break out of an unhelpful self-talk cycle. Keep an accurate record of just how often your unhelpful self-talk occurs. You may want to use counters, notebooks, tape recordings, lists, etc. Listen to others as they talk to themselves. There are certain cues that may signal unhelpful self-talk. For example, feeling anxious or feeling depressed; sudden shifts in emotions, physical symptoms such as fluttery stomach, sweaty palms, tension headaches, etc.,; avoidance thoughts or behaviors. External events such as receiving a compliment or criticism; or beginning a new project may evoke unhelpful self-talk. Listen for it. When you begin to notice the presence of unhelpful self-talk, interrupt your self-critical tirade with the firm statement — "STOP! This is not helping to talk to myself this way. Would I talk to a good friend this way?"

This begins the Evaluation phase of Step 2. As you answer for yourself *Is my self-talk helping*? with the realization that it is not, then you begin to disengage from it. Many of our students have reported that they begin to recognize that unhelpful self-talk produces feelings of anger, depression, anxiety, as well as undermines their problem-solving ability. This recognition is a very important step and helps us to challenge a heretofore accepted way of talking to ourselves. Now it is no longer acceptable.

Step 3 is to identify the driver, stopper, and confuser. As you become more familiar with these, it becomes easier and easier. However, we have students who skip this step except to recognize whether they are driving, stopping, or confusing themselves. In contrast, we have other students who are much more precise about identifying the particular voice. If you can be more specific, then it seems to help pinpoint the source of difficulty and direct you toward an alternative way of speaking to yourself. For example, "I've been calling myself lazy all day. I have the right to do nothing sometimes. This is my day off. I'm not going to spend it "hurrying myself up!"

When our students have moved from unhelpful to more helpful self-talk they often report lightening of feelings; happier, free feelings; more assertion; and feelings of being less driven.

TEACHER D: When I came into this class I was at an all-time low. I had just been through a divorce of a 20-year marriage. I didn't care much about anything. After this class dealing with self-talk, I am feeling a whole lot better. I even bought some new clothes, had my hair cut, and started to laugh again. I never would have dreamed I could help myself like this. I just needed some concrete tools. My sixth-graders have even noticed a difference.

Step 4 is replacing the unhelpful self-talk with permission and self-affirmation. This takes lots of time, practice, and determination. Encourage yourself for small improvements. Be careful not to impose the "Be Perfect" voice as you try to improve your self-talk. No one does or should use only helpful self-talk. The goal is to reduce the amount of unhelpful and increase the amount of helpful. Congratulate yourself on any growth and expect some days to backslide a great deal.

TEACHER E: I was doing so well. I was really using a lot more helpful self-talk and I even noticed I had more energy in the classroom when I quit telling myself how tired I was all the time! But then one day I was a real grump all day and I enjoyed it! I said to myself: "I sure am being grumpy and it feels so good!" I allowed myself that day and was back on track in a day or two.

As a practice exercise for step 4 please reread all the permitter examples shown in Chapter 1, pages 19–22. At the core of all permission is a basic decision to respect and trust one's own feelings. Such trust may fly in the face of some of the things we were taught, such as being unselfish and believing that other people's feelings are more important than our own. However this permission is a means to an end, not an end in and of itself. A prerequisite to nurturing others (end) is the ability to nurture ourselves (means). If teachers do not respect themselves, they often do not respect anyone else either, including their students.

One of the major benefits of a self-supportive position is that it allows us to develop a protective barrier or buffer against unpleasant situations in which we may find ourselves. Teachers desperately need this internal buffer of calmness when they are externally under fire from irate parents or a disgruntled administrator, for example. Teachers need an internal buffer of their own to guard against the detrimental effects of the stressors, inherent in teaching.

The final step, Step 5 is to develop your own guide, instead of the harsh judges, already described in this chapter. A guide affords small, manageable steps; a sensitivity to your own unique environment; a sensitivity to your own feelings, beliefs, and behaviors; and self-reinforcement as you reward yourself for becoming more positive. This step involves the development of a concrete action plan that promotes growth for your unique development without the accompaniment of critical judges.

In some cases, you will need tools to deal with those around you who enjoy the more negative you. Teachers in some schools report to us that they are "Comrades in Complaint" or they are members of the "Ain't It Awful, Ain't It Terrible Club" where the most popular pasttime is to be negative. The more negative teachers often emerge as the leaders of the schools. It is difficult for this "group mentality" to move forward in a growth-oriented manner. It is comforting to know that in our combined half-century of interacting with teachers, this situation is the exception, rather than the rule. Nevertheless, it is worth mentioning that if you are in such a negative environment, you may need "extra effort" to implement a language of self-support.

Two techniques to help you deal with any kind of manipulation from others is the use of (1) I-messages, and (2) the fogging technique. I-messages are discussed in Chapter 2, pages 42–44 of this text. Please refer to this discussion. The fogging technique acknowledges what has just been said without agreeing or disagreeing. For example, a *judgmental comment* such as "Alicia, you really should take that vacation. You may never get another chance." A *hooked-in response* is to say something like: "Well, there wouldn't be much time for me to enjoy sightseeing. After all, I'd have to work some, too. Well, maybe I should go." A *fogging response* is to say something like: "It may seem that way; however, I feel comfortable with my decision."

Maultsby (1975, p. 8) identifies a set of self-questions that may be asked by teachers. These self-questions would make an excellent poster or display for a teacher's lounge or workroom.

SELF-QUESTIONS

1. Is my self-talk helping me to solve problems?

2. Is my self-talk based on objective reality?

3. Is my self-talk optimistic? positive?

4. Is my self-talk being a good friend to myself?

5. Is my self-talk helping me to reach my short and long term goals, personally and professionally?

Watch the overuse of the word "should" in self-talk. "Should" has some first cousins (e.g., must, if, have to) that are also not helpful. "Shoulds" are irrational because when we use the word, the situation has already happened and cannot be changed. If no one in the world ever used the word "should" again, the world might be better. As a challenge, try not to say "should" for an entire week and substitute instead honest preferences, desires, and opinions with phrases such as "I would prefer," "I would like," "I wish." Saying "I would prefer that you not treat me this way" is an honest preference; whereas saying "You should not treat me like this" is a rule-based demand that creates defensiveness and stress in ourselves and others (Edson, 1986).

Irrational beliefs cause teacher stress when teachers talk in maladaptive, unhealthy, non-facilitative ways to themselves. Please refer to the list of irrational beliefs in Chapter 1, page 4. When we catch ourselves saying something like: "What if I can't do this right? That will be just terrible. I'll get in so much trouble. I can't stand this!" we identify that this kind of self-talk comes from one of Ellis's irrational beliefs ("I must be thoroughly competent, adequate, and achieving").

The good news is that changing these irrational beliefs to rational beliefs is possible, within a teacher's capabilities. The best news is that when we change our beliefs to rational, healthy ones, our self-talk is positively affected and also changed. Rational self-talk promotes rational teacher behavior. In addition, rational, healthy self-talk may likely reduce teacher stress. First, the 10 rational beliefs are listed, followed by a discussion of how rational self-talk can reduce teacher stress.

RATIONAL BELIEFS THAT MAY REDUCE STRESS

1. Everybody doesn't have to love me. I don't need approval all the time. If people like me, that's great. If they don't, I will still be a worthwhile person and teacher.

2. Making mistakes is something all individuals do, including teachers. I will accept mistakes I make and mistakes that others make (including my students).

3. Situations and other people are the way they are. I can accept things the way they are and accept people the way they are. Things will not always be the way I want, but I can handle this. I cannot control or change other people. I can only control and change my reactions to situations and to people!

4. I can handle it even if things go wrong. Things usually go just fine and when they do not, I will take care of it. Worrying is a drain on my energies and causes stress.

5. Unhappiness and stress are caused by my reactions to outside circumstances, not the circumstances themselves. I am responsible for how I feel and for what I do. Nobody can force me to feel a certain way. My reactions are my choice.

6. I can be flexible. There are many ways to solve the same problem. There is no "one way." Some ways may seem more sensible to me; however, other people have worthwhile, workable ideas, just as I do (Anderson, 1981, pp. 51–52).

7. I am capable. In most cases, I don't need someone else to take care of me or my problems. I can make good decisions for myself. I am capable.

8. I can change. My past does not have to force me to be a certain way. Every day is a new beginning. It is ridiculous to think human beings can't change.

9. Other people are capable. I don't have to save the world. Helping is helping others to help themselves. It is insulting to others to take away their responsibility to solve their own problems. I don't need to change other people or fix up their lives. I can show concern and care, but I should not own other peoples' problems for them.

10. It is important to try. Avoiding a task does not provide me an opportunity for success and enjoyment.

If possible, take a few minutes and react to and comment on the rational beliefs. A suggested activity that our students have really enjoyed and found helpful is to develop (by orally describing or writing) a potentially stressful teaching situation and the accompanying irrational self-talk. Next, they convert their irrational self-talk to rational self-talk statements and think about the possible benefits. Three examples completed by classroom teachers are as follows:

EXAMPLE 1

Teaching situation: A student in your class calls you, the teacher, an obscene name in front of the whole class.

Irrational self-talk: You have really ruined my day! I'll have to show you who's the boss.

Rational self-talk: I don't like that remark, but I'll stay calm. I can handle this.

Discussion of benefits: The irrational self-statements stem from the irrational beliefs that people should act the way I want and unhappiness is caused by other people. The irrational self-talk is childish and will set up a hostile, combative atmosphere in the classroom. On the other hand, the rational self-talk is a coping self-statement that is problem-focused rather than child-focused. It typifies the educational premise that effective teachers separate the deed from the doer. This kind of self-talk will more likely promote a calm role-model for the students and foster a more cooperative atmosphere.

EXAMPLE 2

Teaching situation: The students point out that you have written the wrong list on the board.

Irrational self-talk: Oh no, what will the parents think when these children go home and tell them about my mistake? What if the principal walked in now? This is really not my day! An awful day is more like it!

Rational self-talk: Even teachers are entitled to human error. I can make mistakes and still be an outstanding teacher. The important thing is to model how to handle one's own mistakes in a healthy manner.

Discussion of benefits: The irrational self-talk originates from the erroneous belief that, "I must not make mistakes and if I do it's awful." The rational self-statements come from the rational belief that it is great to do something without error. However, if mistakes are made, it's not the end of the world—it's not even awful. Some mistakes are unfortunate, but they are not likely to be catastrophic. The irrational self-talk sounds like a "nervous teacher," who has stressed herself unnecessarily by imposing unrealistic demands upon herself. This is not a good role model for children.

EXAMPLE 3

Teaching situation: The teacher next door to you is going through a divorce and she has "dumped" all of her "extra" teaching responsibilities (e.g., bus duty, supervising recess) on you because she "can't handle it."

Irrational self-talk: Poor Alice, she's so upset about all of this. I'll have to watch her children at lunch, too. She can't possibly be strong enough to watch her students. Poor thing.

Rational self-talk: Alice is going through some hard times. I'll lend her a hand on some things I can help with, but she'll have to do some things for herself or get a long term substitute until she gets her life in order. Alice is probably capable of working something out so that her teaching responsibilities are assumed.

Discussion of benefits: Alice is treated like a capable person in the rational self-talk examples. Benefits will be that Alice will likely take responsibility for her own problems. She will not grow to resent the rescuer which often happens when others take over and own a problem that belongs to someone else. Alice is treated as an equal, not as a pitiful, incapable person portrayed in the irrational self-talk examples. In addition, the rational self-talk prevents Alice's friend from assuming an unrealistic workload that may cause the friend additional stress.

Teacher stress can be diminished when we change our irrational beliefs to rational beliefs, use rational self-talk based on our rational beliefs, and reinforce ourselves for using healthy, facilitative self-talk. Rational self-talk fosters teachers who are realistically less demanding (e.g., "Students may not be nice to me all the time."); less likely to cop out (e.g., "Everything is fine even if I have one student that is really difficult: I can handle this."); less likely to overgeneralize (e.g., "The confusion only happens when I forget to remind the student, not *all* the time. I don't *always* blow the lesson. In fact, I rarely do. Just remember to remind the students."); and less likely to catastrophize (e.g., "If I have to get up in front of the whole faculty, I'll handle it. It will not be so horrible, just a challenge!"). When teachers verbally guide themselves and their students with less unrealistic demands, less avoidance of problems, less overgeneralization, and less catastrophizing, these teachers and their students will more likely be less stressed. Irrational beliefs lead to irrational self-talk which leads to stress—self-imposed stress. Rational beliefs lead to rational self-talk which leads to less stress for most individuals, including teachers.

TEACHER ANGER

Since teachers are human they experience anger. However, Thomas Gordon (1974) says that anger is a secondary emotion that follows a primary emotion (e.g., fear, embarrassment, concern, disappointment, panic). He urges teachers to speak to students from the primary emotion felt first, using honest "I" messages instead of angry "you" messages. For example, let's consider the young pupil who is late arriving at the bus when the class is on a field trip to the zoo. While the teacher is waiting for the late child to arrive, what primary emotion is the teacher most likely experiencing? (worry/fear—fear that something may have happened to the child, or at least worry/concern). The most honest "I" message" when the child finally arrives at the bus is to say: "I was worried about you, when you didn't show up on time. What happened?" Instead many of our preservice and inservice teachers have replied that by the time the late child arrives at the bus they would probably respond with an angry "you-message." "You are always late! Where have you been? Didn't you know you were keeping us waiting?" To sum, one way to think about teacher anger is to first determine if another primary emotion preceded the anger. What was I feeling before I became angry? If I can determine that it was fear, worry, disappointment, or embarrassment for example, then I can attempt to speak honestly from the original feeling instead of the secondary emotion, anger.

Teachers often report angry outbursts from themselves in the classroom. They have frequently said that they would appreciate knowing strategies to control these outbursts. A distinction should be made here between "feeling anger" and "expressing anger." We believe it might be beneficial if teachers never felt anger (consciously chose not to feel anger) in their reaction to students. However, this is probably unrealistic when the context of the teaching environment is considered: teachers and students live together usually in one small room for 180 days, approximately 6–7 hours per day. In such intimate, close contexts, we believe it would be highly unusual for there to be a total lack of teacher anger. Therefore, it is the expression of teacher anger that is critical to the climate of the classroom. Frequent angry outbursts from a teacher foster a climate of fear and hostility, and students often demonstrate the same types of angry outbursts, learned first-hand from the teacher. Shouting, out-of-control teachers often have loud, out-of-control classrooms, and occasionally wonder why. Teachers report to us that their out-of-control, often-angry colleagues seem not to associate the link between what children see and hear others do and what children do themselves. In sum, it seems a normal reaction for teachers to feel anger upon occasions; however, the expression of this anger should be monitored carefully.

Teachers need to monitor their visible reactions of anger because we as teachers serve as role models for our students. For example, it should not surprise us if our students shout, rant, and rave at their friends if we, as their teachers, demonstrate angry outbursts while teaching them to be self-controlled students. Meichenbaum (1977, pp. 166–167) provides examples of self-statements used successfully to control anger. We have shared these with many students, and we use them in our own teaching. We hope that you will refer to all the Meichenbaum examples; however, we will only be able to present a few examples from the total list:

SELF-STATEMENTS TO CONTROL TEACHER ANGER

Example 1

Preparing for conflict: "This is going to upset me, but I know how to deal with it."

Impact and confrontation: "I don't need to prove myself. Stay calm. Just continue to relax."

Coping with angry feelings: "It's just not worth it to get so angry. I have a right to be annoyed, but let's keep the lid on."

MAKING A SELF-TALK TAPE EXERCISE #3

1. Use 15–18 examples of positive self statements about any topic that is bothering you. Some examples are provided in this chapter on pages 57 and 58. In addition, Helmstetter (1987) in his book: *The Self-Talk Solution* lists over 2500 self-talk entries for a variety of typical problems, such as procrastination, losing weight, staying calm, etc. On the tape, repeat each of the positive self-statements three times, with a short pause in between each of them. Then go on to the next self-suggestion, again repeating it 3 times, until you have completed your list of Self-Talk phrases.

2. End the tape by asking someone you value to record each of the phrases one additional time, but this time change "I" to "You." "I am a good listener," becomes "You are a good listener." This recognizes our need to have external validation—someone else telling us we are doing a good job.

3. Please listen to the tape several times a day for the next few weeks. The best times to listen to the tape are generally early in the morning, just before you go to sleep, or anytime when a relaxed time is available. Repetition of the self-talk is essential.

4. During your field experience, student teaching, or teaching day read over your list of positive self-statements at least once while you are at school.

5. The tape may be accompanied by background music, if desired.

---

and accomplishing goals through self-talk. His concrete self-talk suggestions, written word for word, may be modified as the particular situation or need requires.

One way for teachers to become less anxious is to become more adept at problem solving. Helmstetter offers some self-talk sentences that provide encouragement and self-direction for efficient problem solving (Helmstetter, 1986, pp. 156–157).

I'm good at solving problems. I like challenges and I meet them head on.

Problems are my teachers. They help me to learn and grow. Without them, I would be going nowhere. With them, I am moving forward in the direction of my own goals.

When I meet a new problem, I do not see the problem as my enemy. I know that finding the solution to the problem will move me forward in my own personal growth.

Because I know that problems are a key ingredient in my spiritual and mental education and preparation, I recognize that all problems are important to me.

I do not fear problems, I solve them. I do not ignore problems, I confront them. I do not avoid problems, I conquer them!

I know that every problem holds within itself the keys to its own solution. Therefore, the better I understand the problem, the clearer I am able to see its solution.

Having problems is not a problem for me. I am confident, self-assured, positive, and determined. I know that I am going to overcome any problem I encounter and I do.

I am good at breaking large obstacles down into smaller pieces that are easier to handle. And I never make any problem appear to be larger than it actually is.

I never worry. I turn "worry time" into positive, constructive, "solution time." I keep my mind alert and open to all solutions—and solutions come quickly and easily to me.

I have learned to recognize that many problems carry with them benefits and potential opportunities which would not have presented themselves had the problem not occurred in the first place.

I do not seek to live a life which is free from all problems. Instead, I choose to live a life of finding solutions and enjoying the benefits which those solutions create.

Challenge, conquer, solution, and win are words which I live by daily. "Challenges" are opportunities. "Conquering them" is the inevitable outcome. "Solutions" are the stepping stones to my success, and "Winning" is my way of life.

Teachers are encouraged to read these examples three or four times each day for a week or two. Many teachers have reported that by the end of the time they begin to see their own problems differently and as a result are much less anxious. The statements mentioned above represent a general problem-solving approach that seems to cut across specific anxiety-producing problems. These examples may also be used to develop your own self-talk tape.

TEACHER FRUSTRATION AND BOREDOM

Rohrkemper and Corno (1988) discuss the need for teachers to refrain from protecting students from frustration and boredom. Instead they recommend that teachers "deliberately promote the development of students' adaptive learning within a supportive classroom environment," (p. 297). They define frustration as the "stress of difficulty" and boredom as the "stress of tedium" (p. 298). The adaptive learning techniques recommended for students might also be helpful to teachers. When classroom teachers are excellent role models for dealing effectively with difficulty and tedium, and many of the teachers we know, are; then, students are more likely to benefit from such role models. Students of all ages are always learning from the significant adults in charge of providing their learning experiences. Effective and ineffective coping skills are modeled by teachers whether or not we deliberately plan to model these skills. Therefore, it appears to make good sense to instruct teachers in adaptive teaching skills for dealing with classroom frustration as a prerequisite to these same teachers' modeling, as well as providing explicitly the same adaptive instruction for students in their classrooms.

Adaptive teaching is dependent upon teachers having realistic expectations for classroom reality. They know ahead of time not to expect the expected and are not undone when they are confronted by the complexity and unpredictability inherent in teaching. For example, adaptive teachers know that one of the cornerstones of teaching is flexibility. Plans more often have to be revised during a lesson, than plans are implemented precisely as the teacher envisioned. Teachers who are adaptive and prepared expect the complexity, multidimensionality, spontaneity, immediacy, simultaneity, and unpredictability associated with classroom functioning. They realize, for example, that lesson plans rarely are implemented exactly as they are written.

Complexity or *multidimensionality* relates to the many facets of teaching. For example a teacher is required to diagnose, revise, develop plans, implement lessons, provide meaningful experiences, communicate with parents, involve all the learners, etc. Teachers have on the average 1000 face-to-face interactions per day (Jackson, 1968), make critical decisions approximately every 2 minutes (Clark & Peterson, 1986), and lose 55% of their instructional time to disruption (Gottfredson, 1989, May, personal communication). These percentages illustrate the complexity inherent in teaching.

Spontaneity and *immediacy* in the classroom are related to classroom demands that require teachers to think "quickly on their feet." Spur-of-the-moment, can't-wait-answers are frequent occurrences in the classroom. For example, a frantic parent calls wanting to know why his/her child is having too much homework. The teacher is called upon to give an immediate answer. Perhaps a student has been hurt on the playground; the teacher must react quickly.

Simultaneity is reflected in the variety of teacher tasks that must be dealt with, all at the same time. This is represented by the skill of the teacher successfully managing more than one task at a time, and performing both tasks reasonably well. Teachers are very familiar with this requirement of teaching; they are often exhausted because of it. Some teachers are very skilled at dealing with the simultaneous demands of the classroom. For example, the teacher who can read a story with expression, while comforting an upset child in her lap, and touching another child to calm him/her down.

Unpredictability means that the events in a classroom are not guaranteed to occur as expected. It is easy to be lulled into thinking that a certain occurrence will happen in an expected manner. And just when we are comfortable with that order, the unexpected happens. For example, the teacher is reading aloud one of her favorite books, that, for the past five years students have really enjoyed. However, for this particular group of children, the responses seem to indicate boredom: sighs, squirms, etc. One child in the group walks forward toward the book in the teacher's hand. The teacher believes that this child is coming closer to see the pictures better. But just as the child reaches the teacher's knee, he grabs his belt and asks "Do you know how much this belt cost?" This example typifies the unpredictability of a teacher's job.

Instead of complaining, moaning, and groaning about complexity, spontaneity, etc., adaptive teachers would be shocked if their school day were simple and predictable. Teachers searching for and expecting calm and tranquil working conditions will stand on the verge of hysteria in most, typical classroom scenarios. Jacob Kounin's work (1970) is an excellent resource for fostering knowledge of teaching reality. He found that certain teacher practices were highly related to effective classroom management. He also identified requirements for teacher coping, necessary for dealing with the complexity, spontaneity, simultaneity, and unpredictability in classroom teaching. Teachers can minimize their frustration and boredom by withitness, overlapping, smoothness, momentum, and group alerting (Kounin, 1970).

Teachers who are aware of what is going on in their classrooms, dealing with student behavior and academic tasks, and who demonstrate this awareness to their students have impressive student involvement with tasks and less student misbehavior. Kounin terms this awareness *withitness*. *Overlapping* practices are also associated with successful classroom managers. Attending to two events or situations at the same time and performing both of these tasks reasonably well comprise overlapping skills. *Smoothness* is exhibited when the teacher stays with the logical organization of instruction. Examples are when the teacher continues with a learning activity without mentioning unrelated topics, being distracted easily, interrupting students when they are trying to work, leaving a lesson in midstream, or reversing directions. Smoothness means that the teacher organizes his/her time in such a way that the teacher's behavior does not interfere with the goal of the lesson. *Momentum* relates to the pacing of a learning activity. An example of lack of momentum is when a teacher overdwells on a point that the students already understand. The last teacher practice that Kounin found to be highly related to effective classroom management is termed *group alerting*. These are teachers' behaviors that keep students alert and "on their toes" as to when or if they will be called upon to demonstrate their skills and/or knowledge. Examples are calling on students at random. Nonalerting practices are those that overprotect students from being held accountable, such as round-robin reading.

If we complement Kounin's work with metacognition, we may greatly increase a teacher's ability to cope with negative emotional reactions, such as frustration. A figure designating Kounin's concepts and examples of accompanying metacognition is provided below.

FIGURE 3–1 Metacognitive Self-Talk Applied to Kounin's Characteristics of Effective Teachers

Kounin's Idea	*Facilitative Self-Talk**
	*These are comments that the teacher makes to herself or himself.

I. Withitness

- Keep alert to sights and sounds in the class
- Arrange students for easy visibility

- Scan the entire classroom when I am working with an individual or small group of students
- At the first detection of misbehavior, use a brief acknowledgment to let the class know that you know of the misbehavior

I. Withitness

- "I can tell they are all on task."
- "Gerry keeps hiding behind that taller person in front of him. Better move him."
- "Glance across the room at everyone. See what the back table of students is up to."
- "I see Jill looking over at Susan. She is writing a note to Susan and trying to distract her. I need to tell Jill to get back to work."

II. Overlapping

- Attend to two events at the same time whenever necessary to keep the classroom functioning moving optimally.
- When instructing one group, acknowledge difficulties that students outside of the group may be having but keep group instruction moving.
- Correct misbehavior but keep instruction moving.

II. Overlapping

- "Listen to the message on the intercom and write Jonathan's mother a quick note about his behavior."
- "I need to get David to keep explaining that math problem outloud to us, while I check Ginger's problem. David, . . ."
- "I can't even hear Stewart read. I need to remind the class quickly to quiet down, so I can hear Stewart."

III. Smoothness

- Preplan the lesson so that extraneous matters are taken care of beforehand
- Once students are absorbed in their work, do not distract them. Leave them alone to work and assist them individually.

III. Smoothness

- "Don't forget to get the overhead for this next lesson and make sure it is working correctly."
- "I certainly would like to interrupt them to tell them about the lunch menu, but that can wait until a bit later when they aren't so absorbed in their projects."

IV. Momentum

- Keep the lesson moving briskly.

IV. Momentum

- "Don't explain this three times, twice is enough."

FIGURE 3–1 *Continued*

Kounin's Idea	*Facilitative Self-Talk**
• Do not overdwell on a minor or already understood part of the lesson.	• "I know they understand this part—move on to the next level."
• Correct students quickly without nagging and return to the lesson promptly	• "It would be better if Brenda put away her toys for right now. Brenda. . . All eyes on the chalkboard for the next problem."
• Have students move from one activity to the next without having to wait for each other on each subpart of the transition	• "I believe everyone should be on page 216. I need to go on with the discussion even if one or two are still looking for the right page."
V. Group Alerting	V. Group Alerting
• Call on students at random	• "I keep calling on the same students over and over. Call on some volunteers."
• Raise group interest by interspersing suspense between questions by such statement as, "This is a very important question? Can you work this one out? You have not worked on this before."	• "I want them to get more interested in this lesson. Remember to tell them motivating clues such as, 'This is a new idea.' "
• Have the entire group or class respond in unison using signaled responses such as Agree/Disagree Cards, Thumbs Up/Thumbs Down, Is It a . ? ! ?	• While Stephanie was answering, this whole side of the room was off-task. I better use some agree/disagree cards to involve them in their peer's thinking.
• Physically move around the room and ask students to show what they have done	• "I need to move over to that back group of girls and take a look at their poster."
• While asking one student to respond, look at other students	• "Beverly is responding but I need to scan the entire room and then come back to Beverly to reassure her that I am listening to her answer."

Teacher behaviors (i.e., stress, anger, anxiety, frustration, and boredom) are all unhealthy emotional reactions that are likely to be diminished if teachers implement a constructive self-talk program. The self-talk serves as a verbal mediator to eliminate or diminish teacher stress, anger, anxiety, frustration, and boredom. The suggested activities (e.g., changing irrational beliefs to rational beliefs, self-talk statements, and affirmation training) can be used to inhibit other negative emotions (e.g., worry, panic), not just the emotions mentioned along with these approaches. It may be helpful to synthesize, adapt, modify, and extend the suggested activities across other negative emotional reactions for your own particular needs. One of our doctoral students, Susan LaFave, who is presently a classroom teacher, developed a teacher's guide for using coping skills. This guide is presented below. It is intended as a guide for teachers to cope with the stress, anger, anxiety, and frustration of teaching.

Teacher's Guide for Coping with the Stress, Anger, Anxiety and Frustration of Teaching

Self-Talk: What Is It?

A. A drive-through taping service.

B. Singing along with the radio in the car.

C. An indication of early senility.

D. The talk you direct to yourself out loud and in your head.

If you chose answer "D," you are right. Think about it—we repeat phone numbers out-loud to ourselves and silently tell ourselves to keep going in the middle of aerobics. We also hear others, including our students, talking to themselves. Self-talk is present in our lives much more often than we realize.

Self-talk includes those things that we say to ourselves aloud when alone and in the presence of others as well as the talk we say to ourselves in our head silently. We have done this kind of self-talk most of our lives. Through an awareness and the monitoring of our self-talk, we can help make our lives more productive.

Remember: Self-talk includes all the things we say to ourselves aloud and silently.

Self-Talk: In What Situations Do We Use It?

A. When we lose our car keys.

B. When we meet someone new.

C. When we are working out.

D. All of the above.

If you chose "D," all of the above, you are exactly correct. We use self-talk in all facets of our lives and in many different situations.

Manning (1991) suggests four domains or main areas in which we may use self-talk: **Emotional, Physical, Social and Cognitive**. Please sort the following situations according to their particular domains. Feel free to add any of your own.

Situations

A. studying	L. working out
B. in traffic	M. parent conferences
C. remembering for recall	N. mistake making
D. expressing anger	O. remembering someone's name
E. when tired	P. breaking boredom
F. problem solving	Q. new social situations
G. coping with non-friends	R. meeting someone new
H. listening	S. feeling guilty
I. rationalizing	T. logical thinking
J. reading	U. time with in-laws
K. getting lost	

DOMAINS

Emotional	Physical	Social	Cognitive
_____	_____	_____	_____
_____	_____	_____	_____
_____	_____	_____	_____

Answers
Emotional: B, D, I, K, N, P, S   Physical: E, L
Social: G, M, O, Q, R, U   Cognitive: A, C, F, H, J, T

Sorting the situations in which we use self-talk creates a new awareness of when we use it. It is somewhat surprising to find out how often we use self-talk without even realizing it.

Each situation gives rise to different interchanges. **Intrapersonal** interchanges are those we have with ourselves. **Interpersonal** interchanges are those we have with others. All situations involve interchanges with ourselves and/or others. We must not only be aware of the situation, but of the type of interchange in which we are involved. With this new awareness, we learn to recognize the types of self-talk we use.

Remember: We use self-talk throughout our lives in at least four different situations: **emotional, physical, social,** and **cognitive** and in two types of interchanges: **intrapersonal** (ourselves) or **interpersonal** (with others). Self-talk is present and available for us to harness to our advantage.

Self-Talk: What Types Are There?

A. Restive and nonrestive.

B. Facilitative and nonfacilitative.

C. Decorative and nondecorative.

D. Suggestive and nonsuggestive.

By choosing "B," we now know that there are two kinds of self-talk: facilitative or helpful and nonfacilitative or unhelpful.

Please note that the terms "positive" and "negative" are not used in this context. These terms do not clearly describe the kinds of self-talk we use. Choosing to speak to ourselves in a "negative" manner may be very facilitative for some of us. Facilitative and nonfacilitative self-talk is very individual and the speaker determines the helpfulness or unhelpfulness of self-talk.

Facilitative self-talk is that which allows us to meet our goal(s) or handle a particular situation. Nonfacilitative self-talk defeats our purpose and may also harm our self-esteem. Self-talk statements are often used for self-questioning, self-guiding, self-correcting, self-coping, and self-reinforcing. We will concentrate on the self-coping statements.

The best way to recognize examples of facilitative and nonfacilitative self-talk is by labelling them. Please read each statement below and label them: "F" for facilitative, "N" for nonfacilitative.

_____ 1. I can't possibly teach this unit in a week.

_____ 2. I may not be able to get through to Sam, but I will try my best.

_____ 3. This is a difficult math concept to teach, but I will be pleased when I have reached my students.

_____ 4. I hate being in school when the weather is so nice.

Answers: (1) N   (2) F   (3) F   (4) N

While these examples may seem obvious, they are not always recognized as we talk to ourselves.

Facilitative statements are best written in the first person singular and in the present tense. Example: I am doing a terrific job. It is usually more meaningful to talk to ourselves in this manner. If we say, "You are doing a terrific job" to ourselves, it may sound as if we are talking to someone else.

Using the present tense is also important. To tell ourselves, "I am doing a terrific job" will help us remain on task much better than "I will do a terrific job." "I will" indicates something that we will do in the future, not something we are doing right now.

As we become more familiar with facilitative self-statements, we will be better able to recognize nonfacilitative ones. Three are listed next. Please rewrite the statements below in a facilitative or helpful way.

1. Darn! I must be the slowest fourth grade teacher since I haven't finished this multiplication unit yet.

   _____

   _____

2. I am so tired. I'll never finish correcting these papers.

   _____

   _____

3. I can't believe the buses are late again. I wish these students would hurry and leave.

   _____

   _____

Sample Answers

1. Even though I am the last to finish this multiplication unit, I know I am doing my best and my children are learning. I'll try to catch up with the other fourth grades in the next unit.

2. I'll correct as many of these papers as I can beginning with the most important assignments. If I don't get them all done, I will finish them when I have time. I am doing the best I can.

3. Even though it's been a long day, I know that the late buses are not the children's fault. I will give them something fun to do while they wait and the time will pass more quickly.

Again, awareness comes into play. Awareness is the key to using more facilitative self-talk. Through our awareness of how and when we talk to ourselves, we will be better able to cope with the day-to-day stresses in our profession.

Remember: Use first person singular statements in the present tense for the most facilitative self-talk.

Self-Talk: Why Do We Need Awareness?

A. To promote more facilitative self-talk.

B. To be accepted socially.

C. To sell insurance.

D. To get a raise.

Answer "A" is right! Awareness is the key to improving one's self-talk. Awareness of our own thinking is labeled metacognition or "thinking about our own thinking." Examples include (a) realizing that you have made an error while adding a column of numbers or (b) recognizing your lack of comprehension as you read the latest memo from your principal.

By becoming aware of our own thinking, we can better control our own thinking. We use metacognition on a daily basis both in the classroom and in our private lives. Through the monitoring of our own thinking, we should be better able to produce facilitative self-talk.

Remember: **Awareness** is the key to more facilitative self-talk. Using our knowledge of metacognition and its relationship with self-talk to our advantage as we cope with day-to-day stresses will increase the likelihood of more productive days and improved mental health.

Self-Talk: By What Is It Influenced?

A. Television

B. The weather.

C. External and internal forces (locus of control)

D. The price of tea in China.

Answer "C" is correct! Our self-talk is greatly influenced by our locus of control: the external and internal forces that exert control over our lives. External forces include the weather, clothes, other people, luck, etc.—all things that are outside ourselves. Internal forces include effort, ability, motivation, etc., which can only be found within. Knowledge of one's personal locus of control is an important step in the use of metacognition.

There are instruments developed expressly for this purpose. Sample items, similar to the ones on the Rotter Locus of Control Scale are found in Chapter 2 on page 40.

Next you will see a drawing of Tillie, the teacher. Tillie has many wonderful strengths. She is, for example, caring, intelligent, organized, etc. After reading all of Tillie's strengths, you may wish to try the "Tillie Exercise" described.

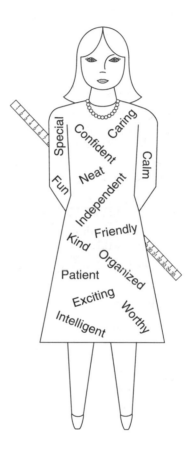

Directions: Please read the following story about Tillie Teacher as you hold her picture. Each time you read something that will affect her self-talk in a nonfacilitative way, rip off a piece of Tillie. Continue in your effort until the end of the story. This story is adapted from *I Am Lovable and Capable* (Canfield, 1980).

Tillie Teacher got up one morning feeling pretty good about herself. She had had a good night's sleep and was ready for the day. Her roommate called from downstairs, "Get up, Tillie, you're always running late. What do you want to do, be late for school? Hurry!"

She tried to hurry, but got her pantyhose on backwards, then she forgot her earrings, and caught her blouse in her skirt zipper. "I am so clumsy," she thought.

When she got downstairs, her roommate laughed at her and said, "Just look at you, do you want to look silly going to school? Let me help you. What would you do without me? And another thing, did you remember to pay the rent? Don't know why I'm asking, of course you didn't—you never remember without a reminder. You better eat your breakfast, and hurry."

"She's right," thought Tillie, "I am very forgetful. I really need to work on that."

Tillie got behind the wheel of her car feeling a little rough, but not completely destroyed. As she reached a four-way stop, she was a little slow taking her turn to go. The driver behind her laid on the horn and gave her an obscene gesture, so she pulled away as quickly as possible. Tillie said aloud, "I am so out of it today. I hope I can get it together."

Arriving late to school she went by the office to sign in and check her box. She picked up the attendance card from her box, signed it, and started to her room.

As she walked by the principal on the way to her room, he looked at her especially sternly. Tillie thought, "Oh, well, here goes" and said, "Good morning, Mr. Filibuster, how are you?"

"Miss Tillie, you're late again today. I hope you aren't going to make a habit of this. You were to be in your room five minutes ago!"

"Sorry, Mr. Filibuster—I was running late again," replied Tillie. Off Tillie trudged to her room to wait for the bell to ring.

"I sure do wish I could get here on time and be a person people could be proud of," thought Tillie.

When class finally started, Tillie couldn't find her attendance card. She started to send a student to the office to check on it when a knock at the door interrupted her train of thought. It was one of the secretaries with her attendance card and a note from Mr. Filibuster. The note read:

"Miss Tillie, you seem to have forgotten your attendance card by the sign-in sheet again. You do this everyday. You need to be more organized! How do you expect to get things done on time? Please come by my office after school today to discuss organization ideas."

Mr. Filibuster

Tillie's day seemed to be going downhill, so she was very glad when it was over. She must have gotten up on the wrong side of the bed because she:

- *had to redo her attendance card*

- *wasn't asked to be on the reading committee about which she knew so much; she was assigned instead to the health committee about which she knew nothing.*

- *dropped her tea at lunch*

- *had to leave school on time in order to pay the rent, but had to stay and meet with Mr. Filibuster which resulted in a late charge with the landlord.*

How glad she would be to get home! When she finally arrived there, her roommate said, "Tillie, don't forget it's your day to clean the oven today!"

Well, what did you think? There's not much left of Tillie Teacher, is there? Did you recognize situations and emotions that occur in your own life everyday? Think about Tillie's day. Was her self-talk facilitative or nonfacilitative? Take just a moment to go back over the story to underline all the facilitative self-talk Tillie might have found if she had monitored her own thinking. If Tillie's locus of control is more internal, she would not have let circumstances affect her as adversely. If you are finding it difficult to find facilitative self-talk, underline all the nonfacilitative self-talk. Tillie's monitoring would definitely have found much more nonfacilitative self-talk, wouldn't it? This would lead us to believe that Tillie has a more external locus of control. It is easy to see through the Tillie Teacher illustration how our lives are influenced by our locus of control orientation. However, we can make the effort to monitor and control our internal forces to overcome the difficult external forces we face everyday. One of the best ways to do this is through recognizing and using facilitative self-talk.

Remember: Awareness of our locus of control and its effect on our self-talk in both intrapersonal and interpersonal interchanges can be facilitative.

Self-Talk: How Do We Use It to Cope?

A. Ignore it.

B. Implement for colleagues of yours.

C. Teach yourself how to use it.

D. Use it in a facilitative manner in coping situations.

Did you choose answer "D"? Absolutely correct! By teaching ourselves how to use facilitative self-talk, we can apply it to situations that require coping skills.

Take a moment to identify at least five situations from your experience that you feel strongly require the use of coping skills. Write them below.

1. _____
2. _____
3. _____
4. _____
5. _____

First, label each situation you chose as predominately Emotional "E," Social "S," Physical "P," or Cognitive "C." Second, label each situation involving an intrapersonal interchange with an "A" and each interpersonal interchange with a "B." Third, label each as requiring verbal mediation in the form of time as "T" or semantics (word meaning) as "W."

Take a moment to categorize your choices through the use of "hash" marks in the organizer below.

Emotional _____   Social _____

Physical _____   Cognitive _____

Intrapersonal _____   Interpersonal _____

Time _____   Semantics (Word Meaning) _____

Did you recognize any one area as being more significant to you? A large grouping of hash marks in one area is a strong indicator of a particular emphasis. If your marks are fairly evenly distributed, then you are not overly concerned about any one area. Through awareness of the area in which you find coping most necessary, you'll be better able to focus your self-talk.

Awareness alone is not sufficient, however. Suggestions (Manning, 1991) that may be of assistance as we attempt to better cope are as follows: (1) self-record, (2) goal story interview, (3) self-talk tape, and (4) cue cards.

Each approach has individual benefits. However, these techniques themselves may assist you or provide a springboard for an idea of your own that better suits your needs. No approach is appropriate for everyone.

Self-Record

This record may be used as coping situations occur. You may also want to use it at set intervals (every hour, etc.), to monitor your coping skills.

Remember to use first person, present tense statements when writing your own self-record. The self-record is to promote awareness of appropriate self-talk.

1. I am aware of my self-talk.   Yes   No

2. I am using facilitative self-talk.   Yes   No

3. I am proud of my self-talk.   Yes   No

4. I am coping through the use of   Yes   No
   my self-talk as verbal mediation.

These few statements should be enough to evoke awareness as necessary. You may want to add more statements of your own that meet your individual needs.

Goal Story Interview (Modified)

This method may be especially helpful when you have particular goals in mind (i.e., teacher of the year, improved test scores, etc.). It is a problem-solving metacognitive strategy developed by Goldman (1982) and modified by Manning (1991).

Step 1   Write about something you want for yourself (i.e., teacher of the year, etc.). Be sure to tell what. Write the accompanying self-talk.

Step 2   Describe why you want this particular thing (i.e., teacher of the year, etc.). Tell why. Write the accompanying self-talk.

Step 3   Write a "Plan of Action." Describe the steps for obtaining your goal. Write how and the accompanying self-talk.

Step 4   Write about wanting this "something" but not being able to obtain it. Write the accompanying self-talk.

Step 5   Write about overcoming the obstacle and still being able to obtain your "goal" in the end. Write how obstacles were circumvented. Write accompanying self-talk. Write self-coping and self-reinforcing statements if the goal is unattainable at this time.

Awareness of our goals and the steps necessary to reach them is sometimes not enough. Through a written exploration of our feelings and self-talk, it will be easier to write facilitative self-coping statements.

Self-Talk Tape

Manning (1991) also suggests the use of self-talk tapes for teachers. By writing your own script of coping statements and listening to them two or three times daily, you are affording both your conscious and subconscious the opportunity to internalize this facilitative self-talk. Remember to use the facilitative self-talk format of first person, singular statements. The steps for making a Self-Talk Tape are presented earlier in this chapter on page 57.

Cue Cards

Cue cards or posters are suggested by Manning (1991) for use in the classroom to help remind students of facilitative self-talk. Some suggestions for cue cards to be used by teachers at their desks as a personal reminder of facilitative self-talk for coping are suggested below. Develop your own cards. You'll be surprised at how effective a quick reminder can be.

- I can do anything I'm capable of if I take my time and do my best.
- I can handle this interruption. I am on task and am keeping the students on task.
- I am calm. I am not losing my temper. I have control.
- I have made a mistake, but I am still a good person. I am not upset. I am doing my best to fix my error.
- I am doing my best. If I can't get it done on time, I'll finish as quickly as I can.
- I am doing a super job. I am taking things one step at a time.
- My students are special. I am lucky to teach them and they are lucky to have me as a teacher. We are a special combination.
- I am doing a g-r-reat job. I have earned praise, but I am not a snob about it.
- THREE CHEERS FOR ME! I am doing my best. I am learning to appreciate myself.

Teacher Survey: Self-Talk and Coping

Education _____   Certification _____
Years of Experience in Present Position _____
Number of Years in Teaching Field _____

Directions: Please rate each opinion statement below using the scale provided. (1=Strongly Agree; 2=Agree; 3=Somewhat Agree; 4=Somewhat Disagree; 5=Disagree; 6=Strongly Disagree)

I use facilitative self-talk when . . .

1. I am teaching my students in front of the classroom   1 2 3 4 5 6

2. I meet with a group of teachers I am familiar with.   1 2 3 4 5 6

3. I meet with the principal.   1 2 3 4 5 6

4. I meet with a group of teachers I am not familiar with.   1 2 3 4 5 6

5. The intercom interrupts my class.   1 2 3 4 5 6

6. My instructional time is interrupted
   (i.e., messenger at the door, etc.).   1 2 3 4 5 6

7. I am beginning a task that is difficult for me.   1 2 3 4 5 6

8. I am completing an ordinary, every day task
   (i.e., walking my class to P.E., eating lunch, etc.).   1 2 3 4 5 6

9. I am trying to meet a deadline.   1 2 3 4 5 6

10. I am confused about something.   1 2 3 4 5 6

11. I am beginning a new, unfamiliar task that is
    difficult for me.   1 2 3 4 5 6

12. I am tired.   1 2 3 4 5 6

13. I feel overworked.   1 2 3 4 5 6

14. I am completing a difficult task.   1 2 3 4 5 6

15. I am trying to relax.   1 2 3 4 5 6

16. I am upset with a student's inappropriate behavior. 1 2 3 4 5 6

17. I am trying to solve a problem.   1 2 3 4 5 6

18. I am trying to understand a problem.   1 2 3 4 5 6

19. I am trying to control my temper.   1 2 3 4 5 6

20. I am bored.   1 2 3 4 5 6

21. I am excited.   1 2 3 4 5 6

22. I am trying to remember something.   1 2 3 4 5 6

23. I am proud of an accomplishment.   1 2 3 4 5 6

24. I meet a new person (people).   1 2 3 4 5 6

25. The buses arrive or leave late.   1 2 3 4 5 6

26. I am criticized.   1 2 3 4 5 6

27. My students are corrected by another teacher.   1 2 3 4 5 6

28. I am taking my students to the cafeteria.   1 2 3 4 5 6

29. I am praised by a peer.   1 2 3 4 5 6

30. I am praised by the principal.   1 2 3 4 5 6

31. I am praised by a student.   1 2 3 4 5 6

32. A student questions my authority or decision.   1 2 3 4 5 6

33. A student argues or disagrees with me.   1 2 3 4 5 6

34. A peer argues or disagrees with me.   1 2 3 4 5 6

35. A supervisor agrees or disagrees with me.   1 2 3 4 5 6

36. I am running late.   1 2 3 4 5 6

37. I get a "see me" note in my box from the principal. 1 2 3 4 5 6

38. I am teaching unfamiliar material.   1 2 3 4 5 6

39. Students are fighting.   1 2 3 4 5 6

40. I am not taken seriously as a professional by
    my peers.   1 2 3 4 5 6

Self-Talk Diary

A self-talk diary for teachers and student teachers provides valuable insight into how we normally talk to ourselves on a daily, routine basis. You may wish to xerox the form on the next page for the number of days you want to keep a self-talk diary.

Please record your self-talk for several days within the contexts indicated.

1. Intercom Interruption

   _____

   _____

   _____

2. Student Misbehavior

   _____

   _____

   _____

3. Walking Class to Special Class

   _____

   _____

   _____

SUMMARY

Metacognitive strategies, intended for the teachers' personal use, are included. Teachers learn metacognitive skills, mentioned in this chapter, as a possible means to inhibit their negative emotional reactions, such as stress, anger, anxiety, and frustration. In addition, procedures for acquiring such strategies and skills are described and detailed. For example, models of self-statements to control anger are presented. Also included are procedures for learning the language of self-support, strategies for converting irrational to rational self-talk, developing a self-talk tape, adaptive teaching, metacognitive self-talk to accompany teacher practice, and a teacher-developed (self-talk) guide for coping with the stress, anger, anxiety, and frustration of teaching.

CHAPTER 4

Understanding Self-Regulated Learning and Teaching

OVERVIEW

First, Vygotsky's theory of verbal self-regulation is explained. Other Vygotskian concepts such as the zone of proximal development and verbal mediation are defined. A brief introduction to several other-regulation teaching/learning models are presented. A more indepth look at these models appears in Chapter 6. To understand self-regulated teaching it is important to first understand self-regulated learning. There is a great deal of information and research on self-regulated learning (see Chapter 1). For example Zimmerman and Schunk (1989) offer six different theoretical views of self-regulated learning: operant, phenomenological, social cognitive, volitional, Vygotskian, and cognitive constructivist. In this chapter each of these is briefly discussed accompanied by a more thorough treatment of the Vygotskian view of self-regulated learning. Finally, the ideas related to self-regulated learning are modified to introduce a new construct: self-regulated teaching.

Self-Questions

1. *Knowledge*. Name two different theoretical views of self-regulated learning.

2. *Comprehension*. Explain the differences between the two views.

3. *Application*. Choose one of the six theories of self-regulated learning and convert the ideas to self-regulated teaching.

4. *Analysis*. Discuss Vygotsky's theory of verbal self-regulation to a peer. Include each of the five parts in your discussion.

5. *Synthesis*. Using the important points of this chapter, build a rationale for why teachers need to be self-regulated in their teaching.

6. *Evaluation*. Your principal has asked you to prepare a critique of self-regulated learning: strengths and weaknesses. What would be included in your critique?

Vygotsky's major goal was to develop a psychology of the mind. Teaching is a mindful task. First in this chapter, we will provide an explanation of Vygotsky's theory of verbal self-regulation and supporting concepts.

THEORY OF VERBAL SELF-REGULATION

Five building blocks comprise and explain this theory. These ideas are as follows: (1) Individuals develop planful speech, (2) Thought and speech converge, creating a qualitative shift from biological to sociohistorical, (3) Cognitive development is determined by language, in particular the social/linguistic experiences of a learner, (4) Speech becomes verbal thought through a development of three stages: external, private, and inner speech, and (5) The major characteristics of verbal self-regulation is purposeful, self-directed speech aimed inward to promote accomplishment of goals. It should be noted that we are Neo-Vygotskian in our explanation of this theory. We do not claim that we have interpreted this theory precisely as Vygotsky meant it. In fact, Vygotsky compared human development to animal development in relation to verbal self-regulation; however, we have chosen not to become this technical. We hope that in our choices, we have preserved the essence of meaning.

Planful Speech

Individuals develop purposeful verbalizations to inform and direct themselves. According to Vygotsky (1962, 1978) this development is curvilinear, with self-regulatory speech-to-self beginning around 24 months in an audible form. This audible speech spoken to and for oneself is known as private speech (Berk, 1985). Private speech increases incrementally from two years old until around age eight, at which time overt speech is mostly internalized and planning speech then becomes a silent guide.

Young children have a tendency to talk aloud to themselves as they go about their activities at play and at school (Berk & Garvin, 1984). This is to say, they sometimes produce verbalizations that do not appear to be intended for, nor adapted to, the listening needs of others, who may or may not be present (Anastopoulos & Krehbiel, 1985). This

---

COLLECTING PRIVATE SPEECH EXERCISE #1

Directions: Choose one to three children (ages 4–6 are best) and observe them during independent school work or play. Try to ensure that conditions are optimal for the use of private speech (e.g., semantic, challenging task performed independently in the presence of a few peers). You can observe children in the school setting or even your own children, nieces, nephews, etc. as they are working on homework or play at home. Children older than 7-years will not be as apt to talk aloud unless they are frustrated by a rather difficult task. Sit near the child and tell him or her that you have to work on something or you just wish to sit close by for a few minutes. After the children realize that you are not there to socialize, but to work, they often will become absorbed in their own tasks or play. As they begin working or playing, they often talk aloud to themselves. If possible collect at least 20 private speech utterances. A private speech utterance is defined as a word, phrase, or sentence separated by a 3–4 second pause from the next word, phrase, or sentence spoken to self or to no one in particular. You might want to hold a small tape recorder to back up your transcriptions of the child's self-talk. Usually you can collect 20 private speech utterances from one child in 4 to 12 minutes. An ideal scenario (based on our experience) has been to catch three or four children working alongside each other or involved in parallel play and sit among them, acting as if you are distracted by your own work. The children are usually talking, but not to each other. With pad and pencil in hand and tape recorder on, focus on one child at a time until 20–25 utterances are collected. Then move to the next child, etc. When you become very proficient at collecting self-guiding speech, you can often keep three separate collections going simultaneously.

tendency is defined as private speech. Vygotsky (1962) viewed private speech as the link in the transition from vocal speech to inner verbal thought. Early in its development, private speech follows children's actions, coming as an afterthought. Then it simultaneously accompanies children's activities. Later, it precedes children's actions and becomes externalized thought where it serves as a tool for self-guidance. Finally during the school years, private speech becomes covert and is internal thought. Berk (1985) stated that in this way, children come to use language to solve problems, to overcome impulsive action, to plan solutions ahead of time, and to master their behavior. For example, Vygotsky wrote, "Speech not only facilitates the child's effective manipulation of objects but also controls the child's own behavior" (Vygotsky, 1978, p. 26), "speech guides, determines, and dominates the course of action, and with the help of the indicative function of words, the child begins to master attention" (p. 35). As children become able to "master this attention", they develop the awareness and conscious control of their thinking. As we have said earlier, this ability to monitor one's thinking is described as metacognition (Flavell, 1979).

Our preservice and inservice teachers often conduct a mini-action research project involving the collection and analysis of children's self-guiding private speech. Exercise #1 is described on page 73, and Exercise #2 is below.

If you choose three children you may only have time to collect a private speech set (20 utterances) once or twice from your group of three. If you are concentrating on only one child, you may wish to collect multiple private speech sets during a variety of contexts (e.g., while the child is working on a task, such as putting a puzzle together; playing with toys, having a snack). You might be wondering why you would want to collect private speech from children. One explanation is that we can learn a great deal about children's thinking via their private speech utterances. Private speech utterances provide a window whereby we can obtain (1) a glimpse of children's past sociolinguistic experiences and (2) a prediction of their cognitive intellectual potential.

CODING PRIVATE SPEECH EXERCISE #2

Directions: Use the coding system described in this chapter on page 75. Categorize each of the utterances according to this coding system developed by Manning (Manning, White, and Daugherty, 1994). Begin by using just the four levels first: Task Irrelevant I; Task Relevant Unhelpful II; Task Relevant Helpful-Cognitive III; and Task Relevant Helpful Metacognitive IV (see page 75, this chapter). After you have categorized each utterance as I, II, III, or IV; then, you have the option of going back and within each category (e.g., III) you further categorize into one of the subcategories listed underneath each major I, II, III, or IV. An example utterance for each of the 13 subcategories is presented in the Figure 4.1. Please refer to this figure in order to code the self-talk utterances.

After you have finished coding all of the utterances for one child, tally how many utterances you have for each of the categories. Suppose your child has 8 task irrelevant (I), 5 task relevant unhelpful (II), 4 task relevant cognitive (III), and 3 task relevant metacognitive (IV); then divide each of these totals by the total number of utterances (e.g., 20). As a result the percentages used by this child are as follows:

$8 \div 20 = 40\%$ Task Irrelevant (I)

$5 \div 20 = 25\%$ Task Relevant, but Unhelpful (II)

$4 \div 20 = 20\%$ Task Relevant, Cognitive (III)

$3 \div 20 = \underline{15\%}$ Task Relevant, Metacognitive (IV)
           100%

FIGURE 4–1   Private Speech Content Classification for Independent School Tasks

	EXAMPLES OF CATEGORIES
I. TASK IRRELEVANT (OFF-TASK)	**Level I**
1. Affect Expression	1. Ohhh-my hand hurts.
2. Commenting (Imaginary others)	2. Batman! Batman!
3. Questioning	3. I see John over there, don't I?
II. TASK RELEVANT (UNHELPFUL)	**Level II**
4. Giving Up	4. I can't do this! I quit!
5. Questioning	5. Why do I have to do this stupid stuff anyway?
III. TASK RELEVANT (HELPFUL/COGNITIVE)	**Level III**
6. Focusing	6. Look at my page.
7. Describing	7. I'm making them blue lines.
8. Questioning	8. Does this go here or here?
9. Directing	9. Put this line right here.
IV. TASK RELEVANT (HELPFUL/METACOGNITIVE)	**Level IV**
10. Correcting	10. No, not this way! The other way! Other Way!
11. Coping	11. It's okay. I messed up. It's okay. Don't worry. I can fix it.
12. Reinforcing	12. Yay! I cut it just right! Nice job!
13. Solving	13. 1-2-3-4-5-6-7-8-9-10. I made 10 straight lines in this maze. I'm right!

Thought and Speech Convergence: From Biological to Sociohistorical

The thought and speech of an individual merge, whereupon thought is verbal and speech is rational. When this convergence takes place a qualitative difference in the heretofore biological development of thinking and speaking takes on a sociohistorical characteristic.

In childhood, the biological development includes a prespeech phase when thought is functional. The actions during the prespeech phase of thought development have been noted in the tenth, eleventh, and twelfth months (Vygotsky, 1962). Examples of prelinguistic thought are purposeful play with toys, planning motor functions such as crawling to a parent, throwing food on the floor.

Another aspect of the biological development that precedes the sociohistorical influence upon thought and speech, is the preintellectual phase of speech development. The child's word play, babbling, perhaps even first words repeated without thinking are examples of emotional forms of behavior, separated from the development of natural thought, or said another way, the intellect. Verbal thought is not predetermined (phylogenetically) but is dependent upon the specific social/linguistic experiences that have accumulated over time (thus history) of each individual (ontogeny). This verbal thought is not subject to the characteristics preset in the natural form of thought and speech.

Knowing this helps us to understand the individuality and uniqueness of inner speech (thought) as it regulates and guides specific human behavior. Once we understand that our self-language possesses the power to motivate, guide, limit, control, and reinforce our own actions, we have a concrete means for restructuring education.

Cognitive Development Determined by Sociolinguistic Experiences

The development of inner speech (verbal thought) is influenced to a great extent by outside social experiences, leaning heavily on the language interactions. These outside factors are outside the natural biological unfolding that comprises each individual's development and usually represent the sociolinguistic experiences between the parent and child, and/or the child and a more experienced peer (e.g., sibling). Rich, substantive, healthy dialogue full of describing, guiding, problem-solving, coping, and reinforcing provides a worthwhile model for children. But beyond a mere model, this verbal environment created within the social transaction between adult or peer and child frames the child's intellectual development. We have known for a long time that the quality of parent-child interaction is a very important ingredient in positive growth and development. This is not new. However, we are underlining and emphasizing that the sociolinguistic experiences create the fabric of a child's mind. If children have models who are excellent language users, who demonstrate clearly verbal problem solving, who cope well and reinforce themselves verbally; then these children will be more advanced intellectually than those in a deprived verbal environment. "The speech structures mastered by children become the basic structures of their thinking" (Vygotsky, 1962, p. 51). This is similar to the idea that expressive language is influenced by receptive language—what goes in, comes out, or garbage in, garbage out. Vygotsky seems to take this a step beyond, when he contends that the language of more experienced members of a cultural unit during social/linguistic experiences of children becomes the means for these children to verbally guide their own lives.

PRIOR SOCIAL/LINGUISTIC EXPERIENCES' EXERCISE #3

In small groups of three or four, recall and discuss with other group members, a growth-producing experience when an important person talked with you a great deal. Describe the situation(s) in which this significant other made a memorable impact upon you. How has this person's words affected your life? What verbal skills did this person model (e.g., problem solving, coping, reinforcing, guiding, defining, identifying)?

Speech Becomes Verbal Thought: Via Three Stages

When children are born, they do not live alone. They develop in a variety of social contexts, often including all or some of the following: parents, grandparents, sisters, brothers, aunts, uncles, and cousins. These more experienced members of the family unit usually talk to the child, albeit in varying amounts, labeling the world and directing the child's activity. The child comes to know the world through the verbalizations of these others. The child is being externally directed through verbalizations. For example, the child soon learns that the configuration of sound "Come here" means a corresponding motoric reaction of walking toward the speaker. The child may come to associate car keys with the parent's directive, "It's time to go ride." The jingle of the keys may prompt the child to find his/her coat even without the usual parent verbal directive. When parents say "bath time," the child may start to shed clothes on the way to the tub. In any event the activity of the child is directed by the verbalizations of an external agent. This is what is termed the "External Stage" of Vygotsky's theory of verbal self-regulation (Stage 1).

The second stage of development is called the "Egocentric Stage." Some researchers object to the name of this stage, "Egocentric," because it is confused with Piaget's meaning of egocentrism. In actuality it is far removed from Piaget's meaning that children see themselves as the center of the universe and are unable to role-take. Vygotsky was interested in the development of verbal self-regulation, instead. We will refer to Stage 2 as the "Private Speech Stage." This is when children have internalized the parents' verbal messages in Stage 1 to the point that they are talking aloud to themselves. They are using words that strikingly resemble the parents' message in Stage 1. Private speech is defined as overt, audible speech-to-self. Within this stage there are three substages. The progression of these stages illustrate the movement of the child from mostly impulsive to much more reflective. This progression is also an account of the term *internalization*. Internalization of the parent message into the cognitive constructs of the child's intellect begins during Stage 1. It is impossible to parcel out exactly when internalization begins and ends. Wertsch and Stone (1985) defined internalization as the relationship between external and internal activity when external activity is transformed into internal activity. The external verbal messages from others are internalized to become an integral part of children's internal cognitive directives.

In Stage 2, children first act and then describe aloud their activity. Next, they act and talk to themselves aloud simultaneously. Finally, they verbally direct aloud, then act in accordance with their verbal guidance. In Stage 2, all substages are in the form of audible self-verbalizations. The child is talking aloud. Gross predictions of age have been ages three (substage a), four (substage b), and five (substage c). Of course, as with any developmental theory, the specific ages are less important than the order of events.

To give several examples, a child in substage 2a will go to a television, turn the knobs, step back, and say aloud to self, "no," "no." This self-direction is actually the parent message which has been internalized by the child, from the External Stage. During substage 2b, the child goes to the television and says aloud to self "no," "no" while at the same time turning the knobs. Finally, in substage 2c, the child has the capability to go to the television, to say "no," "no" aloud, prior to turning the knobs, and to follow this self-direction accordingly.

Another example can be illustrated when asking children to draw a picture. A child in substage 2a will impulsively make scribble marks on the paper and then label aloud the scribbles as "tree." A child in substage 2b will talk aloud to self as he/she draws: "Here's a tree, a sky, under here, etc." A child in substage 2c will talk aloud to self prior to drawing anything, "Now, I will draw a tree, a house, and a bird on my paper." Only in the last instance is the child verbally planning the drawing. The child has moved from reactive behavior (substage 2a) to purposeful, planned behavior based on self-verbalization (substage 2c). Stages 1 (External) and 2 (Private) are alike in the form of verbalizations: both are audible, overt verbalizations. They differ in the source of control: Stage 1 represents external, other-regulation; whereas, Stage 2 represents self-regulated, overt speech-to-self.

Stage 3 is called "Internal Verbal Self-Regulation." In this stage the verbalizations have become inaudible, covert. They are silent. It is important to note that mental problem solving and verbal thought are occurring just as in Stage 2. However, the self-regulatory speech is now spoken inaudibly, rather than audibly. Vygotsky says that the speech-to-self has gone "underground." We prefer to think of it as taking a different form, but being in every way just as instrumental in determining behavior. Therefore Stage 2

(Private) and Stage 3 (Internal) are alike in that they both are characterized by verbal self-regulation of behavior. They differ because Stage 2 is audible, overt; while, Stage 3 is inaudible, covert speech-to-self.

To sum, the three stages of verbal self-regulation are external, egocentric (private speech), and internal. External is when children are regulated by the verbalizations of a more experienced member of society; private speech is when children talk aloud to themselves to bring behavior under their own verbal control. There are three substages in the private speech stage. First children act, then verbalize aloud about the activity. Next they act and speak aloud to themselves simultaneously. Finally they use audible self-verbalization in a purposeful, deliberate way to regulate their subsequent behavior. It is not until "2c" that children are exercising cognitive planning. In Stage 3 they continue to verbally regulate behavior; however, language to self is covert, silent, inhibited speech-to-self. Nonetheless, the power of self-verbalization is still operating in Stage 3 and planful thought is now inner speech.

When individuals are stressed or in disequilibrium, they revert to Stage 2, private overt speech and they talk aloud to attempt to establish equilibrium. Examples are "lost keys," "heavy traffic," or "finding a new location." In all three examples we often talk aloud to ourselves to regulate our behavior: "Where did I have those keys?" "Crazy drivers, look at that!" and "Where was I supposed to turn?" These verbalizations spoken to self are aides to equilibrium or problem resolution.

The progression through the stages is often referred to as movement from an interpsychological to an intrapsychological plane of functioning. In reality, we believe individuals move from intrapsychological, to interpsychological, back to intrapsychological during initial growth and development. To explain, first children are growing from a biological pre-set timetable in speech and thought (phylogenetically). They are very much "within themselves." This is the intrapsychological development. As children shift to the ontogenetic verbal thought as a result of social transaction, they also shift to an interpsychological plane. As they internalize the social messages needed to regulate behavior, they shift back to intrapsychological functioning.

It appears that the progression from intra-to inter-to intra-is more cyclical than linear. Throughout life as we interact with others, especially when learning in a new area of study, we move from what we bring uniquely to the learning situation (intra), to what we learn from someone else (inter), back to how we internalize this information for ourselves (intra), to how this new internalized knowledge impacts on future social transactions (inter). This progression has implications for learning and teaching. We will use these ideas for the foundation of metacognition for classroom processes.

Self-Directed Speech to Accomplish Goals

Inherent in the definition of verbal self-regulation is the concept of goal-directedness. Although there are many areas of confusion and disagreement about Vygotsky's theory of verbal self-regulation, one characteristic of the theory that draws a great deal of consensus has been goal-directed, planful behavior based on verbal thought. If a human purpose is not present, then another area of cognition is operating. Verbal self-regulation does not encompass the entire study of human cognition. It relates more to metacognition, than to cognition. To explain, as mentioned earlier, metacognition is defined as awareness and regulation of one's own thinking. Verbal self-regulation is intrapsychological awareness and control of behavior via speech-to-self as a goal is sought. It is important to remember that verbal self-regulation is not referring to all of the mind's functioning. To sum, the characteristics of verbal self-regulation to remember are (1) awareness, (2) purposeful self-directed speech on an (3) intrapsychological plane aimed at (4) goal achievement. Two other concepts that are germane to a discussion of Vygotsky's theory of verbal self-regulation are the *zone of proximal development* and *verbal mediation*.

ZONE OF PROXIMAL DEVELOPMENT

The zone of proximal development as defined by Vygotsky in *Mind in Society* (1978, p. 86) is "the distance between the actual developmental level as determined by independent problem solving and the level of potential development as determined through problem solving under adult guidance or in collaboration with more capable peers."

This Vygotskian concept has important implications for parenting and teaching. Inherent in the definition is that instruction should precede cognitive developmental levels of children. This learning by social transaction is the means by which children reach higher, more abstract levels. These new levels create more awareness, consciousness, and control over the environment. Vygotsky promoted the idea that social interaction is the means to educating our young. He did not view "good learning" in the paradigm of children, left unaided, struggling to bring about sensible, rational answers that may be meaningless without adult explanation and guidance.

From a Vygotskian perspective, children advance in consciousness and control through the aid of adults and more competent peers. Bruner (1985, pp. 24–25) termed such aid "scaffolding." The tutor in effect performs that critical function of scaffolding the learning tasks to make it possible for the child, in Vygotsky's word, to internalize external knowledge. Skills are mastered first in collaboration with others. Once the knowledge and skills are mastered, children internalize this information as part of their verbal thought. At this point children are able to use speech-to-self dialogues to exercise conscious control over new related learning. The child's language becomes a tool for further learning and deliberate control over the ever-widening environment.

Many researchers (e.g., Ann Brown, James Wertsch) used the "zone of proximal development" concept to formulate systems of educational evaluation and instruction. Brown encourages the use of the zone as an aspect of intelligence testing, beyond the usual way that intelligence is tested (see Brown & Ferrara, 1985 for a complete discussion). She points out that a measure of intelligence is possible when child A (CA = 10; MA = 8) deals with problems up to a twelve year old level with adult guidance, and child B (CA = 10; MA = 8) only deals with problems up to an eight year old's level with the same adult guidance. This is a measure of the capability of children of the same chronological and mental age to perform differentially to a high degree under teacher guidance. Brown proposes that this capability with adult guidance becomes an added dimension to understand and assess learning potential. Traditional IQ measures do not indicate what a student may be capable of when learning is structured and/or aided by a more capable person. Since the instructional process in classrooms is often one of teachers structuring, guiding, and controlling the learning environment to insure optimal gain from learners, it would seem very important to know a student's potential for learning, when aided. As Brown and Ferrara (1985, p. 275) state: "the substantial improvement over initial response (working independently) that is achieved via the interaction of the adult and child (working jointly) is precisely what learning potential methods aim at measuring." These authors discuss three programs which address such an assessment of learning potential. These three programs are Feuerstein's Learning Potential Assessment Device (LPAD), Budoff's Learning Potential and Educability Program, and the Soviet clinical assessments of the zone of promixal development. Readers who wish to know the specifics of these programs are referred to the Brown and Ferrara (1985) reading.

Two important educational implications should be emphasized when considering the zone of proximal development. First, consideration should be given for using this idea in diagnostic intelligence testing previously discussed. Second, instruction should be aimed at the upper, not lower limits of a student's zone. If educational methods/curricula are reserved for only what students can perform independently, then they may be denied the challenge necessary for educational advancement. Both of these implications are extremely important for educational practice.

CONCEPT OF MEDIATION

Verbal mediation is the fundamental unit of analysis for metacognitive processes. For this book mediation is word(s) spoken-to-self to reconcile between stimulus and response. In the case of tutors, the tutors' verbalizations can serve as a social mediator of learning. Later, the verbalizations of the tutor are internalized by the learner and become the learner's self-structures of mediation.

Vygotsky called word meanings, "psychological tools." For him, the word is a "symbol with a definite meaning that evolved in the history of culture" (Davydov & Radzikhovskii, 1985, p. 54). This approach enabled Vygotsky to add a third dimension to the S-R of behaviorism. The "psychological tools" were an intervening link in the behavioristic chain. Meaningful words serve as the determiner that mediates mental functions.

OTHER-REGULATION MODELS

If we combine the definitions of the zone of proximal development and verbal mediation into one understanding, we can envision instructional models. We term these instructional models, *Other-Regulation Models*. Other-regulation models of instruction imply the students' gradual assumption of responsibility for their own learning. This active movement from teacher to learner responsibility is deliberate and planned. Examples of other-regulation models for teaching/learning are proleptic/dyadic instruction, cognitive behavior modification, cognitive self-instruction, and reciprocal teaching (see Chapter 6). In each of these, the adult or peer teacher scaffolds the learning task, models the specific skills and pertinent language, and reinforces learning. Informed training techniques that tell who is likely to benefit, what strategies to use, when to use them, how they are used, and where in the curriculum these strategies might be beneficial are essential components of most other-regulation models. The "teacher" model gradually withdraws instructional and affective support as the student internalizes the self-regulatory processes needed to perform the task.

When children interact with more knowledgeable adults and/or peers, they are often able to accomplish goals that they could not have done on their own. Through social mediation using scaffolding and coaching techniques, instruction should be aimed ahead of a student's developmental level. Vygotsky was critical of the American education tradition of delaying instruction until a student reached "readiness." In contrast, instruction should "rouse to life those functions which are in a stage of maturing, which lie in the zone of proximal development" (Vygotsky, 1956, p. 278, cited in Wertsch & Rogoff, 1984, p. 3). Four "other-regulation" models, using the ideas presented here are explained in greater detail in Chapter 6. The next discussion will center around self-regulated learning theories. These theories serve as the mechanism to develop the framework for self-regulated teaching. To our knowledge, self-regulated learning strategies have never been tailored to the domain of classroom teaching for use by the teacher; self-regulated teaching strategies. Of course, teachers are learners and learners are teachers. In addition teaching and learning are interdependent, reciprocal, and recursive. Because of this, adapting self-regulated learning for teacher behavior in the classroom, is not a difficult task. However, we believe that it is important to make explicit this logical, but often over-looked premise that teachers need to employ and model the skills they are advocating. In fact, one of the reasons that we do not have a large percentage of our students using self-regulated learning strategies may be that a large percentage of our teachers are not using them. We teach what we know and use ourselves. It seems likely to us that if more teachers spontaneously and naturally modeled self-regulated teaching, then more of our pupils would become self-regulated during more tasks, in more contexts, more often. Before we can apply self-regulated learning information to a self-regulated teaching domain, it seems important to describe what we mean by self-regulated learning.

THEORIES OF SELF-REGULATED LEARNING

Zimmerman (Zimmerman & Schunk, 1989) offers six different theoretical views of self-regulated learning: operant, phenomenological, social cognitive, volitional, Vygotskian, and constructivist. Before focusing on differences, the similarities mentioned by Zimmerman (Zimmerman & Schunk, pp. 4–6) are as follows:

SIMILARITIES AMONG SELF-REGULATED LEARNING THEORIES

1. Students can be described as self-regulated to the degree that they are metacognitively, motivationally, and behaviorally active participants in their own learning process. Students are assumed to be aware of the potential usefulness of self-regulation processes in enhancing their academic achievement.

2. Most definitions of self-regulation include a self-oriented feedback loop during learning. This loop refers to a cyclic process in which students monitor the effectiveness of their learning methods or strategies and respond to this feedback in a variety of ways.

3. How and why students choose to use a particular self-regulated process, strategy, or response are assumed by self-regulated learning theorists.

4. Self-regulated learning involves temporally delimited processes, strategies, or responses that students must initiate and regulate proactively. Therefore, students may not self-regulate during their learning when they could.

5. When children reach an age when self-regulated learning processes should occur, their failures to use these processes are attributed usually to one or more of three factors:

    a. students may not believe that a known self-regulation process will work, is needed, or is preferable in a particular learning context

    b. students may not believe that they can successfully execute an otherwise effective self-regulation response

    c. students may not be sufficiently desirous of a particular learning goal or outcome to be motivated to self-regulate

6. Most theorists assume that student efforts to self-regulate often require additional preparation time, vigilance, and effort. Unless the outcomes of these efforts are sufficiently attractive, students may not be motivated to self-regulate.

The differences among the six theories are too numerous to repeat here. A complete discussion appears in Zimmerman and Schunk (1989). For purposes of this text, only the differences in the main self-regulated processes of each theory are provided below:

**DIFFERENCES IN KEY PROCESSES OF SELF-REGULATED
LEARNING THEORIES**

Theory	Key Self-Regulation Processes
Operant	Three major classes of self-regulated learning responses: self-monitoring, self-instruction, and self-reinforcement
Phenomenological	Perceptions of self-worth and self-identity. McCombs (1989) categorizes these as self-system structures, which in turn affect an extensive network of processes like self-evaluation, planning, goal-setting, monitoring, processing, encoding, retrieval, and strategies.
Social Cognitive	Three subprocesses in self-regulation: self-observation, self-judgment, and self-reaction (interact with each other). Schunk (1989) identified two major classes of self-reactions, one personal and the other environmental. Evaluative motivators refer to personal feelings of satisfaction or dissatisfaction. Tangible motivators refer to self-administered stimuli or consequences like work break, food, or new clothes that are made contingent upon task completion or success.
Volitional	Kuhl (1984) identified six volitional control strategies: attention control, encoding control, information-processing control, motivation control, emotional control, environmental control.
Vygotskian	Self-directed speech-to-self, initially acquired from significant others' external speech
Constructivist	Students are hypothesized to function as "scientists," who construct theories to regulate four components of their learning: self-competence, effort, academic tasks, and instrumental strategies. Instrumental strategies refer to deliberate mental and physical "actions" by the learner to process information, as well as to manage time, motivation, and emotions. Students' theory of strategies involves knowledge about what strategies are (i.e., declarative knowledge), how they are used (i.e., procedural knowledge), and when and why they should be used (i.e., conditional knowledge). Paris and Byrnes (1989): Students' theory of self-competence: Can I self-regulate?; Students' theory of effort: Why should I self-regulate? How much effort should I expend on this task?; Students' theory of academic tasks: What is needed to learn this task?

VYGOTSKIAN VIEW OF SELF-REGULATED LEARNING

Recently, a common acknowledgement is that self-regulated learning includes cognitive, affective, and metacognitive components. This does not run counter to the Vygotskian view of learning, instruction, and development. Earlier in this chapter we discussed Vygotsky's theory of verbal self-regulation, zone of proximal development, and the concept of verbal mediation. Although not explicit, the affective and metacognitive domains are critical to Vygotsky's view of learning. For example, the significant other who is interacting, coaching, demonstrating, etc. with the learner needs to be a person the student responds reasonably well to. If the student does not respond to the teacher because of the teacher's poor interpersonal skills (e.g., sarcastic to the child); then, it is not as likely that the student will learn the task at hand. Also, the metacognitive skills of executive planning, monitoring, evaluating, etc. must be modeled by the adult in order for the student to master such skills. Using a Vygotskian approach includes a recognition of a multifaceted, integrated, reciprocal approach that includes cognitive, affective, and metacognitive components. McComb's phenomenological approach (1986, p. 327), categorized by Zimmerman and Schunk (1989) as separate from the Vygotskian view, offers a very appealing schematic diagram bringing together the realistic complexity of self-regulated learning. In order to incorporate a Vygotskian view two additions (i.e., (1) the sociolinguistic experiences that set self-regulated learning into motion and (2) the self-directed speech to self that actualizes self-regulated learning) are included. Other minor variations occur, such as changing the vocabulary slightly (e.g., structure to processes).

The causal model represents the major influence of the sociolinguistic experiences of an individual upon his or her self-directed speech. Language is the main pivotal point within this perspective: the influence of social language upon one's own language. Vygotsky posited that language originates in our social exchanges and acquires two separate functions (i.e., communication and self-guidance). Rohrkemper and Corno (1988, p. 301) explained the role of speech-to-self as it pertains to self-regulated learning (which they term adaptive learning in this particular article):

> *We conceptualize inner speech as the interface between the social/instructional environment of the classroom and the internal world of the student. The self-directive function of inner speech, which reflects both the social/instructional support of the classroom and the individual students' personal resources, leads us to argue that inner speech is the basic instructional unit in the classroom. It guides adaptive learning in that it involves what students tell themselves about tasks and about themselves. Inner speech is directly influenced by instruction and thus is a vehicle*

FIGURE 4–2 Causal Model: From Social Interaction through Self-Directed Speech to Self-Regulation

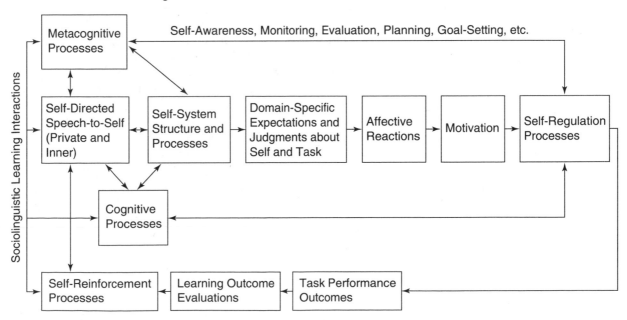

Source: McCombs, B. L. (1986). The role of self-system in self-regulated learning. *Contemporary Educational Psychology, 11,* 327. Copyright © 1986, Academic Press. Adapted with permission.

for learning adaptive behavior. Together, self-involved and task-involved inner speech allow students to modify the self and/or the task when confronted with stressful tasks. Inner speech enables both the initiation and the transformation of tasks. (p. 301)

As can be seen in the model this self-directed speech influences and is influenced by metacognitive, cognitive, and self-reinforcing processes. In addition, the self-system structure and processes (McCombs, 1986) affect and is affected by metacognitive and cognitive processes as well as self-directed speech. The self-system processes of expectations, judgments, affective reactions, and motivation directly affect self-regulated learning processes; which in turn, directly affect task performance outcomes, evaluations of your own learning, and self-reinforcement. Self-reinforcement and self-directed speech-to-self serve in a reciprocal context with each affecting the other. The self-regulation processes per se are influenced by specific cognitive and metacognitive processes and vise versa. In the next section, self-regulated learning strategies will be applied to teachers as they serve in a teaching role (i.e., self-regulated teaching).

SELF-REGULATED TEACHING

Again we turn to an article written by Rohrkemper and Corno (1988) in which they say: "The nature of classroom learning requires students to be adaptive by coping with and modifying stressful situations" (p. 297). We believe that they are exactly on target about students' needs to be proactive and to become responsible for their own adaptive responses by learning to modify tasks, self, and situations when confronted with frustrating and boring school tasks. In addition, the nature of classroom *teaching* requires *teachers* to be adaptive by coping with and modifying stressful teaching situations. Drawing from and modifying the construct of adaptive learning, we would like to propose the construct of adaptive, proactive teaching, which we will call a theory of verbal self-regulation for teachers.

One of the powerful and potent ways to teach is via modeling. It is highly probable that children will not learn to be adaptive, responsible learners in the classroom until the teacher is first responsible and adaptive. Therefore, beginning with self-regulated teaching may be more productive in the long run at fostering the self-regulated learner. This teacher modeling may be operationalized as the teacher "thinks aloud" his/her own coping statements while teaching (e.g., "This lesson is not going so well, I believe I just need to start over again!"). This kind of naturalistic modeling is not simply modeling aloud a suggestion for an adaptive student response, which is also very important, but may not be sufficient for most youngsters. In addition, a natural and spontaneous display of teachers' "think aloud" to cope with the challenging demands of teaching and the sometimes tedious, boring tasks of teaching may be a prerequisite to students' adaptive responses, associated with the frustration and boredom that is sometimes a part of learning. Teachers need to model aloud their everyday teaching situations, as well as model planned instructional "think aloud" to help students use more adaptive responses to school blocks (see Rohrkemper & Corno, 1988). Students often learn higher level metacognitive skills that are modeled, practiced, and cued by adults and peers (Manning, 1988; Manning, 1991).

Teachers teach what they themselves use and know (Goodlad, 1984). Then why are we asking teachers to foster and directly teach "adaptive learning" to students before they themselves have become familiar with and use high level coping skills in their personal lives (Part I of this text) and professional lives (Part II of this text) to deal more efficiently and metacognitively with stress, frustration, worry; and to facilitate their own positive mental awareness, monitoring, regulation, and growth? An immediate response is to ask:

"Well how do you know that teachers don't already know and use these high level mental and affective metacognitive skills?" Perhaps a small percentage do. However, it has been our experience over the past decade of working with and learning from teachers that a huge percentage of them, including us, were not introduced to, did not study, or practice first-hand, metacognition for personal and professional benefit. In our own personal teacher preparation and most likely in theirs, we hear about teaching/learning strategies as if they are failproof. If these strategies do not work in our classroom, we are told that we did not "do them right." We are usually not taught mental coping skills for the frustration of classroom strategies that do not work and for the occasional boring task, associated with the teaching profession. We have witnessed first-hand many cognitive and affective benefits when teachers go from personal to professional exposure and immersion in cognitive/metacognitive restructuring of teacher thought. A recent finding is that simply reading about cognitive/metacognitive therapies has helped some individuals reduce their own depression, anxiety, etc. We do not claim that "metacognitive preparation" for teachers will solve all the problems or help every teacher; however, we do believe that the focus we are advocating in this text will foster more responsible, independent teachers who are better equipped to monitor and regulate their own mental states and behavioral reactions.

SUMMARY

In this chapter, the premises surrounding Vygotsky's theory of verbal self-regulation are detailed. Exercises are suggested to extend Vygotsky's views of planful speech and prior sociolinguistic experiences as shapers of thought and behavior. *Other-regulation models* for teaching and learning possess many recently proclaimed, powerful benefits. Self-regulated learning is the end result of other-regulation efforts. Six different theoretical stances related to self-regulated learning are briefly described, with further elaboration of the Vygotskian view. The construct of adaptive learning, an integral part of self-regulated learning, is used as the basis for introducing a new construct: self-regulated teaching.

CHAPTER 5

Applying the Cognitive Self-Direction Model to Teaching

OVERVIEW

In this chapter, a cognitive self-directional (CSD) curriculum and methodological model for reflective teaching is described which goes beyond the typical definition of teacher reflection. This model is based on higher order mental functioning, emphasizing cognitive awareness, productive teaching, teacher-student interactions, and verbal self-regulation of teaching acts. Studies testing the model and its constituent parts are also described. The CSD model is then applied to the areas of teacher planning, interactive instruction, and classroom management. Metacognitive skills employed by classroom teachers are organized around these three areas. Prototypic examples from classroom situations are used to elucidate the metacognitive processes recommended for classroom use. Future trends and recommendations for this area of research are also suggested.

Self-Questions

1. *Knowledge*. List three researchers in the area of metacognition as it relates to teaching.

2. *Comprehension*. Explain the four steps in Manning and Payne's CSD Methodological Model.

3. *Application*. Develop facilitative (appropriate) teacher self-talk (15 statements and/or questions) for a typical classroom dilemma. Describe the dilemma and then write your 15 verbal reaction statements.

4. *Analysis*. Give several reasons for implementing CSD instruction. Defend putting this instruction in place of a more traditional topic in teacher education.

5. *Synthesis*. Describe the literature using cognitive self-direction and self-regulated teaching as a variable, ten years from now. Describe the answers we may know in ten years and what questions will likely remain unanswered.

6. *Evaluation*. Judge the strengths and limitations of CSD for teaching. What are some major cautions?

METACOGNITIVE SKILLS FOR PROFESSIONAL DEVELOPMENT

Metacognition is a skill that all teachers should be able to demonstrate and use with ease. Teaching requires planning, making quick, important decisions, goal-setting, coping, evaluating, organizing, and managing students' behavior. Processes like these require teachers to monitor and control their own thought processes as these processes impact on planning, interactive instruction, and classroom organization and management. Therefore, one primary reason for promoting metacognition is because teaching, by its very nature, requires metacognitive skill and self-regulated teaching. All of us who are familiar with a typical teaching day, know what happens when teachers act impulsively, rushing through the day without thought and prior mental planning. Many lessons have bombed because teachers did not cognitively oversee them.

COGNITIVE SELF-DIRECTION FOR TEACHING: A CURRICULUM AND METHODOLOGICAL MODEL

Educational researchers Good and Brophy (1984) state that teachers who self-monitor during teaching are more aware of the complexities of teaching. Implicit in this statement is an ongoing self-monitoring that guides and directs teacher behavior. The emphasis is on proactive, deliberate teacher monitoring prior to teaching acts, not simply reactive reflection on a teaching act that has already occurred.

The intent of this section of the chapter is to describe the role of metacognitive monitoring and control activity in self-regulated teaching. We define self-regulated teaching as the use of verbal self-regulation to apply and control higher order thinking. For example, when teachers are confronted with complex classroom problems, they deliberately select and apply certain teaching practices that have been tested by cognitive monitoring and deemed successful.

Good and Brophy (1984) believe that one reason teachers are too often unaware of many classroom events is that they have not been trained to monitor their own thinking and to study their own behavior. We agree; and therefore, for the past ten years, have studied, applied, and evaluated teacher education curriculum and methods to teach preservice teachers to monitor their thought processes prior to teaching-learning interactions. A vital component in this monitoring is cognitive self-direction of teacher behavior. One of the parameters of cognitive self-direction is that it must occur prior to a teaching act. If the teacher cognition occurs along with or after teacher behaviors, a key component of the self-monitoring process is missing. This idea of cognitive self-direction for teachers goes beyond teacher reflection when teachers cognitively react after the teaching situation has occurred. Instead, teachers are taught to cognitively direct their own teacher behavior prior to the teaching act. Cognitive self-direction (CSD) is made known to, modeled for, practiced by, and cued for teachers. Through this model of cognitive self-direction, you come to understand that it is your own cognition that determines the quality of your instruction. You realize that your self-verbalizations serve as the guide for teacher activity.

The overall conceptualization of the CSD curriculum is illustrated in Figure 5.1. The CSD instruction is specific and realistic, and approximates real classroom situations. This means that individual teachers describe specific teaching situations, which can be classified as planning, instructing, or managing. These classifications have emerged from several years of our more informal research as we have talked to inservice teachers about what they say to themselves prior to planning, instructing, and managing situations. In addition, as part of graduate coursework, inservice teachers have collected their self-talk, as it was actually occurring in their individual classrooms. They have reported that they talk into tape-recorders and later transcribe it, or they make notes to themselves about their inner dialogue. Over the years as we have studied this teacher self-talk we have designated the three broad areas of planning, instructing, and managing.

The four classifications of goal-setting, guiding, coping, and reinforcing have served well to categorize the majority of teacher self-talk. An example of each is provided from

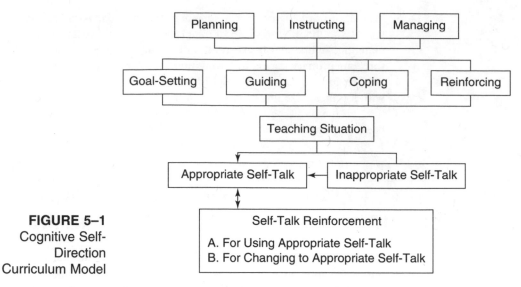

FIGURE 5–1
Cognitive Self-
Direction
Curriculum Model

Source: Manning, B. H., & Payne, B. D. (1989). A cognitive self-direction model for teacher education. *Journal of Teacher Education, 40*(3), 29. Reprinted by permission, American Association of Colleges for Teacher Education, copyright 1989.

the transcripts of a classroom teacher's self talk: *Goal-setting*—"I need to slow down with this information. My students are totally confused." *Guiding*—"Say that again. Say it another way. They look confused." *Coping*—"I'm so tired of this topic; but remember it is new to these students. Come on, be patient." *Reinforcing*—"Some of them have it now. My efforts are starting to pay off." (Individual teachers categorize their own self-talk.) The appropriateness or inappropriateness of what teachers say to themselves about the specific teaching situation is a value judgment made by a particular teacher. The question-to-self is as follows: Is what I am saying to myself helping me solve my problems? If not, what else could I say that might be more helpful?

Located in the center of Figure 5.1 is the Teaching Situation. The situation describes any number of teaching scenarios that are characteristic of a given teacher's or student teacher's day. Moving downward from the teaching situation in Figure 5.1, the teacher's mental problem solving or introspection consists of appropriate, (helpful/positive) self-talk and/or inappropriate self-talk, (unhelpful/negative). For example, if a teacher says, "I can work this out, one step at a time" and the teacher determines that this self-statement helps him/her to cope with the situation, appropriate self-talk (as judged by the teacher) has occurred. If the teacher says, "I can't do this—I will never work this out" an inappropriate/unhelpful self-statement for this particular teacher has been made. As documented by cognitive psychologists (Butler, 1981; Ellis, 1976; Helmstetter, 1986) in Chapter 1, appropriate self-talk leads to more productive behaviors. Assuming this, appropriate self-talk should more than likely facilitate corresponding productive teacher behaviors.

The large rectangle at the bottom of Figure 5.1 represents Self-Talk Reinforcement. Learning to use helpful, self-directed, teacher introspection requires practice, effort and awareness of self-monitoring. Butler, in her book, *Talking to Yourself: Learning the Language of Self-Affirmation* (1992), discusses that learning a new way to talk to yourself is rather like learning a new language. It requires patience. It also requires reinforcement. Reinforcement has the same connotation here as in operant conditioning, except that instead of external reinforcement, the reinforcement is provided internally.

We often require our preservice teachers to develop and report their own facilitative, self-directed speech that serves to guide and direct their teaching decisions during field experiences. In this way, they become more aware and monitor their thought processes, become more proactive as they regulate teaching events, base cognitive self-direction on teacher-student interactions, and use their introspection as a means of verbal self-regulation.

The methodology for teaching CSD to prospective and inservice teachers is illustrated in Figure 5.2 (Manning & Payne, 1989). In brief, the methods include lectures to build a knowledge base of CSD, modeling (Bandura, 1977) using live and videotaped teachers engaged in CSD while teaching; and overt, faded, and covert self-verbalizations practiced by the prospective teachers. The final step teaches cueing techniques to remind prospective teachers to engage in CSD during their student teaching field experience.

More specifically, Step I consists of lectures and discussions of the theory and development of metacognition and verbal self-regulation (see Introduction, Chapter 4) as well as the research related to CSD (discussed later in this chapter). The lectures are intended to build awareness and knowledge of CSD.

Step II consists of modeling, using live as well as videotaped teachers, engaged in CSD while teaching. Initially, a master teacher provides a description of a teaching sit-

FIGURE 5.2   Cognitive Self-Direction Methodological Model*

Step I Knowledge base/ Awareness	Teacher educators provide information about the following topics: a) Theoretical Foundations of CSD[1] b) Nature and Development of Metacognition[2] c) Development of Self-Regulation Through Private Speech[3] d) Research in Metacognition Related to CSD[4]
Step II Modeling of CSD	Master teachers model CSD providing the following: a) Teaching situations and corresponding self-talk: goal-setting, guiding, coping, and reinforcement b) Examples of inappropriate and appropriate self-talk c) Live and videotaped reenactments of classroom situations
Step III Practicing of CSD	Preservice teachers practice steps "a" – "c" and develop step "d" below: a) (Aloud) self-talk statements which correspond to specific teaching situations b) (Whisper/faded) Self-talk statements which correspond to these same teaching situations c) (Silent) Self-talk statements which correspond to these same teaching situations d) Original cognitive self-direction statements for teaching situations
Step IV Cueing of CSD	Preservice teachers learn cueing techniques a) Reminders via cue cards were encouraged b) Examples of cue cards made by inservice teachers were presented as an overhead display

*Steps were adapted from Cognitive Self-Instructional Model (Manning, 1988).

[1]See Vygotsky's (1962) work on the regulatory role of self-talk upon one's own behavior.

[2]See Flavell's conceptualization of metacognition (awareness and regulation of one's own cognition via self-talk) in Weinert and Kluwe (1987).

[3]See Zivin's (1979) historical account and development of self-regulation through self-talk.

[4]See Manning's (1991, *Cognitive Self-Instruction for Classroom Processes,* NY: SUNY) review of research relating to CSD.

Source: Manning, B. H., & Payne, B. D. (1989). A cognitive self-direction model for teacher education. *Journal of Teacher Education, 40*(3), 29. Reprinted by permission, American Association of Colleges for Teacher Education, copyright 1989.

uation while planning, instructing or managing children as well as the corresponding self-talk statements categorized as goal-setting, guiding, coping, or reinforcing. The following is a description of a planning situation.

PLANNING SCENARIO

"It is my second year of teaching, but my first year teaching kindergarten. I am employed by a challenging school district, and I feel the pressure to prove myself as a competent teacher. After returning to school from the holidays, I feel that some changes need to be made in my scheduling in order to meet the needs of my students more effectively. I have found that it is very hard to have enough time in my afternoon to teach all that I feel needs to be taught. I am also concerned about getting to the workbooks in small groups. It is much harder than I had thought to integrate the required curriculum and my own ideas. There just doesn't seem to be enough time in the day! Mornings seem to be going well, but I need to change my afternoon schedule. I need to work in a Science/Social Studies lesson, small group time, storytime, recess, resttime, and nap time. Between meetings and straightening the classroom, the only time left for thought is late in the day."

Following the reading of the planning scenario, the teacher models both inappropriate and appropriate self-talk. According to Vygotsky (1978) behavior is first regulated by the verbal directions of a more capable person. The more capable "other" in this case is a teacher serving as a verbal role model. Both negative and positive self-talk examples are included for a number of reasons. Mcichcnbaum (1977) emphasizes the value of addressing directly and explicitly negative self-talk. This enables the participants to view a negative sequence of inner dialogue from a teacher serving as a model. The objective is that this will enable the participants to become aware of their own negative self-talk. This awareness increases the likelihood of interrupting a series of negative self-talk thoughts or statements that could lead to inappropriate teaching behaviors. The following is an example of the same kindergarten teacher's modeled negative self-talk while planning.

INAPPROPRIATE SELF-TALK

I need to just forget about *their* curriculum and teach what I want to.

Maybe I just can't do this. I'm just not good at this. Why am I teaching anyway?

There's no way to work out this schedule! Nobody ever told me I'd have to squeeze 200 things into one hour!

I'm so sick of this mess!

I'm just going to forget about all this. I'll figure it out tomorrow!

The teacher-modeled inappropriate self-talk is followed by teacher-modeled appropriate self-talk. The appropriate self-talk is incompatible with the previous set of inappropriate self-talk. The next example is of the teacher-modeled appropriate self-talk.

APPROPRIATE SELF-TALK

I know I can work out this schedule—I'm flexible and my children can handle change!

Surely there's a way to fit things in.

I'll just do the best I can. No one can expect more than that.

I shouldn't feel guilty for having to change my schedule; I'm learning.

There are lots of things I do well with my teaching. I have a lot of good ideas and I'm a good teacher!

Our purpose during this step is to have teacher thought (prior to teaching acts) modeled for pre- and inservice teachers. During this type of "modeled" instruction you are able to sit inside the veteran teacher's mind. You observe a classroom teacher invent action on the spot; you hear her think aloud to guide planning, you hear her talk to herself during interactive teaching while responding to children, and you observe her manage the social system of the classroom, while using self-directed speech. You experience the teacher's thinking being shaped by context, speculative teacher thought, hypothetical and probabilistic teacher thought, mental coping, guiding, goal-setting and self-reinforcement. During instruction the abstract principles of teacher cognition are illustrated in context. You are given the opportunity to analyze teacher thought-in-action for explicit situations. Finally, both live and videotaped reenactments of the classroom situation with a teacher modeling metacognition are viewed.

Step III includes the practicing of audible, whispered, and inaudible self-verbalizations by teachers (Meichenbaum & Goodman, 1971). Initially, you practice (aloud) self-talk statements which correspond to specific teaching situations. Second, you practice (whispering) self-talk statements which correspond to these same teaching situations. Third, you practice (silently) self-talk statements which correspond to the teaching situations. Following these procedures, you develop your own teaching situations and generate appropriate self-direction statements using the categories of goal-setting, guiding, coping, and reinforcing to frame reflection.

Step IV teaches cueing techniques to remind you to engage in cognitive self-direction during classroom teaching. You make cue cards with phrases such as, "I can do this" and "Take a deep breath and count from 10 to 1," and keep them displayed in the classroom as visual reminders.

Meichenbaum found in his work that after sufficient practice appropriate self-talk becomes habitual/automatic, is no longer necessary, and in fact is disruptive to complex acts, resulting in reduced performance. He also concluded that after appropriate self-talk becomes automatic it is transferred to self-generation of individualized appropriate self-statements for other tasks, even dissimilar from treatment tasks. When applying the self-directed model to your own teaching, enough practice should occur so that your monitoring and reflection will become habitual, individualized, and improved.

CSD is currently used in our undergraduate teacher preparation program. Each academic year since 1984, the CSD curriculum and methodology have been applied to a random group of preservice teachers to investigate the effectiveness of CSD. The CSD program has been tested against placebo and assessment groups. The CSD preservice teacher group receives lectures on the theoretical/conceptual foundations (see Figure 5.2, Step I) beginning in the first quarter of their professional block of courses. During this quarter they also view videotapes of a master teacher engaged in self-talk while verbally directing planning, instructional, and management situations in a classroom setting. In addition, graduate students who have prior teaching experience serve as CSD role models as they talk aloud to themselves and guide various teaching situations. After viewing live and videotaped modeling of CSD, the preservice teachers practice the use of CSD, following points "a" through "d" in Step III of Figure 5.2. During field experiences at the end of the quarter, the CSD-trained preservice teachers are reminded to use helpful, positive self-talk during planning, instruction, and management. Students are encouraged to use "cueing" cards to inhibit inappropriate teacher behaviors and to initiate and reinforce appropriate teacher behaviors. During the next quarter, the CSD-trained students are reminded to continue the use of helpful verbal self-direction during their field experience. The final quarter is the student teaching quarter. During this 10-week period the CSD trained students meet once every two weeks for one hour in small groups of 6–12 to discuss how they are using CSD in their classrooms. They share specific ways they have verbally set goals, guided, coped, and reinforced themselves. Specifically, they describe situations, how they used appropriate or inappropriate CSD, and the subsequent classroom results.

RESULTS OF THE IMPLEMENTATION

Payne and Manning (1988) have formally investigated the impact of this CSD model with 67 preservice teachers. Students were randomly assigned to one of the three groups: experimental, attention control (placebo) or assessment control (no treatment). The dependent measure used to assess the relative effectiveness of the CSD procedure was Rotter's *Locus of Control Scale (I-E)* (1966). Experimental students received six hours of instruction in cognitive monitoring and the use of CSD strategies for planning, instructing, and managing classroom behavior. The model depicted in Figure 5.2 and the narrative description on the subsequent pages illustrate the CSD curriculum used as the experimental treatment. The attention control group received lectures about cognitive monitoring, but did not actively participate in the use and repeated practice of CSD. They were passive recipients of information about the topics of CSD. They met for the same number of hours, during the same time period of day, month, and year to prevent the Hawthorne effect. The assessment or no treatment control group received the pre-and post-assessments. The results indicated that the self-instructional training was effective in changing preservice teachers' locus of control to more internal orientations.

Previous studies (Rose & Medway, 1981a; 1981b) have documented that teachers with an internal locus of control orientation function better in the classroom than their externally oriented counterparts. In this study, CSD training was powerful enough to alter the locus-of-control of preservice teachers to a more internal orientation.

The CSD model has been applied more recently (Payne & Manning, 1990) to another group of preservice teachers to investigate its effect on preservice teachers' anxiety about teaching. Subjects were again randomly assigned to one of three groups: experimental, attention control (placebo) or assessment control (no treatment). The *Survey of Feelings about Teaching* (SFAT) was used to assess the effectiveness of the CSD procedure. The experimental treatment (6 hours) consisted of three components, representing a modification of Meichenbaum's (1985) stress-inoculation training: (1) discussion of the conceptual framework including a review of the theoretical and empirical literature on the role of cognitive monitoring and self-statements in emotions, feelings, and behaviors, (2) training in cognitive monitoring and modifications of self-statements, and (3) rehearsal and application. Stress inoculation has been defined as a "coping skills therapy" in which individuals are taught ways to respond to stressful events so that disturbing emotions are reduced and behavior adaptation is achieved" (Park & Slaby, 1983, p. 610).

Part 1 included a 3-hour lecture and discussion of the role of self-statements and irrational beliefs on attitudes, emotions, feelings, and behaviors (Ellis, 1976; Meichenbaum, 1977). Initially, a review of research related to cognitive monitoring with children and adults was briefly described. The major focus of the presentation, however, was on the effect of self-statements on emotions and behaviors.

During Part 2 (2 hours) students identified their thoughts, feelings, and concerns about their forthcoming field experiences and then developed positive alternative self-statements to cope with the situation more constructively. For example, a statement such as "I can't do this, I'll never be able to teach" was changed to "I'll do the best I can, I know I can be a good teacher." A solid body of 15 to 18 positive self-statements is needed in order for the self-talk to have the desired effect (Helmstetter, 1986). These positive reactions were rehearsed (Part 3, 1 hour) through imagery, role-play, and cognitive rehearsal. Finally, the individualized self-statements were audiotaped and listened to a minimum of three times a day for 6 weeks prior to and during the field experience. A step-by-step description of how to make a self-talk tape is included in Chapter 3. Students were also encouraged to monitor their own thinking while performing teaching duties, while student teaching.

The results indicated that the cognitive self-direction (affirmation) treatment program significantly decreased self-reported anxiety and stress about teaching. Previous studies have demonstrated that teacher anxiety is negatively related to students' estimates of teacher effectiveness (Rushton, 1985), teacher warmth (Kracht & Casey, 1968), and teacher-student rapport (Petrusich, 1966). This study supports the use of CSD as a procedure useful for reducing teacher anxiety and stress.

Constituent parts of the CSD model have been evaluated with preservice teachers for their effectiveness in altering lesson planning and classroom performance (Neely, 1986), creative problem solving abilities (Riley, 1981), and locus of control (Ekanayake, 1986). In particular, Neely investigated the adequacy of written lesson plans and classroom implementation between experimental and control groups. The experimental group had received training while the control group had not. For both measures (i.e., written lesson plans and classroom performance) the students receiving training in metacognition performed better than those with no training (Neely, 1986, p. 31). Riley (1981) found that preservice teachers trained in metacognitive monitoring and control were better problem solvers when confronted with written classroom dilemmas. This dilemma was similar to the teaching situation generated later for the CSD instruction. Ekanayake (1986) tested the CSD model in its entirety and found that experimental preservice teachers became more internal than their control counterparts in teacher-specific locus of control scores after a one month delay. The significance of the long term effects of CSD on teacher-specific locus of control implies that including cognitive self-instruction as one component of preservice teacher training may be useful in producing more internally oriented teachers.

To sum, benefits of a CSD type instruction for teaching include improved lesson planning, improved classroom performance, improved creative problem-solving ability, more internal locus of control orientations, and less anxiety about teaching. Additional research is necessary to investigate the effects of the CSD instruction on classroom performance, student achievement, and the higher order mental functioning of classroom teachers. Nevertheless, the quantitative and qualitative results are encouraging. By incorporating CSD instruction into teaching, teachers may develop a means of reducing stress and becoming more aware, proactive, self-directed educators.

We will now present some actual examples of classroom situations where CSD has been applied in teacher planning, interactive instruction, and classroom management. The CSD strategies will promote awareness and regulation of your own teaching skills.

METACOGNITIVE SKILLS FOR TEACHER PLANNING

Elementary teachers report that planning activities consume about ten to twenty hours per week, with a lot of planning occurring after school hours (Clark & Yinger, 1979). Some of the planning self-questions required of teachers are as follows: What activities will motivate my students? How long should I spend on each topic? How much practice will be required for mastery? How much instructional time should I allocate for the whole class, small group, and individuals in the classroom? How can I use a multimodality approach? How will I decide who needs to be in a group together? How will I organize my daily, weekly, and grading period schedules? How will I deal with interruptions in my schedule? How will I deal with "catching up" absent or newly enrolled children? How can I plan for non-English speaking children? How can I best communicate my plans to a substitute or to the aide? Such questions should be deliberated by both preservice and inservice teachers. A checklist of self-questions may be a helpful metacognitive aid for teachers when dealing with aspects of teacher planning.

Readers interested in discussions about teacher planning should read the historical and various opinions of Tyler (1950), Taba (1962), Popham and Baker (1970), Zahorik

(1975), MacDonald (1965), Eisner (1967), Jackson (1965), and Peterson, Marx and Clark (1978). As mentioned earlier, Neely (1986) investigated the effect of cognitive monitoring on teachers' lesson planning ability and found that the cognitive overseeing of planning is very beneficial. Very few have continued this line of study. An exception is Hazareesingh (1989) who has applied cognitive self-instruction to Madeline Hunter's planning concepts, with reported success.

If you refer to the CSD model you will see that planning is one of the teaching areas described. Therefore, the following discussion will provide an example of how to incorporate cognitive self-direction for planning activities. First, you begin by reviewing a description of a particular planning situation (actual ones written by classroom teachers are more realistic and contextually sound). You can then read the scenarios yourself or hear the scenario read by a teacher; next you read or hear a classroom teacher (live or videotaped) talk to self. First the model uses inappropriate, unhelpful self-talk. Unhelpful is defined in light of not aiding problem-resolution or movement toward an established teacher goal. Next, the model teacher employs appropriate, helpful self-talk for the same teaching situation. There should be approximately 15–18 complete self-talk units of appropriate self-statements and/or self-questions. Therefore, step 1 is to provide a self-talk metacognitive role-model for planning. An example is illustrated below. We have found it works best for us to videotape the entire process described above, including a description of the planning situation and the modeling of inappropriate and appropriate self-talk. However, the planning scenario may be read by preservice teachers, and the inappropriate and appropriate self-talk may be role played by volunteer students.

EXAMPLE OF PLANNING SITUATION

As an elementary teacher, one of the most important times of the day is small group instruction. Much is accomplished during this time and it gives me the time to individualize and assess my students' progress. Lately, however, I have felt that the gap is widening between my lowest group and the others. The children in the slower group are not mastering important skills, especially letter and number concepts. There are four children in the group, all of them boys. They have very short attention spans, are easily distracted, and are unable to sit still for any length of time. I am very concerned about their progress and lack of skill development. During the art class with the art teacher, I'll have some time to step back and think about ways to help these children. What is my planning strategy? How can I help them make progress and raise their confidence level?

INAPPROPRIATE SELF-TALK

Oh gosh, this group is so far behind the others. They will never catch-up. Why bother thinking about them?

This is so hard—they don't listen during my lessons anyway?

This is an impossible task. They're much too far behind.

I give up. Why did I ever go into teaching in the first place?

I'll never get through all these pages. It's their fault they're behind, anyway.

APPROPRIATE SELF-TALK

Okay. What does this group need? Should I focus on math or reading skills this week? (Self-questioning)

I can't let either of these subjects go? I'll just have to plan strong lessons in both areas. (Self-guiding)

I've got to come up with some motivating activities to reinforce basic skills. (Self-guiding)

Alright . . . relax. I won't accomplish anything by panicking. (Self-coping)

I'm doing a great job with their number recognition and they know all their facts to 10. (Self-reinforcing)

I need to have high expectations for these students. They need to know I believe in them. (Self-guiding)

Okay, these children have very short attention spans . . . and they really need a lot of "hands-on" activities. (Self-guiding)

Let's see: what are their strengths? They are very vocal, they love games and movement activities. Maybe I could use these in my lessons. (Self-questioning)

I'm going to do it. We are going to learn. We can learn together! (Self-reinforcing)

I need to make sure they feel good about themselves, and that they are doing a good job. (Self-guiding)

They have learned a great deal in my class since the beginning of the year — they have made progress. (Self-reinforcing)

I have a lot of good ideas. I need to pull together all my resources and do my best with this group. (Self-reinforcing)

I have these colorful counting blocks. I could bag these into groups of 10, and plan an activity. How long would that take? (Self-guiding and self-questioning)

And the next day, we'll do a similar activity using pictures of blocks. This should help them understand place value. (Self-guiding)

After you see and/or hear or read this teaching situation and corresponding inappropriate and appropriate self-talk, it will be helpful for you to discuss the categories of facilitative (appropriate) self-talk: self-questioning, self-guiding, self-coping, and self-reinforcing. We have found that preservice teachers use almost no self-reinforcing statements to self. It is important for you to keep in mind that it is helpful, and not conceited, to acknowledge objectively one's own teaching strengths. "Objective reporting of strengths" is not synonymous with conceit. Conceit is unrealistic and comparative (e.g., I'm the best teacher in the United States [unrealistic], and I'm so much better than my best friend [comparative]); while objective reporting is realistic and noncomparative (e.g., I have an interesting and motivating lesson for tomorrow).

Another suggestion for planning is that as you develop your written lesson plans try writing your self-talk in the margins of the lesson plans. Evaluation of the metacognitive planning should be as important as evaluation of the written plan itself. Evaluative questions may include the following: Is the self-talk helping or hindering this teacher's planning? How many self-questioning, self-guiding, self-coping, and self-reinforcing statements are there? Are there omissions of any one or more of these self-talk categories? In addition to the recorded self-talk prior to and during planning, a list of self-questions for self-evaluation of the written plan *after* its completion has been helpful for many students. One example is provided below:

LESSON PLAN SELF-EVALUATION

1. Is my goal general and broad?

2. Are my objectives specific to my learners?

3. Does my introduction ensure attention from all or most?

4. Do I have enough activities to provide adequate practice for learning to occur?

5. Do I have materials referenced to their corresponding activities?

6. Do my time estimations seem reasonable?

7. Are the activities appropriate for the grade level I am teaching?

8. Do I have activities planned for various instructional levels represented in my class?

9. Am I trying to cover too much in one day?

10. Is there enough here for one day?

11. Have I balanced learner-centered and teacher-centered activities?

12. Have I used a multimodality approach?

13. What is my rationale for the sequence of my objectives and activities?

14. Is it important for students to know what I am teaching in this lesson?

15. Have I researched this topic well? Do I know my facts? Is the content substantive?

16. Have I pretested the children or somehow assessed their prior knowledge of this material to ensure that I am not teaching material they already know or that is too far over their heads?

17. Is my plan creative?

18. Have I used motivating, unusual dimensions of the lesson?

19. Does this plan represent a concerted effort on my part?

20. Am I pleased with this plan as I have written it? If not, state what parts I am uneasy about and why I am concerned.

Metacognitive Skills During Interactive Instruction

A picture is worth a thousand words and so it is with Figure 5.3. Please refer to this figure. It portrays visually one teacher's representation of teaching.

This figure represents the complexity, spontaneity, multidimensionality, and unpredictability of face-to-face, interactive teaching. Research studies on interactive teaching illustrate that teachers face decision situations at two-minute intervals while teaching. Therefore, teachers are called upon to make hundreds of decisions per day. Many of these decisions call for deliberation within the teacher, and deliberations require metacognitive thought, involving private (aloud) or inner (silent) speech-to-self. In addition to decisions required every two minutes, teachers encounter approximately 1000 face-to-face interactions per day. Teaching is considered an extremely stressful profession. On a lighter note, now we also know why we can't decide whether to exercise or go out to eat after teaching all day in an elementary classroom — who wants to make one more decision after school is over?

Teacher thinking research on interactive teaching has mainly employed "stimulated recall" as methodology. If you are interested in more information on "stimulated recall" please refer to Shavelson and Stern (1981) for a review of this research. In short, studies have indicated that teachers are reluctant to change routines, once they are into a lesson. Their main concern seems to be to keep the lesson moving. Interrupting the flow increases the probability of classroom management problems. During moment-to-moment classroom interaction, teachers must reconcile their thinking about what should be happening with what is happening (i.e., the concrete reality of each teaching situation [Lampert,

• No matter how prepared I am, things always come up that I never expect. You can never predict what 25 different little minds and bodies will do. I guess that's the challenge of it.

• My mind felt boggled as I tried to keep track of everything— what all I needed to do, what all, what all, what all.

FIGURE 5–3
Entry from a
Teacher's Log

1984]). These adjustments often cause frustrations for the teacher. Lampert makes an extremely important point when she says . . . "researchers have tried to separate how teachers themselves think about their work from academic descriptions of practice; researchers have concluded that the language practitioners use is too concrete, too context bound, and too inconsistent to inform good teaching" (p. 15). Language *is* the substance of thought. Because educational researchers often refuse to use the language of classroom teachers, they miss the essence of interactive teacher decision-making. We believe preservice and inservice teachers need instruction within context, using more of a case study approach with particular classroom situations, rather than hypothetical, perhaps unrealistic ones. We have attempted to do this by using teacher-developed scenarios and their accompanying self-talk. In doing so, the language of the classroom teacher is used as the "content" for learning.

As with the area of planning, we use the same steps for teaching CSD during interactive instruction. Since the steps are the same (i.e., cognitive modeling, preservice teacher practice of audible, whispered, and inaudible facilitative self-talk, followed by creative development of self-talk for teaching situations) these steps will not be elaborated again. However, a sample interactive teaching situation will be provided, with accompanying inappropriate and appropriate self-talk, with categorization of self-questioning, self-guiding, self-coping, and self-reinforcing.

EXAMPLE OF AN INTERACTIVE SITUATION

I am attempting to teach my second graders to alphabetize by the second or third letter of a word. Even though I am confident that they will grasp the concept eventually, I realize they are frustrated right now. I can tell by their faces and their posture. When they get this frustrated they often become disruptive. As the lesson moves along, I say to myself:

INAPPROPRIATE SELF-TALK

For heaven's sake. He's already tuned me out. That burns me up.

No! No! Why aren't they getting this — are they just stupid?

Why isn't she listening? She needs this more than anybody in here! I'm not talking to the wall.

I hate teaching!

I wish they'd all look at me when I'm talking! How irritating!

APPROPRIATE SELF-TALK

This lesson is hard to teach, but I can do it. It's important for them to understand this. (Self-coping)

I need to review alphabetizing by the first letter. This seems too hard for several of them. I'll pull them together in a small group later! (Self-guiding)

I should have them look at a visual, like the alphabet across the board. (Self-guiding)

All right, maybe I need to say this in different words. (Self-guiding)

I need to remember, it's not unusual for them to have trouble when I first introduce something. (Self-coping)

Oops, I'm calling on the same children over and over again. I should call on the non-volunteers also. (Self-guiding)

Hmm, three or four seem to have it now; John, Ted, and Felicia have it! (Self-reinforcing)

Maybe this is over their heads. I'm really going to encourage them on this. (Self-guiding)

I need a visual. This is too abstract for them to just listen. They can't seem to deal with this. I'll change the assignment for some of them. (Self-guiding)

Hey! More of them understand this than I thought earlier. I'm making progress. Good. (Self-reinforcing)

I'm going to need to reinforce this in a small group for Sam, Carrie, Todd, and Marcus. (Self-guiding)

What time is it? Oh, ten more minutes until P.E. Not bad! (Self-questioning)

I'm glad I waited and let her answer! She knew what she was talking about. (Self-reinforcing)

I know this must be hard for them. I shouldn't expect mastery so soon. Keep those perfectionistic thoughts to myself. (Self-coping)

I need to wrap up with a short review. (Self-guiding)

Teachers' interactive cognition, resulting in high levels of on-task behavior and higher achievement scores, is typified by rapid judgment and a willingness to change the flow of classroom interaction in midstream when necessary (Clark & Lampert, 1986). Becoming adept at monitoring your thinking, while in the midst of teaching, is a complex skill that requires awareness, practice, and reminders. However, the value of doing so appears to be increased on-task behaviors and higher achievement scores.

Another metacognitive strategy for promoting facilitative mental problem solving during the act of teaching is to wear a microphone (attached to a tape recorder) while teaching. As you teach, your thoughts (inner speech) are spoken into the microphone. The audiotape can be analyzed by transcribing the self-talk, characterizing it as facilitative or non-facilitative. Furthermore, the facilitative self-talk may be classified as either self-questioning, self-guiding, self-coping, or self-reinforcing. This exercise can provide you with a clear picture of how your metacognitive thinking is related to your classroom decision making.

Metacognitive Skills During Classroom Management

Discipline problems are and have been perceived as one of the major educational concerns for the past decade by teachers, parents, students, and administrators. Teachers are called upon to be experts at organizing their classrooms to prevent management problems and to apply management techniques when discipline problems occur. There are no studies known to us that deal with metacognitive teacher cognition to promote either prevention or intervention management in classrooms. However, there is a great need to find out how effective classroom managers verbally guide themselves while managing classroom disruptions, etc., as compared to how ineffective classroom managers use verbal self-regulation during management episodes. This area is wide open for research efforts.

Authors of most current classroom management texts (e.g., Epanchein, Townsend, & Stoddard, 1994; Wolfgang & Glickman, 1986) do not even mention cognitive behavior modification, and certainly not cognitive self-direction. Perhaps in the future they will, because teachers' cognitions impact greatly on classroom climate, organization, and management. Evertson and colleagues (1989, p. 36) provide a checklist of classroom procedures that we believe is an excellent stimulus for metacognitive thinking. In addition to thinking about and writing your procedures for room use, seatwork, transitions into and out of the room, small group work, and general procedures (e.g., distributing materials), it is very helpful for you to write examples of self-questions and self-statements for each of Evertson's areas as a metacognitive checklist for yourselves. In this way, you are learning to be proactive, rather than simply reactive. A few examples are provided below:

Evertson's List (1989, p. 36)	Sample Self-Talk Statements/Questions
I. Room Use A. Teacher's desk and storage areas	1. Where do I want my desk? 2. Is it best in the front or the back of this class? 3. How will I feel about students' getting materials from my desk?
II. Seatwork and Teacher-Lead Instruction A. Student attention during presentations	1. Do I need 100% attention? 2. How do I know if I have a student's attention? 3. What are some strategies to help children foster their own attention?

Management is the third and final area we will discuss. This area is taught via a CSD approach as described earlier for planning and interactive instruction; therefore, these steps will not be restated. Below is an example of a management situation with the accompanying categories of self-talk.

EXAMPLE OF A MANAGEMENT SITUATION

There have been several incidences of "hitting" in my fourth grade class in the past few weeks. It seems that whenever a problem arises between two students, the confrontation usually ends with both students striking each other. I can't believe that this is so prevalent in my class! I had thought that my class rules were stated clearly enough, and that I was setting a good example as a role model; but despite my efforts to change the behaviors, the hitting continues.

It is time for lunch. Just as my students are lining up, and I'm passing out lunch tickets, a child near the back bursts into tears. I rush over, only to find that once again, two students are arguing and have each hit the other. Before I can assess the situation, both students start talking at once, blaming each other, and I have five minutes to get to the cafeteria. I say to myself:

INAPPROPRIATE SELF-TALK

Why are they so awful? They're driving me crazy!

Why do they hit each other all the time? This is really ridiculous.

Ooo, I just want to shake them when they act this way! Every little thing that happens ends up with hitting!

I've told them a million times—there is absolutely *no hitting* in this class, for any reason! What's the problem?

I spend half of my day dealing with this. What is wrong with me?

I must know how to handle them. Other teachers don't have this problem!

We just won't do anything anymore. I'll just keep them all in with their heads down–then they'll remember!

Oh, I just want to go home. I can't deal with this anymore. I just want some peace.

APPROPRIATE SELF-TALK

Calm down. It's not that big of deal. You can handle it. (Self-coping)

I'm going to count to five and speak calmly. (Self-coping)

Not all of them hit each other. It's really just a few of them. It's not that bad. (Self-coping)

I'll just restate the rule, and follow through with the consequences. I've got to be consistent! (Self-guiding)

I need to think about why this is such a problem. There must be a reason. (Self-guiding)

Maybe Betty, another teacher, has a suggestion. Surely she has had a problem like this before. (Self-coping)

OK, I can handle this situation. I need to remember that they are only nine. I don't need to get into a "power struggle" or argument! (Self-coping)

I've got to make strong eye contact. (Self-guiding)

OK, how do they feel when someone hits them? No wonder they hit back! It's probably a natural reaction. I know how they feel! (Self-questioning and self-coping)

They know the consequences for hitting—I've got to follow through. (Self-guiding)

Maybe we should all sit down and talk about this. (Self-guiding)

I've done a good job setting my expectations. (Self-reinforcing)

A quote by Lampert (1984, p. 16) is extremely supportive of using teacher specific situations, generated by classroom teachers themselves (as is the case for the teaching situations presented in this chapter). Lampert says: "Analyzing teacher stories may lead to a reflective language for talking about practice that is more congruent with what teachers do in classrooms. This language could be used by both researchers and teachers for teaching about thinking as well as thinking about teaching. Finding such a language is of critical importance for curriculum change."

CSD EXERCISE

A sample teaching scenario focusing on a management dilemma follows: Begin by writing down five inappropriate comments you might make to yourself if you were confronted with this situation. Follow this with 15 to 18 appropriate comments to self. After the self-comments are written, you should share them in groups and help each other designate each appropriate comment as either self-questioning, self-guiding, self-coping, or self-reinforcing. The final step is for you to repeat the appropriate self-talk aloud, whispered and silently to internalize the metacognitive process of management.

An assignment sheet used to gather "teachers' stories" in the areas of planning, instructing, and managing is illustrated in Figure 5.4. This is just one example and may be modified as needed or not used at all. We have used it as a review of metacognition for these three teaching areas.

FIGURE 5–4 Teachers' Use of CSD Assignment Sheet

Directions: For each of the three areas listed below, write a description of a recent teaching experience and what you said to yourself. Write at least five inappropriate statements or questions and fifteen appropriate statements or questions. Label each self-talk thought as either self-questioning, self-guiding, self-coping, self-reinforcing, or other.

I.   While Planning Situation   II. While Instructing Situation   III. While Managing Situation

Inappropriate Self-talk   Inappropriate Self-talk   Inappropriate Self-talk

Appropriate Self-talk   Appropriate Self-talk   Appropriate Self-talk

Future Trends in Metacognitive Study Applied to Teaching

It certainly seems logical that self-regulated teaching would enhance the teaching profession. We need self-directed teachers for their own benefit, and also as self-directed role models for students. This line of research is young, very young. It is not an easy phenomenon to research: the most valid and reliable ways to tap into teacher verbal introspection during the teaching act, as that act occurs, have not been uncovered yet. Researchers need to continue to pursue ways to find out how teachers verbally direct their own behaviors. What variables affect this verbal self-guidance? Do master teachers talk to themselves differently than poor teachers? What are the categories of teacher self-talk? Is there a developmental progression of self-talk categories as teachers gain experience in the classroom? Can teachers be taught new ways to talk to themselves to improve their abilities to cope with stress, control anger, become more creative? Other populations, discussed previously in this book, experienced benefits when their self-talk was modified (e.g., Meichenbaum, 1975; 1977). This leads us to believe that these gains are also possible for classroom teachers. An entire body of research studies and systematic, concerted efforts are necessary because we have almost none of these answers. After answers are found, replicated, and confirmed, preservice and inservice teachers should be assisted in acquiring these valuable metacogitive skills for planning, instructing, and managing their classrooms. The research and follow-up activities in this chapter are a start in this direction.

SUMMARY

The use of metacognitive strategies for monitoring and regulating teacher behaviors will most likely become a major area of research. In general, metacognitive strategies have been used successfully to help various populations learn to think before they act, to employ mediational processes, and to develop verbal control of behavior. All of these seem important for classroom teachers. These general benefits motivate our attempts at specific application to the preparation of classroom teachers through use of the cognitive self-direction model. Teachers, both preservice and inservice, have and will continue to benefit from CSD processes for planning, interactive instruction, and classroom management. These particular strategies comprise self-regulated teaching and are meant for teachers' professional classroom skills. Cognitive self-direction strategies promote awareness and regulation of these skills. As the CSD processes are internalized, they become automated and routinized with repeated use. Eventually these self-regulated processes enable teachers' metacognition so that they are cognitively aware and able to deliberately choose facilitative self-guiding verbalizations. At this point, they are much more likely to model rich, substantive verbal self-guidance for their students. The "modeling" itself is viewed as the transition when teachers externalize their internal guidance. Students learn vis-a-vis this modeling. For example, the teachers do not simply give directions, they cognitively model the directions. Students are more likely to understand such "direction-giving behavior." CSD programs for teachers are the prerequisite to fostering cognitive self-direction in students. As a result, the educational product will likely be more self-regulated learners capable of directing their own learning and behavior.

CHAPTER 6

Using Other-Regulation Models for Teaching and Learning

OVERVIEW

An integral part of teaching is to structure, monitor, and evaluate the learning tasks for others. In fact guiding the learning of others lies at the very heart of teaching. In this chapter four models of how this social/instructional guidance influences cognitive and metacognitive development are described. We term these teaching/learning models *other-regulation models* (first introduced in Chapter 4). Proleptic/learning instruction, reciprocal teaching, cognitive behavior modification, and cognitive self-instruction comprise the examples of other-regulation. Informed training whereby teachers explain to students what, when, how, where, and why certain cognitive and metacognitive strategies should be implemented is included as a type of scaffolding within each of the four other-regulation models. The underlying assumption for this chapter is that social contexts provide the foundational core of cognitive and metacognitive development.

Self-Questions

1. *Knowledge.* State the definition of cognitive self-instruction.

2. *Comprehension.* Explain the concept of other-regulation.

3. *Application.* In the research literature, find another example of other regulation, as defined in this chapter.

4. *Analysis.* Write a lesson plan using all the components of reciprocal teaching. Label the components.

5. *Synthesis.* Write a proposed research study using informed training as an important thrust.

6. *Evaluation.* Support the use of proleptic instruction within a regular education classroom setting, rather than a clinical, research setting.

Before addressing the four other-regulation models of instruction, commonalities across all four models are discussed. In contrast to Piaget's view that developmental levels determine the instructional match, Vygotsky took the reverse notion that learning was the driving force enabling development. Recall from Chapter 4, Vygotsky's idea of development occurring in collaboration with adults and more advanced peers—the disparity between the learning performance that individuals can demonstrate independently and that which they can display within the support of others. As you may also recall, from

Chapter 4, the distance between independent and supported activity is termed the zone of proximal development. This zone is created by learning. The abilities and skills that individuals can perform independently is thought of as completed development; whereas, learning performance displayed in socially supported contexts are in the process of being mastered. Later, these abilities and skills will become internalized and reflected in the individual's independent behavior. As educators we might refer to the independent condition as *level of mastery* and the socially-scaffolded condition as *level of instruction*. Level of instruction is defined in this chapter as supportive learning contexts in which teachers (adults and more advanced peers) "organize the learning environment (e.g., by making some objects available and others not), interpret and give meaning to events, direct attention to relevant dimensions of experience, provide ways to cope with the environment, and regulate on-going problem-solving efforts" (Day, French, & Hall, 1985, p. 34). In addition the teacher models critical metacognitive processes so that the learner can begin to internalize such processes for him or herself. During these instructional episodes of joint participation and shared learning the learner's cognitive and metacognitive abilities are socially transmitted, constrained, nurtured, and encouraged (Day, French, & Hall, 1985, pp. 33–34). The following information expands upon these four instructional responsibilities.

SUPPORTED INSTRUCTION

Teacher Responsibility	Examples of Instruction
Transmit	Explain, demonstrate, structure, question, correct, monitor, and reinforce (Teacher models these processes.)
Constrain	Limit, chunk the learning pieces, and frame (Learners demonstrate skills that they are not able to perform when working alone.)
Nurture	Teacher reduces some of the cognitive and/or metacognitive responsibilities by assuming responsibility for certain components of a task while the learner concentrates upon and gains complete mastery of another component. Reducing the cognitive/metacognitive workload while the learner gains secure footing.
Encourage	Teacher gradually relinquishes more and more responsibility for the task as the learner demonstrates increasing competence. Teacher verbally encourages by pointing out the improvements as children gain more and more cognitive and affective mastery of a specific task.

SUPPORTED INSTRUCTION EXERCISE #1

Directions: In pairs, plan a role play in which the four aspects of supported instruction (i.e., transmit, constrain, nurture, and encourage) are demonstrated. Choose any learning task that seems to lend itself to these processes.

Another concept common to the other-regulation models in this chapter is informed training (Brown, Campione, & Day, 1981). The term *informed training* was derived from research studies in which individuals were provided information about the reason for, and expected benefits/outcomes of the instructed procedures. When students are told what learning strategies to use, when it is important to use them across various content areas

Reflecting on the conflict:

    a. *When conflict is unresolved*: "These are difficult situations. Thinking about it only makes me more upset. Think about something else."

    b. *When conflict is resolved or coping is successful*: "I actually got through that without getting angry."

Example 2

Preparing for conflict: "Try not to take this too seriously."

Impact and confrontation: "For someone to be that irritable, he or she must be awfully unhappy."

Coping with angry feelings: "I can't expect people to act the way I want them to."

Reflecting on the conflict:

    a. *When conflict is unresolved*: "Can I laugh about it? It's probably not so serious."

    b. *When conflict is resolved or coping is successful*: "My pride can sure get me into trouble, but when I don't take things too seriously, I'm better off."

Example 3

Preparing for conflict: "This could be a testy situation, but I believe in myself."

Impact and confrontation: "Just roll with the punches; don't get bent out of shape."

Coping with angry feelings: "My muscles are starting to feel tight. Time to relax and slow things down."

Reflecting on the conflict:

    a. *When conflict is unresolved*: "Try to shake it off. Don't let it interfere with your job."

    b. *When conflict is resolved or coping is successful*: "I guess I've been getting upset for too long when it wasn't even necessary. I'm doing better at this all the time."

TEACHER ANXIETY

In Chapter 5 an affirmation training program for reducing anxiety of student teachers during their field experiences is described. Please refer to pages 92–93. The program includes making a self-talk tape using at least 15 positive affirmations written in the present tense (e.g., "I am a relaxed, calm teacher"). Instructions for making a self-talk tape are described on the next page (Helmstetter, 1986).

It should be noted that since anxiety levels are often high about field experience observations, and other teaching stressors, it has been our experience that student teachers and teachers are eager to use the tapes and learn self-coping skills for themselves. Many have reported how much the tapes help them to cope with field experiences and student teaching complexities and requirements; and in the case of classroom teachers, anxieties associated with teaching (i.e., dealing with disgruntled parents, excessive paperwork, discipline problems).

Other affective variables (e.g., eliminating worry) may be approached, using similar affirmation training procedures. Another excellent resource for starter self-talk statements is found in Helmstetter's book (1986) entitled *What to Say When You Talk to Yourself*. He provides excellent chapters on changing habits, attitudes, solving problems, and school and home settings, how to use the strategies, who is likely to benefit from this use, and why it is important to apply these strategies; then educational benefits have resulted. Informed training is thought of as the intermediate levels of instruction. Informed training translated to an educational realm, is similar to the practice of providing our students with "a purpose" or the reason for learning certain concepts or acquiring specific skills. Based on the research results gained from informed training studies (e.g., Burger, Blackmon, Holmes, & Zetlin, 1978; Ringel & Springer, 1980), this educational practice is a sound one.

Beyond telling, explaining, and demonstrating directly the who, what, when, how, and why to use various learning strategies, benefits have also occurred when students were (1) indirectly informed, (2) required to display successful strategy use during instruction, and (3) the teacher checked to make sure that students realized the benefits of using certain strategies. In order for students to be consciously aware of benefits, metacognitive awareness has to be operating within the students. If students are unable to state benefits of strategy use for their own learning, then teachers tell students directly what possible benefits might occur if the students apply certain strategies, such as saying to students: "rehearsing information aloud usually helps us remember that information."

Brown, Bransford, Ferrara, and Campione (1983) indicate that there are benefits of informing students indirectly about the many uses of a strategy. To do this, a given strategy is demonstrated across a variety of contexts. When individuals see more than one context use, they are better able to transfer and use this skill in an unfamiliar instructional context. In addition, when students are required to show mastery of a certain strategy during scaffolded instruction, they were able to use the strategy longer. This practice is similar to guided practice sessions in direct instruction approaches. Finally, metacognitive awareness of strategy benefits may be the reason the informed students continue to use a strategy after instruction.

To sum, Vygotsky (1978) claimed that learning appears on two planes: first on an interpersonal level and then later on an intrapersonal level. From the Vygotskian viewpoint, cognitive development is a dynamic process that does not evolve out of social isolation during passive assimilation. Instead, budding skills emerge and are sharpened as learners actively interact in scaffolded contexts that are expressed, constrained, nurtured, and encouraged by teachers. The next four sections present types of other-regulation models that comprise examples of such scaffolded contexts. The examples are proleptic/dyadic instruction, reciprocal teaching, cognitive behavior modification, and cognitive self-instruction. In this chapter we will only deal with explanations and definitions of these models, except in the case of cognitive self-instruction. Due to the characteristics of cognitive self-instruction, classroom application is inherent in the definition and explanation. In Part III, classroom application using these other-regulation models as a basis will be presented.

PROLEPTIC/DYADIC INSTRUCTION

Prolepsis is defined in a dictionary as "anticipating difficulty." In assisted learning, teachers structure situations and transfer responsibility gradually. The teacher scaffolds the learning event in such a refined way that difficulties or blocks to learning are anticipated by the teacher and are cleared out of the path for the most efficient learning. The ability to structure and transfer learning creates the various gradations of teaching ability from poor to outstanding. Teachers' involvement in students' learning can motivate, focus attention, guide steps, provide coping techniques, correct errors, and reinforce learning. Wood, Bruner, and Ross (1976) cited in Rogoff (1990) provide six functions through which teachers "extend current skills and knowledge to a higher level of competence" (p. 93). These scaffolding functions are as follows (p. 94):

PROLEPTIC/DYADIC FUNCTIONS

1. Recruiting the child's interest in the task as it is defined by the teacher.

2. Reducing the number of steps required to solve a problem by simplifying the task, so that the learner can manage components of the process and recognize when a fit with task requirements is achieved.

3. Maintaining the pursuit of the goal, through motivation of the child and direction of the activity.

4. Marking critical features of the discrepancies between what a child has produced and the ideal solution.

5. Controlling frustration and risk in problem solving.

6. Demonstrating an idealized version of the act to be performed.

As you become familiar with these six functions, observe pairs of individuals as one guides the learning of another. See if you can identify the six functions when they occur in real-life teaching or tutoring contexts. Begin by informally observing everyday instruction between two individuals, such as someone helping another learn (1) a computer skill, (2) how to choose a good tomato, (3) how to fax a message, (4) how to work the VCR, or (5) how to prepare a meal or certain recipe and make note of the examples of the six functions of Proleptic Instruction. Next, you may wish to conduct an in-depth study of a mother-child dyad or teacher-child dyad learning a particular skill such as putting a puzzle together or performing a long-division algorithm. In any event, try the following exercise for a better understanding of Proleptic/Dyadic Instruction.

PROLEPTIC/DYADIC INSTRUCTION EXERCISE #2

Directions: Observe a dyad of parent-child or teacher-child in an instructional session. You may be able to observe in a home of a friend or relative, or in a school. Gain written permission to conduct your mini-action research project. Videotape the session if possible. In addition use the prepared sheet (shown below) and fill in as much evidence as you can gather. Before and after the instructional session, you may wish to interview both the teacher and the learner to understand their perspectives about the session. A few questions are suggested; however, you may wish to generate your own list of questions. Depending on the ages and other factors (e.g., learning disability) you may need to modify these questions accordingly.

INTERVIEW QUESTIONS FOR THE LEARNER

Before Instruction
1. What do you expect to learn from _____ today?
2. Do you like to learn about _____?
3. What do you usually do when _____ is teaching you?
4. Is this going to be difficult, okay, or easy to learn?

After Instruction
1. What did you learn?
2. Can you do this by yourself now?
3. Can you teach this task to someone else?
4. Was this as (easy, difficult) as you thought?
5. What would have helped you learn this better?

INTERVIEW QUESTIONS FOR THE TEACHER

Before Instruction
1. What are your teaching plans for today?
2. How did you decide what and/or how to teach this concept or task?
3. How will you decide how fast to proceed?
4. What will you do if _____ seems completely lost?
5. What will you do if _____ seems bored and seems to already know how to do this?

After Instruction
1. How did it go?
2. What would you change if you could teach this again?
3. What parts of the task could _____ perform with minimal or no help from you?
4. What parts of the task (if any) did you have to continue to perform?
5. What was the most exciting aspect of this instructional session?

MINI-ACTION RESEARCH WORKSHEET EXERCISE #3

Directions: As you observe two people interacting during an instructional session write examples of the six functions of Proleptic/Dyadic Instruction.

1. Recruiting the learner's interest in the task:

_____
_____
_____
_____

2. Reducing the number of steps required to solve a problem by simplifying the task:

_____
_____

3. Maintaining the pursuit of the goal, through motivation of the learner and direction of the activity:

_____
_____
_____

4. Marking critical features of discrepancies between what a learner has produced and the ideal solution:

_____
_____
_____

5. Controlling frustration and risk in problem solving:_____
_____
_____
_____

6. Demonstrating an idealized version of the act to be performed:

_____
_____
_____

Proleptic/Dyadic Instruction was initially investigated in mother-child interactions. Researchers observed mother-child dyads as these two worked together to solve novel problems and then correlated maternal teaching patterns with their children's competence (e.g., Hess & Shipman, 1965, 1967). Hess and Shipman found that mothers who used more specific, varied, and precise language for a greater time period tended to have children who performed better on cognitive abilities' tasks and who were more verbal. Although these early studies documented the relationship between social contexts and cognitive development, they were not instructionally informative. The specifics of exactly how tasks were taught by the mothers were not indicated.

In the late seventies and early eighties, some research activity, stemming from a Vygotskian perspective, filled in some of the instructional void surrounding dyadic instruction (e.g., Gardner & Rogoff, 1982; Wertsch, 1979; Wertsch, McNamee, Budwig, & McLane, 1980). The studies conducted by Wertsch and his colleagues detailed how mothers foster the development of self-regulatory skills in preschoolers as they jointly solved jigsaw puzzles. Four levels of joint participation were documented by the Wertsch studies. These four levels are outlined below:

WERTSCH'S FOUR LEVELS OF PROLEPTIC INSTRUCTION

Level One
a. Learner's understanding of the task is severely limited.

b. Communication is difficult.

c. Learner may not understand the relationship between verbal explanations and the task at hand.

d. Regulation of activity by the adult is practically nonexistent.

Level Two
a. Learners perceive in part that there is a relationship between verbal instructions and the task.

b. Since there is not a complete connection made between others' speech and activity, implicit and indirect instruction may be missed (e.g., questioning may be an inappropriate technique).

c. This partial lack of understanding necessitates that adults state directions explicitly, such as with direct statements or imperatives.

Level Three
a. Inferences from adult instructions are possible.

b. Implicit messages, such as questions, are interpretable by the learner.

c. The problem solving remains primarily social.

d. The learner begins to regulate some of the problem-solving activity when the task solution becomes more obvious.

e. The shift from other-regulation to self-regulation continues to the next level.

Level Four
a. Learners are capable of regulating their own problem-solving behavior.

b. During this level, the learner usually uses (audible) private speech, causing the self-regulation to be observable.

In addition to these specific levels, Gardner and Rogoff (1982), Moss (1990), and Sonnenschein, Baker, and Cerro (1992) offer excellent descriptions of precisely how parents assist their children's learning. Moss (1990) and Sonnenschein, Baker, and Cerro (1992) studied the transfer of metacognitive skills from parents to their children. Moss found that mothers of gifted children linguistically structure their children's learning in a way that is recognizably different from nongifted parents' teaching styles. Sonnenschein, Baker, and Cerro posited that middle class parents did not transfer metacognitive skills to their children because they did not model them in problem solving. Morris's case study (1993) of a kindergarten child, using self-guiding speech, at home and at school confirmed this finding.

At the same time that Wertsch and his colleagues were conducting research on mother-child dyads, others began the study of teacher-child dyads (e.g., Hood, McDermott, & Cole, 1980), and peer-child dyads (Cazden, Cox, Dickinson, Steinberg, & Stone, 1979). Similar findings as compared to those of Wertsch, were evident. Basically, the teacher began instructional sessions with explicit directions, clarifying the exact goals of the task, and checking to make sure each step was understood and completed correctly. Next, the teacher became less directive as students gradually understood the task. Finally, teachers often asked students who had demonstrated sufficient mastery, to explain the task to a peer. Interestingly, the peer serving in the role of teacher followed the same pattern, moving from explicit, detailed instructions to less elaboration as their classmates gained their own understanding of the task.

The previous research on proleptic/dyadic instruction clearly points to the significance of social interaction to cognitive and metacognitive development. Adults (parents and teachers) and more experienced peers are able to explain, demonstrate, model, limit, correct, nurture, and encourage cognitive strategies that promote task completion. They can model metacognitive awareness, monitoring, and regulation of thinking related to the task at hand. These cognitive and metacognitive functions of other-regulation are the precursors to self-regulation of the same functions within a learner. Therefore, the degree and quality of self-regulation are dependent upon the degree and quality of other-regulation.

The next other-regulation model to be discussed is called *reciprocal teaching*. It is directed toward listening and reading comprehension, using a scaffolded approach whereby students gradually assume the role of the "teacher."

RECIPROCAL TEACHING

As is evidenced by the the proleptic/dyadic model previously discussed, metacognitive strategies can be taught to students who for some reason do not develop them on their own. Since the early 1980s, Ann Brown and Annemarie Sullivan Palincsar have investigated a successful metacognitive strategy they call "reciprocal teaching" (Palincsar, 1986; Palincsar & Brown, 1984). Reciprocal teaching is best characterized as a dialogue between teachers and students in which they take turns in assuming the role of the teacher. In this approach, students who are having problems with reading comprehension, are taught four critical metacognitive skills through interactive dialogue (Palincsar, 1986, p. 118).

1. Summarizing: identifying and paraphrasing the main idea in the text.

2. Question-Generating: self-questioning about the type of information that is generally tapped on tests of comprehension and recall.

3. Clarifying: discerning when there has been a breakdown in comprehension and taking the necessary action to restore meaning (e.g., reading ahead, reading, asking for assistance).

4. Predicting: hypothesizing what the structure and content of the text suggest will be presented next.

FIGURE 6–1   Example of a Reciprocal Teaching Lesson

TEACHER:	The title of this story is "Genius with Feathers." Let's have some predictions. I will begin by guessing that this story will be about birds that are very smart. Why do I say that?
FIRST STUDENT:	Because a genius is someone very smart.
SECOND STUDENT:	Because they have feathers.
TEACHER:	That's right. Birds are the only animals that have feathers. Let's predict now the kind of information you might read about very smart birds.
THIRD STUDENT:	Parrots or blue jays.
FIRST STUDENT:	A cockatoo like the bird on *Baretta*.
TEACHER:	What other information would you want to know? (*No response from students.*)
TEACHER:	I would like to know what these birds do that is so smart. Any ideas?
SECOND STUDENT:	Some birds talk.
FOURTH STUDENT:	They can fly.
TEACHER:	That's an interesting one. As smart as people are, they can't fly. Well, let's read this first section now and see how many of our predictions were right. I will be the teacher for this section. (*All read the section silently.*)
TEACHER:	Who is the genius with feathers?
FIRST STUDENT:	Crows.
TEACHER:	That's right. We were correct in our prediction that this story would be about birds, but we didn't correctly guess which kind of bird, did we? My summary of the first section would be that it describes the clever things that crows do, which make them seem quite intelligent. Is there anything else I should add to my summary?
FIRST STUDENT:	How they steal corn?
TEACHER:	That's a detail that described one of the ways in which they are clever. For our summary we will not include details. I think I found a word that needs clarification. What does "resourceful" mean?
ALL STUDENTS:	(*No response.*)
TEACHER:	If I say you are a resourceful person, I mean that you are able to deal with problems and difficulties easily. Being resourceful is another way in which crows are intelligent. I would like to make a prediction now. The section's last sentence says, "One major reason they have mastered survival against heavy odds is the amazing communication system." My prediction is that the next section will describe this communication system. How do you think crows communicate with one another?
ALL STUDENTS:	Caw-Caw.
FIRST STUDENT:	With a special song.
TEACHER:	Let's read on. Who will be the teacher for this section? (*Dialogue follows in which the student Jim is chosen to lead the discussion, with the teacher providing corrective feedback.*)
JIM:	How do crows communicate with one another?
TEACHER:	Good question! You picked right up on our prediction that this is about the ways crows communicate. Whom do you choose to answer your question?
JIM:	Barbara.
BARBARA:	Crows have built-in radar and a relay system.
JIM:	That's a good part of it. The answer I wanted was how they relay the messages from one crow to the other crow.
TEACHER:	Summarize now.
JIM:	This is about how crows have developed a system of communication.

FIGURE 6–1 *Continued*

TEACHER:	That's right. The paragraph goes on to give examples of how they use pitch and change in interval, but these are supporting details. The main idea is that crows communicate through a relay system? Jim?
JIM:	It says in this section that crows can use their communication system to play tricks, so I predict the next section will say something about the tricks crows play. I would like Sue to be the next teacher.
TEACHER:	Excellent prediction. The last sentence of a paragraph often suggests what the next paragraph will be about. Good, Jim.

Source: From Annemarie S. Palincsar, "Reciprocal Teaching: Working within the Zone of Proximal Development." Paper presented at the annual convention of the American Educational Research Association, New Orleans, April 1984. Reprinted by permission of author.

These four steps are taught to students as a routine sequence to follow in reading text. Initially, the teacher does most of the modeling, questioning, and explaining. Gradually, more and more instructional responsibilities are turned over to the students, until they eventually take turns acting as the teacher, leading small group discussions of the texts. The rate at which this transfer occurs will vary among students, but no matter how slow the rate, each learner must always be challenged at his or her level of competence. When necessary, the teacher provides prompts, cues, questions, and encouragement (Bruner refers to this as scaffolding) until students master the strategies themselves. Palincsar (1986) emphasized that each student is given the support needed to execute the strategy successfully, and the support is gradually withdrawn as the student indicates increased competence with comprehension.

It is important to note that reciprocal teaching is not the same as teaching skills. Rather, the primary goal is that students actively participate in discussions of text (Palincsar, 1986). Figure 6.1 provides an example of dialogue from a reciprocal teaching lesson that will help illustrate the nature of the instructional procedure.

Research studies have found that reciprocal teaching methods significantly increase the reading comprehension of low-achieving middle grades students (Palincsar, 1987; Palincsar & Brown, 1984). When students use reciprocal teaching in small groups or pairs, in addition to cognitive benefits, they also gain many social and affective benefits as a result of interacting with their peers. Respect for others' opinions and collaboration toward common goals are examples of such benefits. Positive results were also found in a more recent adaptation of the method with first graders (Palincsar & Brown, 1989).

In an article in *Instructor* magazine, Palincsar (1987) provided some key tips to teachers when considering the use of reciprocal teaching that include:

1. Even though reciprocal teaching was designed for middle school students who were adequate decoders but poor comprehenders, it can be adapted and used with students as young as six years of age. In first grade the teacher should demonstrate the importance of being an active listener and reader. In third grade, try reciprocal teaching as a read-along activity. With middle schoolers, emphasize study strategies for science and social studies.

2. Small groups of six to eight students during group reading time work best.

3. Older children can use reciprocal teaching for peer-tutoring.

4. Carefully monitor the dialogues.

5. Frequently measure changes in each student's ability to read and answer comprehension questions.

6. The teacher's introduction of reciprocal teaching should run 20 consecutive school days.

The dialogue that is emphasized in the reciprocal teaching method provides an important message to classroom teachers that sociolinguistic interaction is essential to learning. This language format is simply conversation with an informed purpose and provides a familiar and useful vehicle for improving reading comprehension. Reciprocal teaching strategies are important not only because they promote reading comprehension but because they also increase students' awareness and regulation of their own comprehension instruction (Palincsar, 1991). Cognitive behavior modification, to be discussed next, is another way that the transfer from other to self-regulation can be accomplished.

COGNITIVE BEHAVIOR MODIFICATION

Teaching individuals to manage their own behavior is a primary goal of cognitive behavior modification (CBM). CBM is a rubric for a number of theories and interventions including anger control, problem solving, self-instruction, self-control, self-monitoring, self-evaluation, and self-reinforcement training. Cognitive behavioral interventions have been used to modify social, affective, and cognitive behaviors such as attentional deficits, anger, impulsivity, depression, social skills, metacognition, and reading, writing, mathematics, and spelling deficits. CBM techniques typically incorporate self-regulation of cognitive and metacognitive strategies, self-verbalizations as important tools for achieving self-regulation, and emphasis on the active role of the individual in the learning process (Harris, 1982; Harris, 1986). Cognitive behavior modification (CBM) brings together, according to Meichenbaum (1976), the clinical concerns of semantic therapists (e.g., Ellis & Beck) and the technology of behavior therapy (e.g., operant conditioning and modeling).

Origins of Cognitive Behavior Modification

Behavioral Psychology

Historically, programs to change behavior were characterized by the close application of operant learning principles, involving the systematic use of reinforcement to strengthen desired behavior. Based on the operant conditioning paradigm of Skinner (1953), the central tenet of behavior modification holds that behaviors are primarily learned and maintained as a result of people's interactions with their environments. The behavior change may be achieved by manipulating or modifying either the antecedent conditions for behavior or the consequences following behavior. Therefore, an individual's behavior can be changed and reshaped by directly changing the environment (Bandura, 1969; Blackmon & Silberman, 1975; Homme, 1970). Behavioral procedures include such techniques as reinforcement, punishment, stimulus control, contingency-contracting, time out, saturation, extinction, etc. For true behaviorists, cognitions and feelings were denied, ignored, or considered irrelevant to the task of changing behavior. The behavioral approach to teaching was basically the idea that a child will move toward positive reinforcement and withdraw from negative reinforcers.

During the 1970s there was a growing dissatisfaction with behavioristic interventions for several reasons. First, traditional behavior modification techniques emphasize external control by the teachers, rather than trying to foster internal control by the child. A second disadvantage is that because the focus is on systematically manipulating consequences of behavior, teachers are not as likely to examine their own teaching methods as possible contributors of students' misbehavior. Finally, a single teacher cannot possibly systematically reinforce and punish a class made up of twenty to thirty children (Brophy, 1983). Due to the ongoing dissatisfaction with behavioral techniques, a shift toward more cognitively oriented interventions began during the 1980s. This changing view acknowledged that behavior and learning are influenced by an individual's cognitions.

Albert Bandura (1969, 1974) posited his social learning theory that views behavior as resulting from a reciprocal relationship among individual characteristics, behavior, and environmental influences. Neither overt behavioral nor covert mediational processes can be considered in isolation. Rather, a mutually interdependent network of cognitions, behaviors, and environmental factors must be considered in cognitive development. Bandura (1974) added a vital assumption: humans are active and self-regulatory and initiate many behaviors. He hypothesized that people observe their own behavior, judge it against their own standards, and reinforce or punish themselves. Bandura's work in social learning laid the groundwork of what was to become cognitive-behaviorism (Meyers, Cohen, & Schlester, 1989).

The movement toward cognitive behavior modification was also furthered by research on the processes of self-control and self-regulation (Harris, 1982). The new trends of contemporary cognitive behavior modification are attempts to teach students to control themselves rather than be controlled externally; to elicit behavior through different strategies instead of shaping through post-response reinforcement (Brophy, 1986).

Cognitive Psychology

The cognitive view of learning, unlike the behavioral perspective, sees people as active processors of information who initiate experiences that lead to learning, seek out information to solve problems, and reorganize what they already know to achieve new learning (Woolfolk, 1993). The determinants of human behavior lie within the individual.

Craighead (1982) credits the cognitive therapies of Albert Ellis (1973) and Aaron Beck (1976) as important influences on cognitive behavior modification. Both are considered cognitive-semantic theorists who believe that mental disorders are fundamentally disorders of thinking. Ellis (1962) emphasized cognitive factors that contribute to mental illness and focused on altering the patients' maladaptive self-verbalizations. Ellis' rational-emotive therapy (RET) is based on the assumption that emotional suffering is largely due to the ways that people misconstrue the world. Such misconceptions lead to internal dialogue which is often self-defeating and which has adverse effects on behavior. To help the individual overcome the disorder, he or she is made aware of the negative self-statements and images and of the negative consequences of such thoughts. (For a more detailed explanation of RET, see Chapters 1 and 3.) Beck's (1976) cognitive therapy asserts that problems are often the result of misinterpreting events. Individuals often have distortions in their thought patterns that result in selectively attending to and inaccurately anticipating consequences, and making logical errors. Cognitive therapy includes (1) clients become aware of their thoughts, (2) they learn to identify distorted thoughts, (3) these distorted thoughts are replaced by accurate, more objective cognitions, and (4) feedback and reinforcement are a necessary part of the process.

Soviet Psychologies

In addition to the historical-theoretical underpinnings of both behavioral and cognitive psychologies just described, Meichenbaum (1977) and Craighead (1982) cite the Soviet child development theories of Vygotsky (1962) and Luria (1959, 1961, 1962) as significant influences on the development of cognitive behavior modification. As we have discussed previously in Chapter 4, Vygotsky proposed a theory of development of intellect and thought in which the development and internalization of private speech played a critical role in a child's establishment of voluntary control over behavior. To briefly summarize again, he theorized that, self-regulating private speech results from social interactions between the child and adult and saw such speech serving the cognitive functions of orienting, organizing, and structuring behavior. Luria, Vygotsky's student, recognized the role of speech in the regulating of thinking, the importance of social interaction, and the movement of speech to thought from an interpsychological plane to an intrapsychological one. While Vygotsky focused on the semantic aspect of self-verbalization, Luria was interested in the motoric aspect of speech. Luria (1961) described the three stages in the development of self-regulation which are recognized as the foundation of self-instructional approaches: (a) the child's behavior is initially controlled by the verbalization of others, (b) the child's own overt verbalizations direct his or her own behavior, and (c) the child's behavior is controlled by his or her own covert self-verbalizations. The theories of Vygotsky and Luria serve as the building blocks for most self-instructional interventions.

Techniques of Cognitive Behavior Modification

Cognitive behavior modification, as described by Meichenbaum (1977), refers to techniques designed to develop in individuals the capacity for controlling their own behavior. Techniques often utilized with CBM consist of methods of self-control, self-guidance, self-verbalizations, self-instruction, self-monitoring, self-assessment, self-recording, and self-reinforcement. The CBM techniques typically feature self-treatment, verbalization, a strategy, modeling, and evaluation of alternative choices (Lloyd, 1980). CBM procedures require the individual to be an active participant and responsible for his or her own learning (Zimmerman, 1990; Zimmerman & Schunk, 1989).

Cognitive behavioral strategies involve training individuals to alter thoughts and speech-to-self in an attempt to produce constructive emotions and behaviors (Meichenbaum, 1977) and have been successful in reducing students' anxiety (Payne & Manning, 1990; Warren, Deffenbacher, & Brading, 1976), improving academic performance of behavior-problem students (Lovitt & Curtiss, 1968), improving reading comprehension, strategy use, and attitude toward reading (Payne & Manning, 1992), increasing on-task behavior (Manning, 1988), as well as altering the attributional traits of various populations (Manning, 1988; Manning, 1990b; Payne & Manning, 1988).

The focus of CBM is to teach individuals how to think, not what to think. CBM self-instructional strategies are geared toward teaching individuals to spontaneously produce and use cognitive strategies and self-instructions. Meichenbaum (1977) defines self-instruction as verbalizations and images to oneself that initiate, guide, or maintain one's own nonverbal behavior. Said another way, the self-instructional CBM training aims at teaching individuals to employ mediation responses that represent a general strategy for regulating one's behavior under various situations. We can do this for students by providing them with specific statements they can make when confronted with specific, frustrating situations.

In CBM, students are taught directly how to use self-instruction in order to change emotions and behavior. Meichenbaum and Goodman (1971) developed a self-instructional training regime to teach hyperactive, impulsive children to talk to themselves as a means of developing self-control. This program was extremely successful in reducing impulsivity and promoting reflectivity which in turn fostered self-control. The remedial sequence in Meichenbaum and Goodman's self-instructional training had five basic steps (Meichenbaum, 1977, p. 32):

1. An adult model performs a task while talking aloud to self (cognitive modeling);

2. The child performs the same task under the direction of the model's instructions (overt external guidance);

3. The child performs the task while instructing self aloud (overt self-guidance);

4. The child whispers the instructions to self as he/she goes through the task (faded, overt self-guidance); and finally

5. The child performs the task while guiding his/her performance via inner speech (covert self-instruction).

Inherent within Meichenbaum and Goodman's (1971) process was the use of several performance-relevant skills:

1. problem definition ("What is it I have to do?")

2. focusing attention and response guidance, which is usually the answer to the self-questions ("Now, carefully stop and draw the line down.")

3. self-reinforcement ("Good, I'm doing fine.")

4. self-evaluation, coping skills ("Okay, I can start over again.")

Meichenbaum and Goodman's CBM approach was an innovative method using games, problems, etc., to teach children to use self-instruction to control their own behavior. The procedures were designed to encourage students to slow down, approach tasks systematically and reflect on information (e.g., feedback) from task performance. The CBM approach has been extremely successful in helping various populations learn to think before they act. These individuals then have a cognitive strategy that can benefit them for a lifetime. The individuals are taught and learn to help themselves, rather than having to be dependent upon an external agent. In Chapter 7 we will revisit CBM and provide some classroom examples of its application.

An approach that draws heavily from the ideas of cognitive behavior modification is called *cognitive self-instruction*. Cognitive self-instruction, as presented here, takes a more instructional approach with an emphasis on classroom practice. As with the three *other-regulation models* previously discussed, the adults (teachers or parents) model the skills of self-instruction initially. Then there is a gradual transfer of responsibility for one's own instruction to the learner.

COGNITIVE SELF-INSTRUCTION

Cognitive self-instruction (CSI) is defined as instructing yourself, using your own cognition. Usually the cognition is in the form of audible and/or inaudible self-talk. Talking to yourself in order to question, guide, cope, correct, and reinforce your own learning and behavior are the subskills comprising cognitive self-instruction. If students have had significant adults in their lives who have modeled, explicitly taught, and/or demonstrated implicitly such skills; then, they will more likely have a head start on the educational process because they will be more knowledgeable about how, when, where, and why to facilitate their own learning. However, even these students can profit from instruction aimed at improving and/or increasing the use of their self-instructional skills. In addition, your classrooms will be filled with students who have experienced impoverished social/linguistic environments, where models of cognitive and metacognitive self-instruction were wholly lacking. Such students will be more likely to lack knowledge of when, how, what, where, and why to use self-instructional language and strategies.

The explanation of cognitive self-instruction is based on the classroom research conducted by Manning (1988, 1990b). Manning (1988) taught CSI to 28 elementary students, grades 1 and 3, with a behavior modification comparison group of 27 students, grades 1 and 3. After four weeks of CSI instruction, the CSI group improved significantly more than the comparison group in on-task behavior and teacher ratings of classroom conduct. In addition, locus of control orientations became more internal for the CSI group as compared to the behavior modification group. Findings were consistent at the one month and three month follow-up evaluations. The benefits of CSI instruction transferred to the students' art class as rated by the art teacher and also to home behaviors as rated by their mothers. In an in-depth case study (Manning, 1990b) with a fourth grade student exhibiting severe concentration problems, CSI was taught to improve school work habits. After four months of instruction the student improved significantly in her ability to focus, follow through, and finish classroom tasks assigned as independent work. Manning's CSI approach that includes the three components of modeling, practicing, and cueing is illustrated in Figure 6.2.

MODELING

Modeling of CSI is essential because of the abstractness of thought processes. It is much easier to teach overt behaviors than to teach metacognitive thinking strategies to regulate overt behaviors. Students need to hear first hand how teachers and productive peers guide themselves verbally to regulate behavior. Do not assume that all students understand and can spontaneously use CSI since it appears to occur very naturally and easily for some individuals.

To overview first, the CSI modeling can be presented spontaneously by adult or peer models, or presented as audiotaped modeling, or videotaped modeling. Students should hear CSI models during school work habits (e.g., concentrating, staying on task) and during social responsibility (e.g., waiting turns, sharing materials). The CSI self-talk categories that need to be explicitly modeled for students are problem defining, attention focusing, self-guiding, self-coping, and self-reinforcing. Please refer to Figure 6.2 for the modeling component.

Teacher modeling is a viable way for students to learn. Optimally, teachers' modeling needs to occur on four levels within the Manning approach. These four levels are as follows: (1) Spontaneous teacher use of CSI for teacher need (e.g., self-guiding speech to correct the situation when the overhead projector will not work); (2) Role-play CSI for teacher need (e.g., staying calm while being observed by the principal); (3) Spontaneous teacher use of CSI for student need (e.g., teacher sees some students looking on other students' tests and he/she models on the spot the choice between cheating and not cheating), and (4) Role-play CSI for student need (e.g., after several days of pushing in the line for water the teacher subsequently sets up a role-playing situation in which he/she models self-talk for waiting in line for water even when thirst is great). Examples of each of these types are presented below:

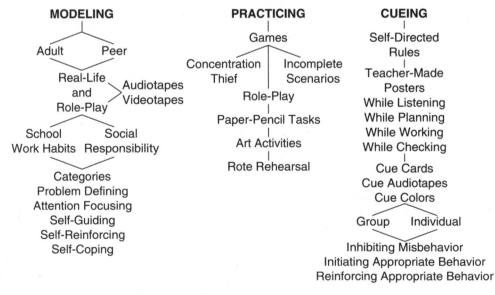

FIGURE 6–2
Manning's Classroom Approach to Cognitive Self-Instruction

Source: Manning, B. H. (1988). Application of cognitive behavior modification: First and third graders self-management of classroom behaviors. *American Educational Research Journal, 25*(2), 193–212. Copyright 1988 by the American Educational Research Association. Reprinted by permission of the publishers.

SPONTANEOUS TEACHER USE OF CSI FOR TEACHER NEED

Categories	CSI
Problem defining	Why won't this overhead turn on?
Attention focusing	Let me see. I'll try all the switches again.
Self-guiding	This arrow points to the right. Did I turn left or right. Try again.
Self-coping	It is easy to get frustrated. Take a deep breath and relax. There must be a solution.
Self-reinforcing	Success: Hey! I stuck with it and found the outlet is faulty. I'll try this other outlet. Yay! It works.
	No Success: I've tried all I know. I'll either show you this information by putting it on the board or call the media specialist to help fix the machine. Which would be the fastest?

ROLE-PLAY CSI FOR TEACHER NEED

Categories	CSI
Problem defining	Why am I getting so uptight about being observed?
Attention focusing	Now put a lid on this. Stop panicking myself. Calm down.
Self-guiding	Count slowly. Concentrate on the students. Forget the principal is here.
Self-coping	I may make a few mistakes. It won't be the end of the world even if I do! Things will be fine.
Self-reinforcing	Success: I knew I could get through this observation calmly.
	No Success: My heart never stopped pounding and I didn't teach my very best. Next time I'll be better prepared so I can stay calmer. Learn something from this.

SPONTANEOUS TEACHER USE OF CSI FOR STUDENT NEED

Categories	CSI
Problem defining	I forgot to study for my test. Should I look at my friend's test?
Attention focusing	I can see her paper easily. But, is that right?
Self-guiding	Just do my best. I'll feel better about myself if I don't look.
Self-coping	This is hard. I know some of my answers are wrong. That's okay. I've done the best I can. Next time I won't leave my book at school.
Self-reinforcing	Success: I'm glad I didn't take answers that didn't belong to me. I feel good about that!
	No Success: I looked at someone else's answer. I feel terrible. I'll just turn in my paper and tell the teacher. I hate this feeling. I'm too important to treat myself this way. Make better choices next time.

ROLE-PLAY CSI FOR STUDENT NEED

Categories	CSI
Problem defining	What if I push in line or jump in front of someone? How can I follow the rule to wait my turn when I'm so thirsty?

Attention focusing	Look, everyone else is thirsty too. They don't want to wait either.
Self-guiding	Just think about something else. There are just three more people and Mrs. Dollard is moving people along quickly.
Self-coping	I don't like to wait. But who does? I can do it.
Self-reinforcing	I'm proud of myself. I didn't push and I didn't jump in line. I can wait my turn. I like that about me.

After spontaneous teacher or other adult modeling, review with the students "what," "why," "how," and "when" CSI needs to be employed. Ask students questions such as: "Did anyone notice what I was doing when the overhead would not work? Why was I talking to myself? Sometimes I do this aloud and sometimes I do it inside my head. Either way, it helps me to plan what I need to do." Ask students if they ever talk to themselves? "When? What kinds of things do you say to yourself?" List these on the board or poster. "Why do you use this self-talk? When I was talking to myself about cheating, what did I say to myself? Who remembers something I said?" Continue and prompt if necessary until they have named most or all of the teachers' self-talk and have discussed benefits of guiding themselves verbally. Since the self-talk occurred spontaneously and was used as a teaching tool after the fact, this modeling will most likely not be available on audio or videotape.

Role-playing sessions of CSI can be used for instruction just as any role-play situation can. Prepare the students. Describe the scenario and the self-talk script they will hear. Tape the session. Show the self-talk sessions and teach directly the CSI categories of problem defining, attention focusing, self-guiding, self-coping, and self-reinforcing if you deem that this type of direct instruction is appropriate for your group of learners. For example, we would not teach categories to most kindergarten groups that we know. Use teacher judgment.

Peer modeling of CSI logically follows teacher modeling. It is important for students to experience how their productive classmates verbally guide themselves at school. There are numerous ways that teachers can use peer models of CSI.

In our previous research, we have been impressed with the students' positive reaction to videotapes of elementary school children their age or older using self-instruction to guide on-task classroom behaviors during seatwork. The students participating in our research studies internalized and used similar CSI after viewing and discussing the tapes for only two weeks, twice per week for fifty minutes. Teachers can easily make their own videotapes. First, you film your class during independent seatwork time, or for older children, during study sessions. Write a script of self-talk (after interviewing students about what they were saying to themselves) and audiotape the self-talk script using a male and female reader to coincide with male and female students on the screen. Dub the self-talk over the original audio soundtrack. Here are some examples of self-talk from a videotape we have used:

Problem-defining CSI
What am I supposed to be doing?

Was I supposed to be sitting in my seat paying attention?

Let's see, what was I going to put there?

Attention-focusing CSI
Mrs. Bowersett is telling me what to do. I need to listen carefully.

I better get back to this writing if I want to finish.

Self-guiding CSI

Let's turn back and see if I can get some help from the directions.

I need to be careful while cutting this.

Self-coping CSI

This is a lot of work today, but I'm going to go slowly.

Oops, I made a mistake, but that's okay. I need to slow down.

Self-reinforcing CSI

Yeah! I think I'm getting it.

I did that problem well. No one had to help me.

As students become proficient at identifying categories of self-guiding speech, they become more enabled to supply their own self-talk needs in each of the categories (e.g., Student identifies frustration over a task and then identifies the need to use self-coping statements, "I'm having trouble here, but I can figure this out if I take my time.").

STUDENTS' CATEGORIES OF COGNITIVE SELF-INSTRUCTION
EXERCISE #4

Directions: Listen to one student talk to him or herself during independent school work. Younger children (ages 4–7) may talk to themselves aloud spontaneously while working on an assigned task or at home while playing alongside a peer. With children older than 7 you may have to request that they think-aloud as they work or play. In either instance record and/or write at least 20 self-talk utterances (a word, phrase, or sentence spoken aloud to self, separated by a 3- or 4-second pause). Then classify each of the 20 utterances as one of the following categories. After data are collected, share your results in groups of three or four. In this way, if you have a category with no representative utterances someone else may have an example in that category. As a class, you can make a graph of how many utterances were recorded for each of the five categories listed below.

1. Problem definition (e.g., What did the teacher say to do next)?

   _____

   _____

2. Focusing attention (e.g., Now get back to work on this math.)

   _____

   _____

3. Self-guiding (e.g., Watch carefully here.)

   _____

   _____

4. Self-coping (e.g., Even if I do not get all the answers correct, I will do my best.)

   _____

   _____

5. Self-reinforcing (e.g., Good, I remembered to wait my turn.)

   _____

   _____

PRACTICING

It is not enough to just model CSI for students, even if a large amount of modeling occurs and creative development of modeling episodes are used in the classroom. Students need to practice CSI themselves in order to internalize the processes. Practice is crucial for transfer and maintenance of such strategies. Students must create their own metacognitive reality. They need to sensorially experience CSI for themselves. Therefore the following practice examples are provided. The best ideas for practice, however, come from individual teachers who know the needs of their students. These examples have worked for the teachers who developed them. They may require some modification if used by other teachers.

Please refer to Figure 6.2, Practicing. The practicing is intended for students. Students must be directly involved and experience enough repetition to incorporate self-guidance into their present way of thinking about school behavior. The practice strategies are classified as games, role-play, paper-pencil tasks, art activities, and rote rehearsal. Each of these will be briefly addressed. It is hoped that these "starter suggestions" will spark teacher creativity and motivation.

Games

Three *games* that have been tried and endorsed by teachers are "Concentration Zapper," "Incomplete Scenarios," and "Can We Play." In Concentration Zapper, the teacher initially (and later a concentrating student) goes about the room attempting to break students' concentration on an academic task. Students often do not understand what it means when the teacher says "Concentrate on your work." After students are given a certain school assignment to complete, they are told to concentrate on the assignment which means "Keep my mind on my work." As the students repeat aloud with or echo after the teacher, "Keep my mind," they point with their fingers to either side of their head, "on my work," they point down to their papers. The kinesthetic/tactual experience of moving hands from the head to the work seems important in helping young students understand the concept of "concentration." Students are directed to say to themselves in whisper or silently, "Concentrate on my work." The game itself helps them to understand the role they must assume to insure the quality of their own concentration. The concentration zapper carries a pretend container "Concentration Bucket" and tries to take away (zap) somebody's concentration. The teacher (zapper) walks among the students making noise, rattling papers, tapping students on shoulders, whistling, laughing, dropping books, trying in any acceptable manner to cause a distraction. If a student looks toward the zapper or away from the work, or laughs, that student has just lost his/her concentration to the zapper. The zapper says, "I just zapped your concentration; you'll have to ignore me next time which means don't look at me, think about your work." Students still remaining when time is up (time set by teacher) are designated "Great Concentrators" and a new zapper is chosen from among them. In the busy classrooms of today, filled with many interruptions, children have to be able to help themselves concentrate on the task at hand and selectively ignore distractions. A game such as Concentration Zapper teaches them to do this.

In addition to the game, some teachers report teaching the use of cue cards (to be explained in detail later in this chapter) during Concentration Zapper. Teachers give each student a laminated index card that says "Concentrate on my work." Students are instructed to read the cue card to themselves when the "Concentration Zapper" is trying to distract them. In this way students learn to remind themselves to concentrate even during distractions. One teacher, Susan Jones, developed a catchy slogan that she uses as a visual reminder to children to concentrate. It goes like this: I AM AS BUSY AS A BEE,

THE CONCENTRATION ZAPPER WON'T GET ME!!! The last time we were in Susan's classroom, this slogan was displayed prominently in the front of her class. Mrs. Jones's young students know how to concentrate.

The second game, the "Incomplete Scenarios" are geared more toward school/social responsibility. The teacher describes a situation such as "Your class has just come in from recess. It is a very hot day and the line for water is long. The teacher has talked to you about waiting your turn, but she is nowhere in sight. Your best friend is next to get water and she offers to put you up in line, what will you say to yourself?" After children respond to the incomplete scenarios, role-play can be used with an emphasis on the five categories (e.g.,self-coping) of self-talk. Focus on self-guidance of appropriate choices. The following self-talk utterances were developed for this scenario. They are written in large letters on a comic-strip bubble, accompanied by the students' favorite fictitious character, looking as if he/she is saying these self-talk statements. This display appears in the hall over the water fountain and serves to remind students to verbally guide themselves in an appropriate manner. Teachers say this display has really helped to decrease pushing in line, etc., at the water fountain.

"I wait patiently in line for my turn at the water fountain."

"I stand quietly at the water fountain."

"I do not push and shove while waiting my turn at the water fountain."

"It's hard when I am so thirsty to wait patiently. But I can do it."

"I am happy with myself when I wait my turn."

"My teacher is proud of me when I stand quietly and wait patiently at the water fountain. Good for me!"

Another example of an incomplete scenario is focused on lunchroom behavior: Billy wants to get Tim's attention. Tim is sitting several spaces down from Billy. Billy says to himself, "I think I'll yell at Tim, or even better, I'll throw my roll at him to get his attention." What can Billy say to himself to help in this situation?

"I need to eat my food while in the lunchroom."

"After I eat my lunch, I talk quietly to those people sitting beside me."

"I eat my food quietly in the lunchroom."

"I do not play with my food."

"When I want to talk, I talk quietly to my neighbors."

"The lunchroom is a nicer place to come to when I eat my food and talk quietly."

"I feel better when I eat my food slowly and don't rush through my lunch." "I am proud of myself when I eat my lunch quietly."

(The water fountain and lunchroom scenarios were developed by teacher, Dr. Peggy Dagley [1988, p. 163].)

A third game is called "Can We Play?" This game was adapted from Markman (1977/1979). The teacher instructs the students to ask themselves (self-questioning) three questions: "Does this make sense to me?" "Is there anything missing?" "What else do I need to know?" The teacher writes these questions on the board or poster and displays them as a stimulus/reminder. Sets of complete and incomplete directions for games and activities are given. Students play the game (with incomplete directions) when they can supply the missing instructions. Any usual classroom games (e.g., Dog and the Bone, Five

Up) can be used by simply omitting essential parts of the directions and then asking the students "Can We Play?" Why or why not?" Remind students to ask themselves the three questions on the board.

Role-Play

The focus here has changed from modeling in a role-play situation to practicing CSI in a role-play situation. Any of the incomplete scenarios might be used as a stimulus to practice the use of CSI through role-play. For example, students may role-play walking to the lunchroom appropriately using a silent self-talk statement (e.g., "As I go to lunch, I won't disturb others") before they actually go to lunch for the first time in a given school year. Any school procedure (e.g., fire drill) needs practice, with *accompanying CSI,* to facilitate cooperativeness and a healthy school climate.

A form of role-play that is more appropriate for older students is called "soliloquy," a sociodrama technique (Torrance & Myers, 1970). A volunteer subject is asked to speak aloud his/her thoughts about a school-related problem to aid problem resolution via CSI. The setting for this particular soliloquy is as follows: You have a test in social studies tomorrow. You are really uptight about the test. You know when you get like this you don't make very good grades. Talk to us about what you are saying to yourself about this problem. Other students listen for self-talk categories (e.g., self-reinforcing).

STUDENT'S SOLILOQUY

"Well, I've been really paying attention in Social Studies but did I go over my questions every day? Sometimes I don't ask the teacher questions about the things I don't understand. Why do I do that? I need to ask right then, but the others would think I was a dummy. Well, I better start studying. But I don't know where to start. Do I have in mind what to study? Guess I better call Samantha; she always makes high marks. Maybe she'll tell me what to study. Why do we have stupid old tests anyway? They make my stomach hurt. My mother thinks I'm lazy. I am not very smart in Social Studies. Did I bring my book home? What if I make a zero and everybody finds out. I'm really going to have to think hard tomorrow. I wish my teacher wouldn't call out everybody's grade. Don't worry so much. I can't study if I worry, and I'll make a zero if I don't study. I better call Samantha. I can do this if I will first calm down, stop saying horrible things to myself, get organized and STUDY. I'm just wasting my time. Get with it. Do the best I can—that's all anyone can ask for or do! I feel better. I can do this. I trust myself."

Paper-Pencil Tasks

These tasks include such things as self-talk journals, CSI booklets, cartoon characters, and handwriting. Each is explained separately as follows:

Students are required to keep *self-talk logs or* journals. This assignment can be varied to fit the age level and specific student needs. Students will have a tendency to describe external events instead of describing their internal talk, unless the teacher spends quality time preparing the students. In classrooms where teachers have been using many CSI strategies, promoting metacognitive skills as vital to learning, the students are more apt to find self-talk journals a natural, creative outlet. Students write in first person what they have been saying to themselves during math class or during recess, or during morning work, or any time agreed upon by students and/or teachers. During or after these classes once every day, or at least once per week, the students write down their self-talk. Many follow-up activities can occur at the discretion of the teacher based on "knowing the students." One example is that students classify their self-talk entries for their math lessons after one month in one or more of the following ways: (1) Positive-neutral-negative, (2) helpful-unhelpful, (3) adult-parent-child, (4) problem defining, attention focusing, self-guiding, self-coping, self-reinforcing, (5) task relevant-task irrelevant, or (6) on task-off task. As a result the students and teachers gain insight into student frustration, apathy, motivation, boredom, etc. Teachers can learn a great deal about students through "self-talk logs" that they may not discover in any other way. Also, students may convert some of their negative self-talk into neutral, positive, task-relevant self-talk. In essence, they learn new, more helpful ways to guide their own learning. The greatest challenge to the teacher will be to get the students to externalize internal thoughts into written journal entries. It can be done with persistence and a creative teacher's touch. We know a wonderful kindergarten teacher who has her students (in the last half of the year) use their invented spellings and drawings to convey their inner thoughts about various assignments. Readers would be impressed with what these young children have learned about verbal expression of their own thought.

The next paper-pencil example is to have students make a *CSI booklet.* One teacher asked students to make CSI booklets to emphasize when to use CSI across the school curriculum. Manning (1984a, 1984b) designated four school uses of CSI. Teachers spend the majority of each day engaging students in academic work. In order to help students of all ages increase their achievement in academics they must *listen* well, *plan* effectively, *work* efficiently, and *check* their work accurately. These four school uses of CSI: listening, planning, working, and checking were identified and discussed in Manning (1984a, 1984b). The booklet is centered around students learning, reinforcing, and extending these four times when CSI is especially required. On the cover of the booklet, the students write WHEN TO USE CSI and draw themselves with a balloon-caption (comic bubble) over their heads saying something helpful to themselves at school (e.g., Do I have all my materials together to start my assignment—a sharpened pencil and paper?). Each of the next four pages of the booklet is devoted (one each) to listening, planning, working, and checking. Each page is labeled with a word, (e.g., LISTENING) to aid students' association with the corresponding self-talk for listening times at school. Depending on students' ages, they draw or cut out pictures of people or they write examples of self-talk for each "time to use CSI." Over each person's head they draw a bubble (like in the comics) and write a task-relevant, helpful self-talk message to self. Some teachers have modified this and used familiar cartoon characters first, then magazine cut-out people, then self-portraits or their own school pictures (movement from an external to an internal focus). The purpose of the booklet is to familiarize students with appropriate school times to remember to use CSI. Some examples from a second-grade class are presented next:

Listening	Planning
What is she saying?	Do I know what to do?
Do I understand?	What should I do first?
Does this make sense?	I'll do my best on this.
I need to listen carefully.	Let's get going.

Working	Checking
I need to slow down.	Does this look good to me?
This looks sloppy. I can do better.	Did I skip anything?
I need to quit staring out the window and get back to this work.	Can I do it a better way?
	I have all the sentences.
Looking better.	I'm proud of this work.

Another paper-pencil task is to use *commercial comics* and ask children to rewrite them, based on what the characters are saying to themselves, rather than to each other.

This requires monitoring by the teacher and students to make sure they are using private speech and not social speech. This is not an appropriate written activity for K–1 students. This activity may be modeled for them as a discussion of the cartoon characters' self-talk, with a follow-up language experience story using self-talk as the focus. In addition, even second-to fourth-grade teachers have reported that their students respond best to this activity when they begin with a comic strip that has only one character per frame. This way it makes more sense that the character might be talking to self, rather than to someone else. However, it is a fun activity for students to write in self-talk when there are two or more characters per frame—it is a challenging and usually a humorous activity. Students enjoy sharing their creations. Teachers begin by saving comic strips. Cut out the strips that appeal to the teacher. Cut out white paper bubbles to glue over the original captions or "white-out" the original words and photocopy the cartoon for students. Laminate about forty of these for a classroom set. Try to select ones with one character per frame to be used at first and then progress accordingly. Each student receives a strip on which to write the character's self-talk. This activity can be completed in dyads or small groups. One teacher uses an opaque projector for follow-up discussions of each self-talk cartoon.

A first-grade teacher provides a set of questions (shown next, Example 1) at each work station in her classroom. The teacher reports that these questions cause students to reflect on their own school tasks, as they practice metacognitive thinking.

EXAMPLE 1

TAKING CARE OF MY BUSINESS

Name _____

Date _____

Work Station _____

Listening   Yes or No

_____   Does this make sense to me?

_____   Is there anything missing?

Planning and Working   Yes or No

_____   Am I ready to begin?

_____   Do I have all of my supplies?

Checking   Yes or No

_____   Did I stay on task?

_____   Is this my best work?

_____   Is my work complete?

_____   Is my name on all my papers?

Note: Students respond by writing "yes" or "no" in the blanks and hand in this sheet along with their work pages when their morning work is completed.

EXAMPLE 2

PRACTICING SELF-TALK: LISTENING TO TEACHER DIRECTIONS (THIRD GRADE)

1. I'm supposed to repeat the teacher directions inside my head.

2. I read the directions along with the teacher.

3. I say each direction over in my head.

4. Does that make sense to me?

5. If it doesn't, raise my hand, and ask for help.

Another paper-pencil task to reinforce CSI is to ask students to make *written posters* for the class. These posters can include anything related to CSI that the teacher and students want to display in the room. One example is to have four groups of students make a helpful poster for each of the four school uses of CSI. Each group is assigned one of the times to use CSI (i.e., listening, planning, working, and checking). They write a draft list of task relevant, helpful questions and statements-to-self for each of the four areas and propose this list for acceptance. The drafts are evaluated by members of the other three remaining groups to validate the helpfulness of each self-talk entry. If an entry is considered unhelpful or task irrelevant by a majority of students then that entry is deleted. The remaining self-talk entries are written neatly on a poster and displayed as a CSI bulletin board. Four posters, as developed by a fifth-grade class are provided below:

POSTER 1

While Listening:

1. Does this make sense?

2. Am I getting this?

3. I need to ask a question now before I forget.

4. Pay attention.

5. Can I do what he's saying to do?

POSTER 2

While Planning:

1. Do I have everything together?

2. Do I have my friends tuned out for right now?

3. Let me get organized first.

4. What order will I do this?

5. I know this stuff!

POSTER 3

While Working:

1. Am I working fast enough?

2. Stop staring at my girlfriend and get back to work.

3. How much time is left?

4. Do I need to stop and start over?

5. This is hard for me, but I can manage okay.

POSTER 4

While Checking:

1. Did I finish everything?

2. What do I need to recheck?

3. Am I proud of this work?

4. Did I write all the words? Count them.

5. I think I finished. I organized myself. Did I daydream too much?

In a final example, the teacher writes a language experience story (to be used later as a handwriting lesson), illustrating how students are successfully using CSI. The story, using the students' names for characters, illustrates examples of how the students were able to maintain concentration on their school assignments even in the midst of classroom conversation, etc. Focus on the students' self-talk. On one day "Concentration" may be the theme. Another day "CSI for Listening" may serve as the theme. Other themes may include "CSI for Planning," "CSI for Working," "CSI for Checking," "CSI for Completing Tasks," etc. The students are more motivated to practice handwriting if it is personalized. In the meantime, they are also having their CSI skills positively reinforced.

Art Activities

Please refer to Figure 6.2 to locate where we are at this time on the CSI model. Art activities are used here to insure that students practice the CSI strategies they have heard and seen modeled for them previously. Art activities and CSI are integrated because students often enjoy expressing themselves through art. They are motivated by the drawing, painting, etc., while CSI is squeezed into the art activity as reinforcement and practice of

CSI strategies. Next are some examples of how classroom teachers use art activities to practice cognitive self-instruction. Students draw self-portraits with a cartoon bubble over their heads illustrating a CSI statement: "I will remember to wait my turn." Students may also paint their portraits and add a touch of self-talk. Students may be divided into four groups to illustrate on four different murals the four school times to use self-guiding statements (i.e., listening, planning, working, and checking). These murals usually consist of drawings or paintings of students in a school environment with a bubble over each head, with the self-talk written with magic markers. These make beautiful wall displays in the room. One principal was so impressed that she asked to use them in the school foyer for everyone to enjoy and to learn. The last example is to divide a sheet of drawing paper into four sections: "listening," "planning," "working," and "checking." The students are asked to draw themselves for each section and write a CSI statement-to-self or question-to-self.

Rote Rehearsal

The last practicing component is rote rehearsal. Students practice the modeled CSI, following Meichenbaum and Goodman's steps (1971) described previously in this chapter. For classroom use this means that students practice self-statements aloud, softly, and silently to themselves in order to internalize the process. Meichenbaum and colleagues were successful in improving impulsivity and promoting creativity when subjects were taught helpful, facilitative self-talk. It will not be adequate to stop after teachers or peers have modeled CSI statements. Instead the three steps of student practice in sequence are: (1) practice CSI speaking aloud, (2) whisper CSI statements to themselves, and finally (3) silently rehearse the statements-to-self. Use teacher judgment in the application of these three steps because some children will not need this much repetition. If students already have efficient self-guiding language, requiring too much repetition often causes boredom and frustration. On the other hand, some students are severely lacking in a battery of self-regulated learning strategies and will, therefore, require a great deal of repetition.

This process may be conducted with the whole class, small groups, or individuals. Meichenbaum used CSI with individuals to reduce impulsivity; therefore, working with individual students is not repeated here. A description of using students' rote rehearsal for large group instruction is included. The same classroom process can be used for small groups as well as large groups. The example is "hallway behavior." The class has just returned from lunch and they were excessively noisy, pushing each other, opening doors to other classes, and running over smaller children who were also in the hall. The sixth-grade teacher decides to use a CSI strategy. She's tried everything else. Therefore, she begins by expressing her dissatisfaction with their hallway behavior using I-messages. Next, she describes her expectations clearly: "As you go down the hall tomorrow I'd like you to do five things. They are (1) walk, don't run; (2) remain silent, don't talk; (3) stay together, don't leave the group; (4) stay in a line, don't run into others; (5) keep your hands and feet to yourself, do not touch another. I am going to talk about each one of these separately because they are very important. We must stop disturbing the whole school each time we leave this room. I'll talk to myself as if I were one of you going down the hall. First I'll talk about the need to walk, instead of running. Please listen carefully. Tell yourself to listen to every word I say. If I were you I'd talk to myself like this: 'I walk quietly down the hall. When I run, I endanger my own safety and those I may meet. Sometimes I forget this safety rule. I will remember to walk, not run. I'll monitor my feet by saying, "Walk feet—no running feet allowed. I can do it!"' Now class I'd like you to repeat each one of the statements I just said to myself. I'll write them on the board. We will repeat all the statements aloud together, then I want you to whisper all the statements, and then say all of them silently to yourself. The first one is 'I walk quietly down the hall.' Starting with this one, and reading down the list, repeat aloud together until we finish the last one which is 'I can do it.' Altogether, . . . " The students repeat together using all three forms: aloud, whisper, and silent self-talk. The same process is repeated for the other four rules for hallway behavior which the teacher described to the students. After each hallway rule is verbalized, following Meichenbaum and Goodman's (1971) steps, the students and teacher return to the hall and practice using CSI statements for hallway behavior.

One reason students do not follow class procedures and rules is because the procedures and rules are not specific, nor have they been explicitly taught by the teacher, modeled by the teacher and perhaps peers, and practiced by the students with accompanying self-guiding speech to self. You may be saying, "Too time consuming." It isn't too time consuming if one observes how much time is spent policing, nagging, and pleading with students to behave. Recent statistics revealed that teachers lose approximately 55% of their instructional time to disruption. In addition to being less time consuming over the long-run, students are learning a means for life-long self-control via explicit, quality exposure to a "self-talk" role model. We believe strongly that if all teachers took the initial time at the beginning of the school year to teach, model self-talk, and instruct practice for all classroom rules and procedures, classroom discipline problems would no longer be the number one or number two problem in our nation, as they have been for the past fifteen years. This process, using Evertson's rules and procedures, coupled with self-guiding speech was mentioned previously in Chapter 5.

For each school function (e.g., lunchroom, hallway, bathroom, water fountain) that requires teacher planning and deliberation about procedures, teachers should also do something resembling a task analysis for each classroom procedure. The sixth-grade teacher-model for hallway behavior (presented earlier) represented this kind of teacher thought. The behaviors she required in the hall were (1) walking, (2) quiet, (3) staying together, (4) staying in line, and (5) keeping hands and feet to self. Therefore, her task analysis of hallway behavior consisted of these five behaviors. If teachers will take the time to (1) analyze other procedures in their classroom, (2) conduct a task analysis to decide what they really mean by appropriate behavior (e.g., in the lunchroom), (3) clearly articulate these behaviors, (4) model accompanying, facilitative self-talk, (5) insure practice from students using the three forms (aloud, whisper, and silently), (6) role-play the procedures, and then (7) monitor and encourage the use of CSI, a great improvement in classroom management should result. But better still, a means for self-control is fostered.

CUEING

Referring again to Figure 6.2, the last component of Manning's approach to CSI is cueing. Students have now experienced "teacher and peer modeling" of self-management. They have had first-hand practice of self-management. Now students may need prompts and reminders to insure continued and sustained use of CSI. Prompts can take the form of posted class rules written from a self-management orientation, rather than the traditional other-control orientation, posters, group and individual cue cards, cue audiotapes, and other cueing signals.

The first suggestion is to write classroom rules and procedures in "first person, present tense." For example instead of a rule that reads "Wait your turn" the rule reads "Wait my turn." This facilitates responsibility toward oneself. When second person is used, it is not really a self-reminder; it is a reminder made by someone else. Especially young children, who view the world from an I-orientation, respond much better to rules stated from their own perspective rather than from an external directive. Often when young children read the rule "wait your turn" they read it literally to mean that you should wait your turn but I don't have to. When the rule reads "wait my turn," young children are more likely to realize that the rule includes them as well. Also, older children respond more personally to self-directed rules, using "I" and "my" in place of "you" and "your." In addition to first person, rules should be written in present tense: "I raise my hand" or "Raise my hand." Future tense rules, such as "I will raise my hand" foster futuristic thinking and may cause students to postpone adherence to a later date. Many of our creative student teachers have developed outstanding thematic rules that accompany units of study. One example is a first-grade animal unit when the rules were posted on climbing monkeys. One monkey had the rule "I don't monkey around," while another monkey had "I go bananas over finishing all my work" written on their stomachs. The students were very motivated to follow the "monkey rules" stated in a self-directed manner. Nothing can replace the creativity of individual teachers to make CSI really work to foster self-control. Another example of self-directed rules, using pictorial cues to accompany the rules is provided below. These picture rules are very helpful for nonreaders or young learners.

Written Class Rule	Cue Picture
I raise my hand.	(Show picture 1: student with hand raised.)
I listen.	(Show picture 2: a large ear.)
I wait my turn.	(Show picture 3: two students—one waiting for lunch while the other is getting a tray.)
I stay in my seat.	(Show picture 4: a student sitting quietly, listening to the teacher.)

The teacher-made posters on page 129 for the four school uses (i.e., listening, planning, working, and checking) are similar to the posters made by students to practice CSI statements-to-self. In this place on the model (see Figure 6.2) these posters serve a cueing role to remind students to use CSI. Teachers are encouraged to use student-made posters to represent the best self-talk examples for cueing purposes. With younger students (grades K–2), these posters should be introduced one poster at a time and practiced for approximately two weeks to one month before the next poster is introduced. Use teacher judgment as to how fast older students (grades three to twelve) can process the information effectively. One fourth-grade teacher says she puts all four uses on posters—with examples of exemplary CSI—over her chalkboard to guide work habits of students all year. Her posters contain the following information:

WHILE LISTENING TO INSTRUCTIONS

1. Goal setting: I will listen carefully.

2. Coping statements: I can understand, if I don't daydream.

3. Guiding statements: She is telling us what to do first.

4. Self-questioning: What do I do when I finish?

5. Self-reinforcement: I know what to do now. Good for me!

WHILE PREPARING TO WORK

1. Goal setting: I will get everything organized.

2. Coping statements: I don't have all the crayons I need. What should I do about that?

3. Guiding statements: Put all my materials on my desk.

4. Self-questioning: Am I ready to begin?

5. Self-reinforcement: I have everything ready.

WHILE WORKING

1. Goal setting: I want this to be my best workday.

2. Coping statements: This is hard for me, but I'm trying.

3. Guiding statements: Be careful—don't skip a line.

Picture 1

Picture 2

Picture 3

Picture 4

4. Self-questioning: Is this looking right to me?

5. Self-reinforcement: This is really looking super. I'm working hard.

WHILE CHECKING FINISHED WORK

1. Goal setting: I check over every paper.

2. Coping statements: I'm tired of looking over this. Just two more problems, though.

3. Guiding statements: Yes, that's right.

4. Self-questioning: Where do I put these?

5. Self-reinforcement: I finished all my work and checked over it once. Good for me!

The next discussion will center around cue cards to remind students to use CSI strategies. In the regular classroom, students have behaviors they need to improve. Almost every child has some behavior that needs improvement. Each week, students may decide individually what behavior they wish to address via a cue card reminder. Of course, the regular classroom is not conducive to students talking aloud to themselves all at once. The students are instructed to whisper the self-instructions or to read them to self silently. Examples of cue cards might be, "Stay seated now," "Don't daydream—concentrate," "Try to answer." Cue cards can be individualized to meet the needs of each class member. One teacher uses a clear plastic shoe bag in which she puts categories of behavior reminders on laminated index cards. All are stated from an internal perspective (e.g., "Finish all my work"). The students are free to get a card when needed and tape it on their desk as a reminder. Occasionally this teacher will choose a cue card for a particular child; however, the emphasis is on child initiative for self-correction. For nonreaders, Palkes, Stewart, and Kahana (1968) training pictures may be worthy of consideration (see Chapter 7). In any event, the cue card serves as a stimulus/reminder to mediate behavior.

Cueing may be used in the form of small index cards for individual children, large posters, group cue cards, and other display methods. One teacher uses a large cue card which simply says "I CAN TRY." This card is suspended from the ceiling on poster board. She introduced the card because her first-grade children had begun the unfortunate habit of saying "I can't," even before they had heard all of the directions. She reports that the card has been very effective in practically eliminating shouts of self-defeating "I can't! I can't!" She points to the card. Further, she says some of the students point to the card for their peers. The group cue card reminds the children not to defeat themselves before they even attempt tasks. This works extremely well in changing attitudes about what children are able to accomplish and about the corresponding accomplishments, themselves.

Individual cue cards are used to remind single students. This cueing system is used for three types of classroom reminders. These types are to (1) inhibit inappropriate classroom behaviors, (2) initiate, and (3) reinforce appropriate behaviors. Depending on grade level and maturity of students, one of these types may be introduced at a time and practiced until students follow their own cues quite easily. However, teachers in third grade and above report that they introduce all three types at once. Some teachers make a set of cue cards for each type and give them to students who exhibit a need for them. Other teachers have asked students to make their own cue cards as needed. These are usually taped on the student's desk and used as a reminder (e.g., "raise my hand") until the students and/or teachers believe that students no longer need them. When the appropriate behavior has become automatic, the cue card should be removed. Of course, modifications of cue cards are often made by teachers to suit their own particular needs. Modifications of cue cards have included paper bracelets with cueing on the bracelet, group cue cards displayed in the classroom (e.g., "I try my best") and cueing folders kept at desks to self-record appropriate behaviors at the sound of a buzzer or timer in the room (e.g., "Am I on task? If not, tell myself to focus on my work").

It should be emphasized that in most cases students should work on only one behavior at a time. Therefore, only one cue card should be visible on the desk. A string of cue cards taped to the student's desk is inappropriate and will probably be unhelpful.

Cue cards may be represented as drawings of animals, stick figures, people, or imaginary characters demonstrating the target behavior the teacher wishes the student to perform (e.g., listening to others). These cue cards are sometimes drawn by teachers or commercial cut-outs may be used. Cards are usually laminated and are the size of a 3 x 5 index card. However, cue pictures may be reduced or enlarged. Pictorial drawings (e.g., a smiling face with one oversized ear to cue "listening") may be used with or without a written prompt (e.g., "I listen well") accompanying the picture.

In addition to teacher-made cues, there are some commercial cueing techniques available. The Ralph Bear Training Figures (see Chapter 7) in the Bash and Camp research (1975) are extremely popular with teachers, as well as the Palkes, Stewart, and Kahana training pictures (1968) mentioned earlier. Teachers like to modify these and then enlarge these for bulletin boards and other learning displays. They also make excellent individual cue cards singly and collectively.

Long (1984) demonstrates teaching self-control and pro-social behavior by using therapeutic signs and sayings in classrooms for emotionally disturbed children. Some of these are easily adapted or used as they are in regular classrooms. Most of these are stated in the second person (e.g., Listen to Your Controls) and should be changed to first person (e.g., Listen to My Controls). To illustrate how cue cards may be adapted for individual school needs, consider one particular school faculty who were not satisfied with lunchroom behavior. Children were throwing food, screaming, and getting under the tables. Therefore, the teachers and/or students made large colorful cue cards, (written in present tense, first person) and posted them in the lunchroom; they prepared center pieces for the tables containing cue cards; they made cue card place mats for the lunch tables; and they prepared reinforcement cards or buttons for children to wear when they demonstrated appropriate lunchroom behavior. They reported a great deal of improvement in their lunchroom atmosphere.

Cueing of CSI may also be conducted using teacher-made audiotapes. Hallahan, Lloyd, and Stoller (1982) have compiled a very helpful manual for teachers to improve attention of students. The materials needed are a self-monitoring tape and a self-monitoring card. In self-monitoring studies, the Hallahan et al. method was found effective for increasing on-task behavior and academic productivity. Benefits continued even after students stopped using the tape. Tapes with earphones may be used for individual children or tapes may be used with whole classes or small groups experiencing difficulty with attention and concentration. We might call this a "Tape Cueing Activity" for the purpose of encouraging student(s) to concentrate throughout the day and to be aware of their own concentration abilities. The directions for making such a tape are as follows:

1. The teacher prepares a 60-minute tape periodically recording the sound of a bell or melodious tone. The ringing of the bell or tone should be recorded at different intervals throughout the 60-minute period. Vary the length of the intervals.

2. The teacher plays the tape throughout the day as needed.

3. When the students hear the bell or tone on the tape, have each student ask him/her self the question, "Was I concentrating or not?"

4. Supply each student with a record sheet. Have each student mark "yes" if he/she was concentrating and "no" if he/she was not concentrating. Beside the "yes" response the student reads a self-reinforcement comment such as: "I was concentrating, that's good." Beside the "no" response the student reads a self-guiding comment such as: "I need to pay attention to my work now. I can daydream later."

5. This procedure may continue until the students' concentration improves (1–2 weeks). It can then be used periodically throughout the year if you so desire.

The final discussion about cueing of CSI is the use of color for cueing attention. Zentall and Kruczek (1988) found that color placed on the part of the word, difficult to remember, increased performance for hyperactive, nonattentive students. Color may be used to draw attention to relevant stimuli within tasks. Please note that color used just to make a task more attractive can actually disrupt the performance of many students. However, color may be placed strategically on difficult words in a passage or even near difficult to remember objects (e.g., bright yellow dot placed over the light switch to cue children to turn off the lights in their room). A classroom example is to put a large, bright red circle over the classroom door to remind young children to wait at the door for further instructions from the teacher before exiting. One teacher used a red dot to cue students, who were hopping up every few minutes, to stay seated for a reasonable period of time. She placed a cue card on the desk with a red dot, picture of a student sitting at a desk, and the words "Stay seated" on the card. She also placed a large red dot on the floor where the child would turn her foot to get out of her seat. The child was instructed that when she felt the urge to pop out of her seat at inappropriate times, she was to touch and read her cue card in a whisper and to look down at the red dot on the floor as she turned in her seat. This child was soon regulating her own "in-seat" behavior and had grown in feelings of self-efficacy.

Cueing is a method used to encourage students to remind themselves to bring their own behavior under their own control. This frees the teacher from excessive policing and allows more time for academic pursuits. The teacher is not continuously reminding students to raise hands to speak, to sit down, to wait their turns, to lower their voices, and so forth. Instead, a system of cueing is implemented whereby students prompt themselves. Cueing is never administered as punishment. Cueing, as with most management strategies, may be abused if used incorrectly by teachers to control students. The aim is just the opposite. It is a means to help children learn to control themselves. Cueing is nonpunitive self-reminders. As students learn to manage their own classroom behaviors, they need reminders. Self-reminder cue cards are nonpunitive tools for the promotion of the self-controlled, self-managed student.

SUMMARY

The concept of other-regulation implies a gradual progression from other-regulation to self-regulation. Four models (i.e., proleptic/dyadic instruction, reciprocal teaching, cognitive behavior modification, and cognitive self-instruction) are outlined in this chapter. In all four, the adult or more experienced learner structures the task verbally and nonverbally for the less experienced learner. This "guided practice" period of time is critical to what the learner will be able to perform independently. This assisted, supported learning by others is conducted to insure that the learner is understanding the task accurately and to provide the initial step of mastery. When students are left to self-regulation prematurely, asking too much too soon, the learner often becomes frustrated and/or performs the task incorrectly. Meichenbaum (1977) recommends that coping skills be modeled for the student as part of other-regulation to preempt predictable obstacles inherent in the task. Therefore, in addition to modeling the cognitive steps of a task, the healthy emotional side is addressed for the learner to teach both cognitive and emotional actions and reactions. After the modeling stage, the learner practices overtly and covertly the internal dialogue that accompanies a specific task. It is important to communicate to the learner the how, why, what, and when certain procedures and thinking processes are beneficial to goal achievement. What a learner is able to accomplish, with help, should be considered as a viable measure of assessment, just as teachers value the measurement of what a learner is able to accomplish independently.

CHAPTER 7

Researching Metacognitive Strategies for Classroom Use

OVERVIEW

The goal of CBM research has been to train subjects to bring their overt behavior under their own control through the self-regulatory function of inner speech. Research in cognitive behavior modification has focused on both children and adults in both personal and academic areas. In section two we addressed metacognitive research and strategies with teachers; therefore, this discussion will focus on relevant research studies using cognitive-behavior modification with children. No attempt is made to present an exhaustive review of the CBM literature. Rather, research studies were selected for review when they represented "classics" or "landmarks" in the field or if they were particularly appropriate for application with school-aged children. Studies selected include CBM for children in various cognitive areas (e.g., memory, problem solving), for various academic areas (e.g., reading, mathematics), and in various settings (e.g., classroom, clinical). Following the review of published research studies are descriptions of CBM and other metacognitive strategies, based directly on this research literature, that some of our teachers have developed and used in their own classrooms. In Chapters 8 and 9, we provide additional classroom strategies developed, implemented, and evaluated by teachers.

Self-Questions

1. *Knowledge.* List the five steps in Meichenbaum and Goodman's self-regulated model.

2. *Comprehension.* Explain how basal reader instruction can be enhanced through prereading activities, guided reading activities, and postreading activities.

3. *Application.* Describe a reading group's activities using Brown and Palincsar's notion of reciprocal teaching.

4. *Analysis.* Compare and contrast the elements of reciprocal teaching with the five steps of the self-regulated model described by Meichenbaum.

5. *Synthesis.* Develop an argument for using CBM as a classroom management option. Present the arguments to someone who supports traditional behavior modification.

6. *Evaluation.* Support the use of cognitive behavior modification with regular education, average learners rather than a clinical population.

Metacognitive Research on Self-Control

Early laboratory studies conducted by Palkes and her colleagues investigated the use of self-directed verbal commands with hyperactive nine-year-old boys (Palkes, Stewart, & Kahana, 1968). The boys were taught to verbalize a set of self-directed verbal commands, "I must stop, look, listen, and think before I answer." The cue cards illustrated in Figure 7.1 served as a stimulus/reminder to use the self-statements. The results of the study indicated that the boys who used the self-directed verbal commands improved on posttest performance on the Porteus Maze compared to controls who simply practiced the training procedure.

In a follow-up study Palkes, Stewart, and Freedman (1972) compared the silent reading of instructions to verbalizing aloud the self-instructions by hyperactive children. The overt self-verbalizations were significantly more effective in enhancing self-control of impulsive behavior.

Drawing from the theoretical foundations of Luria and Vygotsky, Meichenbaum and Goodman (1971) in a classic study, developed a five-step approach of self-guidance to decrease impulsivity and increase performance in primary aged children identified as impulsive. You may recall the discussion of this model in Chapter 6; however, it is repeated here because of its importance to self-regulated research. The study included two parts with early elementary students who were identified as being impulsive. Subjects were assigned to one of three groups, namely, the cognitive self-guidance group, an attention control group, and an assessment control group. The attention control group was exposed to identical materials and engaged in the same activities, but did not receive any self-

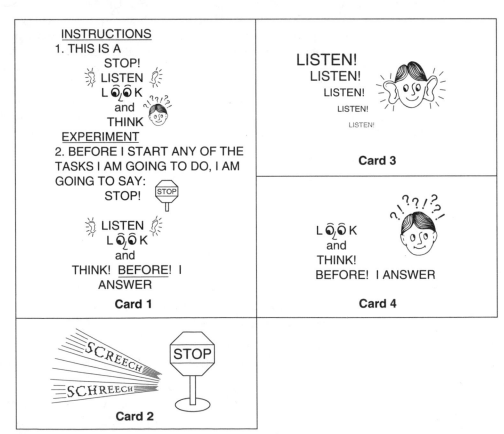

FIGURE 7–1
Training Pictures

Source: Palkes, H., Stewart, M., & Kahana, B. (1968). Porteus maze performance after training in self-directed verbal commands. *Child Development, 39.* Copyright © The Society for Research in Child Development, Inc.

instructional training. The assessment control group, on the other hand, received only the pretreatment, posttreatment, and follow-up assessments that the other two groups received. The students in the cognitive self-guidance group were trained to use self-instruction to perform tasks while coping with errors and appropriately reinforcing themselves. The Self-Regulated Model consisted of four half-hour, individual training sessions over a two-week period and was administered as follows: (a) the instructor modeling a task while describing aloud the thinking process; (b) the instructor modeling each self-statement verbally as the child rehearses with or performs the corresponding motor behavior; (c) the instructor prompting the child by saying the first word of each self-statement as the child verbalizes the complete self-statement and performs the corresponding motor behavior; (d) the instructor whispering as a cue for the child to whisper the complete self-statement and perform the corresponding motor behavior; and (e) the instructor modeling thinking aloud each self-statement as the child is encouraged to "think" each statement while performing the corresponding motor behavior. Meichenbaum (1977) further explained that:

> *In this thinking-out-loud phase, the model displayed several performance-relevant skills: (1) problem definition ("What is it I have to do?"); (2) focusing attention and response guidance ("Carefully . . . draw the line down."); (3) self-reinforcement ("Good, I'm doing fine."); and (4) self-evaluative coping skills and error-correcting options ("That's okay . . . even if I make an error I can go on slowly.") (p. 32)*

The tasks employed to train the child to use self-instructions to control his nonverbal behavior varied in complexity. The simpler sensorimotor tasks involved copying line patterns and coloring figures within boundaries. These tasks provided both the model and the child the opportunity to use self-statements, first overtly and then covertly, in the form of a narrative description of the behavior, both preceding and accompanying performance. These activities were followed by more cognitively demanding tasks such as reproducing designs, following sequential instructions, completing pictorial series, and solving conceptual tasks. The results of this study indicated that the self-instructional training groups significantly increased their total decision time and had fewer errors on tests measuring impulsivity. Meichenbaum concluded that a self-guidance training program can significantly alter impulsive children's behavior.

In a related study, Camp, Blom, Hebert, and VanDoormick (1977) examined the use of self-instructional training with aggressive children. Camp et al. utilized Meichenbaum and Goodman's (1971) self-instructional training methods to prompt aggressive boys in controlling their own behavior. The primary purpose was to teach aggressive children to engage in *coping* self-instructions when responding to provocations. A thirteen-session *Think Aloud* program was developed to train aggressive boys in using self-instructions in a problem-solving sequence. The children were introduced to the program with a "copycat" game, which required the child to ask himself/herself the following four basic questions: "What am I suppose to do?" "What are some plans?" "How is my plan working?" and "How did I do?" Cue cards, using Ralph the Bear, were introduced to remind the child to self-verbalize (see Figure 7.2). The CBM training yielded significant improvement relative to control groups on a variety of measures, including Porteus Maze, Matching Familiar Figures Test, Weschler Intelligence Scale for children (performance IQ), reading achievement, and classroom behavior. The Think Aloud program was evaluated and found effective for cognitive and problem-solving outcomes. It should be noted, however, that initial evaluation studies (e.g., Camp, 1977; Camp & Bash, 1981) were conducted by the authors of the program. Nevertheless, Hughes (1985) in a more recent study reported positive results from two case studies when parents served as cotherapists in a social/cognitive problem-solving Think Aloud program. This program involving parents as co-trainers, was a modified version of the Think Aloud, and included twenty-three lessons covering problem definition, generation of alternative solutions, predicting and evaluating consequences, monitoring plan implementations, and self-evaluation.

FIGURE 7–2
Training Figures

Source: From *Think Aloud: Increasing Social and Cognitive Skills: A Problem-Solving Program for Children* (Classroom Program, Grades 1–2; pp. 334) by M. A. S. Bash and B. W. Camp, 1985, Champaign, IL: Research Press. Copyright 1985 by the authors. Reprinted by permission.

Manning (1988) utilized self-instructional training with first and third grade students whose behavior was identified as inappropriate by their teachers. The subjects were randomly assigned to either the experimental or the control group. The groups differed in that the training received by the experimental group focused on an internal source of behavior control and the training received by the control group focused on external sources of control. The self-instructional training was adapted from Meichenbaum and Goodman's model (1971) and consisted of adult modeling of appropriate self-guiding speech to encourage positive school work habits. The adult modeling was then followed by peer modeling; next students practiced appropriate self-statements; and finally they were cued to use relevant self-talk. Treatment resulted in improved teacher ratings, increased on-task behavior, and an increase in internality of locus of control.

Metacognitive Research for Academic Uses

In addition to self-instruction for behavior control, researchers have explored cognitive control of academic learning (e.g., Brown, Campione, & Day, 1981; Corno, Collins, & Capper, 1982; Manning, 1984b; Schunk, 1988). Inquiries have been made in areas such as memory, comprehension and problem solving, and in academic areas such as reading, writing, and mathematics. These innumerable studies relate results on the benefits of self-instruction within various subjects, various ages, and different settings.

Whereas the initial work in CBM with children focused on problems of self-control, more recent efforts have been directed at applying the cognitive behavior self-instructional approach to academic tasks. Other content areas for which self-instruction has led to benefits are handwriting (Blandford & Lloyd, 1987; Robin, Armel, & O'Leary, 1975); creative writing (Trimbur, 1987); and general creativity (Meichenbaum, 1975). The first content area we will discuss is mathematics. This discussion is followed by research related to metacognition for listening comprehension, reading comprehension, and handwriting.

Mathematics

Meichenbaum and Goodman's model has also been used successfully with exceptional children. Leon and Pepe (1983) examined the effectiveness of a self-instructional training program designed to teach exceptional children mathematics. Ten special education teachers were randomly assigned to a self-instruction group or a contrast group. Both groups of teachers received training in the use of diagnostic mathematics materials. In addition, the self-instruction group received instruction for utilizing self-instructional strategies with their students, ages nine through twelve, who were at least two years behind in mathematics achievement and were classified as learning disabled and mildly mentally handicapped. Both groups of students received diagnostic mathematics instruction, but the students in the self-instructional group received additional instruction based on Meichenbaum and Goodman's Five Step Method.

First, the teacher modeled the computation while verbalizing the steps aloud as the student listened. Second, the teacher verbalized the computation as the student performed the computation. Third, as the student verbalized and performed the mathematics computation, the teacher observed and monitored the work. Fourth, the student whispered the self-instruction as the teacher monitored the students' computation. Fifth, the student internalized the procedures and computed the problem. As students progressed through each mathematics module, they were tested over the skill taught and the skill to be taught in the following module to determine if they were able to generalize the skill. The results indicated that both the self-instructional and the traditional remediation approaches were effective, but the self-instructional approach required less direct training time and was more generalizable to similar types of arithmetic problems.

Lovitt and Curtiss (1968) investigated the effect of verbalizing a mathematics problem aloud before making a written response for an eleven-year-old boy versus simply writing the answer to the problem. It was found that this middle schooler, who had previously experienced difficulty in mathematics, scored more correct answers, with a decrease in error rate, as a result of verbalizing the problem aloud before making a written response. The improvement was stable over time and supports rehearsing aloud as a helpful learning aid for some middle grades students experiencing difficulty with school tasks. Students' self-verbalizations seem to activate the mind to remember and reinforce correct problem-solving strategies, which in turn increase accuracy. Overt self-verbalizations force children to attend to strategies and form a type of self-rehearsal.

Listening Comprehension

Schunk and Rice (1984) examined the effects of overt self-verbalization on the listening comprehension of children in grades two through four and investigated the influence of self-instruction on self-efficacy ratings. Forty-two remedial reading students were randomly assigned to either a self-verbalization or a no self-verbalization group. The subjects received two weekly 30-minute instructional sessions over a four-week period of time. The self-verbalization treatment included the following listening strategies presented on poster board: "What is it I have to do?" "I must find the correct picture." "How will I do it?" "I'll look at each picture carefully to see if it matches the story I heard." "When I find the answer, I'll mark it." The instructor read each strategy aloud and the students verbalized them afterwards. Several stories were completed per training session. The no strategy self-verbalization training was identical to the self-verbalization training except the students were not required to verbalize the strategy. Results indicated that students in the self-verbalization group judged themselves more efficacious. In addition, third and fourth grade students in the self-verbalization group outperformed their counterparts in the no verbalization group on the listening skills test. It was concluded that self-verbalizations can help children focus and maintain their attention on important task components.

Manning (1984b) investigated the effects of four programs on reading disabled students' listening comprehension. One hundred reading-deficient third grade students were randomly assigned to one of four conditions: cognitive monitoring, creative problem solving, and a combination of cognitive monitoring and creative problem solving, and no treatment. Each group received instruction from the researcher for 30 minutes for ten consecutive days. The cognitive monitoring group was taught to use cognitive monitoring while planning, working, checking for mistakes, and while listening. The creative problem solving group learned a creative problem solving procedure. The combination group received briefer versions of the cognitive monitoring and creative problem solving instruction. The control group worked on art projects. Two listening tests of basic concepts, read aloud to the subjects, were administered to assess listening comprehension. Pairwise comparisons revealed significantly higher effects on one of the listening tests for the combination group. On the other listening test, both the combination and the cognitive monitoring group had significantly higher effects than did the control or the creative problem solving group which had limited value when utilized alone.

Reading Comprehension

Reading comprehension is an area which has been enhanced through the use of a self-instructional program (Bommarito & Leon, 1980). Learning disabled students in the fourth grade were shown how to break down reading tasks into manageable units, how to determine the hierarchy of skills needed to do the tasks, and how to translate skills into self-statements. The results indicated that the self-instructional training group was significantly superior to the control group at the time of post-teaching. The superiority of the self-instruction group was maintained one month later.

Comparison of the prose texts was the focus of a study conducted by Elliott-Faust and Pressley (1986). The purpose of the study was to train children to compare different parts of text in order to detect errors. In addition, these researchers examined the effects of a self-control treatment on the comparison processing strategies of third grade children. Self-control training consisted of the instructor modeling the strategy and students practicing the strategy and receiving corrective feedback. Practice began with overt verbalizations and was gradually faded to covert practice. Students were taught to ask themselves questions that elicited responses concerning the nature of the task, the appropriate strategy to use, evaluation of correct implementation of the strategies, and self-evaluation of performance. Results indicated that the self-control and self-instruction conditions were more effective interventions in text comparison processing. The subjects in the self-control group detected more errors in texts and improved significantly in their comprehension monitoring.

Handwriting

A study conducted by Robin, Armel, and O'Leary (1975) attempted to assess the role of self-guiding verbalizations with children who had deficiencies in handwriting. Thirty kindergarten children were randomly assigned to one of three groups: (1) self-instruction, (2) direct training, and (3) no treatment. Students in the self-instruction group were exposed to Meichenbaum and Goodman's (1971) model. Overt verbalizations of an adult were followed by the child's overt self-verbalizations, which were then followed by the child's covert self-verbalizations which resulted in the child's verbal control of non-verbal behavior. Self-instructions included questions about the nature of the task and answers to the questions in the form of planning, guiding, correcting, and reinforcing. A significant main effect for self-instruction treatment was identified. In addition, a significant main effect for direct training was also found. It was concluded that self-instruction plus direct training was more effective than direct training alone for remediating handwriting deficiencies.

In summary, the research on cognitive monitoring and cognitive behavior modification indicated that children's overt behavior can be brought under their own control through self-instruction. This self-instruction was most effective when overt verbalizations of an adult were followed by the child's overt verbalizations. The child's verbal control of non-verbal behavior was then a result of the gradual fading from overt to covert self-verbalizations.

In the next section, some examples of classroom applications derived from the literature are outlined. In each of the examples, the teacher's suggestions for using these ideas with learners are not altered, and in some cases, are presented verbatim so as not to distort the teacher's original intent.

STUDENT USE OF METACOGNITIVE STRATEGIES

Young children, passive learners, and poor learners often have a particularly difficult task in the pursuit of learning. They often times fail to use organized, goal-directed, metacognitive strategies when approaching a specific learning task. In order to be more successful in the classroom, children should be taught to engage in metacognitive skills. Children should be taught to become aware of their own learning processes, monitor their current task performance, and gain control of academic tasks. The use of metacognitive skills requires **active** participation of the learner which enhances the likelihood that students can then translate them into improved academic performance.

Without direct teaching of metacognitive strategies to students, a major gap in metacognitive instruction exists. Classroom teaching of metacognitive strategies in the example areas of language arts, writing, reading, and mathematics, is now described. These strategies can serve as stimuli for the development of other creative activities intended for specific students under specific conditions and for other content areas across the school curriculum. When these approaches are introduced to prospective or practicing teachers, they should be (1) presented as a knowledge base, (2) practiced as examples in role-play, micro-teaching, or field experiences in actual classrooms, (3) used as stimuli for the creative development of other metacognitive strategies, formulated and implemented during student teaching or classroom teaching, and (4) evaluated by teacher education faculty and classroom teacher supervisors and/or self-evaluated.

Language Arts

Many students fail to learn any strategies for recall of information. They fail to remember capitalization and punctuation guidelines, spelling words, important dates, etc., not because they lack cognitive ability but because they have never learned appropriate strategic metacognitive skills necessary to commit these items to memory. The following metacognitive approach pinpoints a step-by-step process that requires the active participation of the student in his or her own learning.

STEPS FOR REMEMBERING HOW TO SPELL WORDS

1. While looking at the word, I say it and then spell it aloud.

2. Without looking at the word, I spell it aloud.

3. I check for accuracy.

4. I spell the word aloud while I write it.

5. I spell the word softly while I check for accuracy.

6. I spell the word in my mind.

This cognitive self-instructional strategy (Figure 7.3) relies on teacher modeling as the mode of instructing, and consists of a cognitive modeling phase, an overt guidance phase, and a covert self-instructional phase. The teacher begins by modeling the self-talk statements for learning each spelling word and then provides children the opportunity to practice the statements.

POSSIBLE DIALOGUE:

"Karen (student's name), when I want to learn to spell a word, I look at the word and say it aloud. Then as I am looking at it, I spell it aloud. Next, I spell the word aloud without looking at it. I check myself. If I am correct, I spell the word aloud as I write it. As I recheck the written spelling, I spell the word softly to myself. Finally I spell the word in my mind."

This is followed by the overt guidance phase in which the student's actions are guided by the teacher.

"Let's try it together. This time as I say what I do, I want you to demonstrate it."

The student then demonstrates the six steps for spelling a word while the teacher instructs him/her.

Next the student repeats the entire sequence of steps independently. Students may practice the techniques in dyads or triads. A cue card containing illustrations of each step for learning how to spell words may be used in all phases of the cognitive self-instruction (see Figure 7.3). The cue card encourages children through visual reminders to verbalize for themselves each statement.

Verbalization helps the student to attend to the information, transfer information for understanding, and monitor actions. Our goal in cognitive self-instruction is for students, themselves, to provide self-feedback in much the same way another individual would provide it for them.

This procedure may seem rather cumbersome at first. Students who are already good spellers may not want, nor profit from this type of instruction. However, many students never learn any strategies for recall. They fail spelling tests week after week, not because they are cognitively limited or poorly motivated, but because they lack the strategic knowledge to recall the spelling of words. Teachers in grade two through eight have

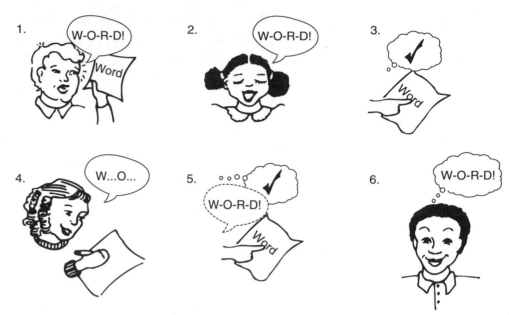

FIGURE 7–3
Self-Instruction
for Spelling

reported great success using the metacognitive strategies prescribed above. Teachers should not be hesitant to modify these steps based on their own style and student needs. This is just an example. The main idea is to promote verbal rehearsal because, consistently, rehearsers retain more information. In addition, it should be noted that these strategies to recall spelling can easily be used for any subject matter, requiring recall (e.g., geography terms and definitions, mathematics facts).

Mathematics

STEPS FOR LEARNING MATHEMATICS FACTS

1. While looking at the mathematics fact, I say it aloud.

2. While looking at the mathematics fact, I whisper it aloud.

3. While looking at the mathematics fact, I silently say it to myself.

4. Without looking, I say the mathematics fact aloud while I write it.

5. Without looking, I whisper the mathematics fact to myself.

6. Without looking, I say the mathematics fact silently to myself. I check it for accuracy.

7. I visualize the mathematics fact in my mind.

8. I say the mathematics fact silently in my mind. I double check for accuracy. Do I know this mathematics fact now?

Reading Comprehension

In Chapter 6 we discussed a metacognitive strategy to improve reading comprehension called reciprocal teaching (Palincsar & Brown, 1984). As a review we will list the basic procedures in a reciprocal teaching lesson (Palincsar, 1986, p. 119).

RECIPROCAL TEACHING METHOD

1. Each day, before the dialogue, the teacher uses informed strategy training. Review *what* strategies students are learning, *why* they are important, *how* to use them, and *when* to use them (the context in which the strategies are useful).

2. The teacher, using the title of the text brings out background and prior knowledge. Students make predictions about what they will learn in the text; students indicate what they are interested in learning.

3. A teacher is appointed for the first section of text.

4. Teacher and students read the section (silently and/or orally).

5. The "teacher" (student or adult) asks a question about the material to which the others respond.

6. This teacher then summarizes the main points and asks for elaborations on the summary from other members of the group.

7. The students and teacher discuss clarifications that came up during the reading of the text.

8. The teacher and students make predictions regarding upcoming text. A new "teacher" is appointed.

One of our inservice teachers, Rebecca Martin, developed and implemented her version of reciprocal teaching with her class of second graders. She claimed that this method was extremely successful and helped even her "slowest readers." Following is a description of how this procedure was developed, introduced, and implemented in her classroom.

GOAL

To introduce the strategy of reciprocal teaching to students the teacher must first model the procedure, explaining that students will be taking turns being the teacher and reminding them that they will be using the steps of the monitoring process. The students then read a specific selection, stopping at an appropriate interval depending on the levels. The teacher then models the monitoring process and summarizes, clarifies, questions, and predicts based on the material that has been read. Students and teacher are actively involved in answering the questions generated both in the questioning portion and in the part the teacher wishes to clarify. Once students understand the steps involved, the teacher selects another student to act as the "teacher." Students read another section of the material and the process continues.

SUGGESTIONS FOR APPLYING RECIPROCAL TEACHING—LARGE GROUP*

Reciprocal teaching was first introduced through the use of literature in a large group situation. Everyday I read to my students for 15 to 20 minutes in the morning, 30 to 40 minutes after lunch, and at the end of the day if time permits. I first ask students to predict what they think the book will be about based on the book or chapter title. As we complete a chapter, we check our predictions and forecast the next passage. I ask two students at the beginning of the reading to prepare a question about what I have read. They generate these questions and select students to answer at the appropriate time. I frequently stop after a particular passage and ask if we need to clarify anything, especially if a passage is difficult to grasp. Occasionally, I have comprehension problems and I use this opportunity to question myself and reread for clarification. Summarizing is a difficult task for most second graders. They have problems judging what is important, and usually tend to

*As described by teacher Rebecca Martin.

report stories verbatim. When reading chapters in books, we first read the summary that is given on the back cover and this helps students to understand the idea of telling "What the story is mostly about."

Another method for presenting the four processes to all students is to use posters (Figure 7.4) that list the steps along with a question that can help students monitor their reading. When reading to large groups or when working with small groups these visuals help students become more aware of these steps as self-questioning. These strategies do not constitute reciprocal teaching in themselves. They are not steps to be mastered, although it is easier to introduce them this way. This approach is not the same as teaching skills, and should not be viewed as a prescription. The aim of reciprocal teaching is that students actively participate in discussions of the text. Dialogue serves as the scaffold—

FIGURE 7–4   Cues for Monitoring Reading (adapted from Bash & Camp, 1985)

a mechanism that provides temporary and adjustable support to instruction. This "talk" allows teachers to adjust instruction to students' needs.

SUGGESTIONS FOR APPLYING RECIPROCAL TEACHING—SMALL GROUP*

Since this dialogue seems to be so crucial to the success of reciprocal teaching, I felt that my poor comprehenders would have more opportunity to become active participants in a small group situation. I selected a group of four students who were identified as adequate decoders but poor comprehenders, based on teacher opinion, standardized and informal measures of reading comprehension. These students scored below or near the 49th percentile on a standardized test of reading comprehension. Three of the four students are considered to be passive learners. Two are almost nonverbal in the classroom. One of the students is considered to be verbal and an active learner, but test scores and teacher observation indicate underachievement in reading comprehension. I felt that this student would benefit from this direct strategy instruction. With these students it seemed essential to present reading as a meaningful activity. They must discover that to understand what one hears or reads, it is essential to become an active listener and reader.

The first few times I tried reciprocal teaching, I assumed the primary responsibility for directing and sustaining the dialogue. My four students and I worked for about 30 minutes each day, three days per week to practice these strategies. The other students in the classroom were involved in "reading workshop." They were reading books of their choice alone or in groups of twos and threes. Although basals are still used in my classroom, the emphasis is now on a more "holistic" approach and students have the opportunity to select their own text. My ultimate goal for reciprocal teaching is to have students working together in small groups and using these strategies to make meaning of the text they are sharing.

Initially, I modeled the use of the four strategies, thinking aloud about the process used to understand what is read. For the first day or two, I put the primary emphasis on question-generation. My students have had previous experience with questioning and are more familiar with this task. However, many students ask questions concerning unrelated and rather trivial information. Having read a paragraph explaining the cause of lightning, a child asks: "What is the longest lightning bolt ever seen?" The paragraph dealt with the "cause of lightning," while the child's question had nothing to do with the cause of lightning. They need guidance in identifying important information in the text or main idea information. The more practice they have in formulating related questions the more they improve. I often have partners make-up one or two questions after seeing a video or after listening to a resource person. I remind them to ask themselves—What question could a teacher or text ask about this material? Many times I later use their questions for assessment.

The next strategy we work on is summarizing. Forming a summary is troublesome for second graders. They often focus on unusual ideas rather than on important ones. Knowing how to condense is also foreign to young children. From time to time, I ask my students to record in their reading log a summary about a book they read in reading workshop. Only a few had even limited success. My four students were more successful when we used a short selection. Summarization of narratives seemed less difficult than expository text. I just kept directing them to try and tell what they had read in their own words.

The clarifying strategy helps students notice when there has been a breakdown in understanding. It focuses on the ability to make sense of something by using context clues. After some initial teacher modeling, my students were quick to engage in clarification. We compare this strategy to a cloudy day that becomes sunny—clearing it up. When given permission to find the text confusing, they were willing

*As described by teacher Rebecca Martin.

to admit their misunderstanding. Some reacted with genuine surprise to discover that adults may find a passage unclear. Clarification aids students who are unable to form a summary or ask appropriate questions because it encourages them to identify which part of the text is hindering their understanding.

Occasionally, a student is hesitant to call attention to his or her own comprehension difficulty. I ask the student to pick out information in the text that he/she thinks might be hard for a younger child (kindergarten partner) to understand. This proposal usually draws out the most reluctant child.

Predicting serves many purposes. Most importantly, it supplies the connection between what students already know and the new knowledge they acquire. Children's predictions give you a picture of students' prior knowledge. Encourage students to use several sources of information when forming predictions. The first clues, of course, are the title of the passage and the pictures that appear throughout the story. Guide students to tell what they already know about this subject, and ask them what they would like to learn about the topic. Probing questions for predicting from narratives might include:

1. *What do you know about this character that helps you predict what he will do next?*

2. *Given the situation in the story, what might happen next?*

3. *In stories like this, what usually happens next?*

4. *Predict how the story will end.*

Have students apply these techniques with shared reading of predictable books. For informational selections, try these:

1. *What do you know about this subject that can help you predict what will be covered next?*

2. *What hints do the pictures provide about what will be presented next?*

3. *Why do you think the author wrote this? On that basis, what information will be presented next?*

The accuracy of the prediction is less important than the level of thinking needed to make it. Remind the students that predicting can be compared to a "very good guess." There may be some passages that do not have enough clues to support a prediction. Because many second graders have an immature knowledge base, I believe they experience more success predicting from narrative rather than from informational books.

SAMPLE LESSON USING EXPOSITORY TEXT

TEACHER: Today we have an information story called "Remarkable Reptiles." Information stories are read to learn new facts about something. What might this story be about?

S4: I think this story might give strange facts about alligators, snakes, and about reptiles. Doesn't remarkable mean strange?

TEACHER: Yes, I would say unusual or peculiar.

S1: (reading) Reptiles are animals that have scales and a backbone. Reptiles are cold-blooded animals. This means they have no way to keep their body temperature the same at all times. Reptiles are warm if the place around them is warm. They are cool if the place around them is cool. Because they cannot keep their bodies warm in very cold places, reptiles do not live in the coldest part of the world. Snakes, lizards, turtles, crocodiles, and tuataras make up the five groups of reptiles.

TEACHER: Why are reptiles described as cold-blooded?

S2:   Because their bodies are warm if in warm places and cold if in cold places.

TEACHER: Who can ask another question about the information we just read?

S1:   What are reptiles covered with?

S3:   Scales.

TEACHER: Can you summarize now, J?

S3:   This is about reptiles and why they are called cold-blooded animals.

TEACHER: Right. This paragraph is mainly about why reptiles are called cold-blooded. Are there any clarifications we need to make?

S4:   Do snakes have a backbone?

S1:   Yes, because snakes are reptiles.

TEACHER: Are there any predictions?

(no response from the students)

SAMPLE LESSON USING NARRATIVE TEXT

TEACHER: The name of our story today is called "The Sociable Seal." Can anyone predict what the story will be about?

S1:   It's about a seal that needs a home. It looks like it is hurt.

TEACHER: Do we know what sociable means? Have you heard the word social?

S1:   I've heard of social studies, but I don't know what it means.

S2:   I think we need to clarify.

TEACHER: Do you think reading ahead might help to clarify this?

S3:   I believe that it means friendly.

S3:   (reading) Mr. and Mrs. Kelly were spending a summer at the beach. They owned the Kelly School of Music in the city. They had been eager to leave their home because they had very few pupils in their school. The Kellys thought that a summer beside the sea might help them forget their troubles.

    One day they found a sick seal pup on the beach. It had been carried away from its home and its mother by high waves. Mr. and Mrs. Kelly took the seal pup to their summer home.

TEACHER: Can someone tell us what has happened so far in the story?

S1:   It is about some people who own a music shop and go on a summer vacation.

TEACHER: Where do they go?

S2:   To the beach.

TEACHER:	When we tell the main parts of the story in a few words we are what?
S3:	Summarizing.
S4:	Why did they take the seal to their house?
S3:	They are going to help it finds its mother.
S1:	To help it get well.
S2:	They are going to nurse it and then put it in a band.
TEACHER:	What are you doing when you tell what you think will happen next?
S2:	Predicting.

These were some of our earlier attempts in the use of reciprocal teaching. After several lessons I concluded that it would be more effective if I grouped my students who were considered poor comprehenders with some more capable students. I discovered that these heterogenous groups were more effective than having four below average comprehenders together. The more capable students served as additional models or catalysts in the instructional group and motivated the at-risk students to participate.

The literature suggests that one way to know if the instruction is working is to monitor the dialogues. With each passing day of instruction, discussions should occur more easily, with students gradually assuming more responsibility. If individual students show no improvement, conference with the child to determine why this might be the case. Is the student working with material that is inappropriate? Is the student contributing to the discussions? Is further instruction and modeling of the separate learning strategies required?

Reciprocal teaching offers frequent opportunities for diagnosing the sources of students' comprehension problems. As you are thinking aloud, so are students, displaying the way they are processing the text. Using only worksheets, we could assess the product but not the process. Based on this "kid listening as well as kid watching" you are able to adjust objectives and materials to meet the needs of each individual child.

In summary, I would conclude that the second grade students in my classroom benefitted from the strategies used in reciprocal teaching. The strategies were useful in helping students understand what "good readers" do to make meaning of what they are reading. The students responded very positively to these ideas, easily picked up the new vocabulary, and demonstrated that they understood the process as they participated in small and large group instruction and when reading on their own.

The reciprocal teaching methods used in my classroom improved the reading comprehension of my second graders. The strategies helped students to focus on what they were reading to insure the words had meaning for them. These strategies are easily adaptable to various types of reading material, including basals and trade books, and can be used to promote understanding of any content area.

What makes reciprocal teaching so successful is its focus on active discussion and critical thinking rather than on isolated reading skills. Children need to be assisted to learn the "how to" of the reading process rather than specific, sequenced bits of information presented in isolated ways. Instruction focused at the strategy level takes into account the complexities of the reading process and individual differences in students. The reciprocal method is compatible with the practices now employed by many classroom teachers of active, engaged learning. By guiding students to apply appropriate strategies we are helping them to "learn how to learn."

Reading Comprehension with Basal Readers

Improving instruction in reading comprehension is a concern shared by most educators. One of the promising areas of teaching reading comprehension has been comprehension monitoring, or discerning whether what is being read makes sense and, if not, knowing strategies to correct the problem. Good readers monitor comprehension. They identify when they are not understanding and they use self-instructional strategies to overcome their problems. Some strategies are knowing when to reread, when and how to use context clues, and use of a dictionary. These have been referred to as "fix-ups"—knowing how to fix up one's comprehension problems.

Traditional basal reader instruction can be enhanced to promote and develop metacognitive abilities. Schmitt and Baumann (1986, pp. 23–31) clearly describe how to incorporate comprehension monitoring into basal reader instruction. The methods are based on an adaptation of reciprocal teaching, just described. The authors break down a directed reading activity into prereading activities, guided reading activities, and postreading activities.

PREREADING ACTIVITIES

1. Activate background knowledge: Do this by finding out what the students already know about the topic to be read. Discuss the title and pictures to ascertain what the group already knows and has brought with them to the story.

2. Make predictions about the content: Use the title, pictures, and prior knowledge to hypothesize what might happen in the story. Record the group predictions or allow individual members to record their own predictions.

3. Set purposes for reading: Tell students they should read with a purpose in mind to help their attention and comprehension. Often the students' predictions serve well as the purpose(s) for reading (i.e., find out if the apple really did turn into a mouse).

4. Generate questions: Ask students to develop questions that they want answered as they read. Students tell what questions they want answered. These too can be listed, to be answered later.

GUIDED READING ACTIVITIES

1. Summarize at various points: At strategic places in the story, after a main element has occurred, ask the students to stop and review the main points of their reading.

2. Evaluate and make new predictions: As students read and know more facts, they should verify their predictions and make new ones if necessary.

3. Relate new information to prior knowledge: As new facts are presented students should discuss how this new information fits in with or relates to something they already know about.

4. Generate questions: Encourage students to ask themselves questions about the story as they read.

POSTREADING ACTIVITIES

1. Summarize total selection: Students review the whole story stressing the main points. Individual students may summarize the story or group summaries may be sought.

2. Evaluate predictions: Go back to predictions made before and during the story to validate predictions, what caused changes in their predictions, how accurate were they, etc.

3. Return to the purpose set for reading: Provide children with self-questions: Did I find out what I needed to know? Did I meet my purpose for reading?

4. Generate questions for the total selection: Teachers and students ask questions about characters, plot, situation, goal, solution, etc. Students ask each other questions, students ask the teacher questions, and the teacher asks the students questions. Throughout the prereading, guided reading, and postreading activities the teacher tells the students the rationale for these processes (e.g., "stopping reading to review main points periodically is a great way to check your own comprehension").

Classroom Literacy

Corno (1989) defines "classroom literacy" as knowing what it means to be a student within a classroom setting. Some of the skills that comprise classroom literacy are ability to (1) focus on the task at hand, (2) screen out distractors in order to continue working on a school task, (3) persist at a task, (4) seek help when needed, and (5) finish a task with a reasonable amount of accuracy and promptness. Students have varying degrees of classroom literacy as a result of a number of variables. Some variables that impact classroom literacy are (1) nature of the assigned task, (2) emotional climate of the classroom, (3) teacher's personal affect, (4) teacher's professional skills, (5) student motivation, volition, and cognitive competency, (6) time of day, (7) family values, and (8) competing environmental distractors. You may be able to think of others. Some students have a great deal of classroom literacy while others seem extremely deficient in this kind of literacy. These latter students seem unable to regulate their own concentration, do not focus attention to an assigned task unless they are prompted excessively by the teacher, do not follow through on tasks, and do not finish school work in a timely fashion. These are the students who day after day do not get their work done. Teachers often try many things to get these students to a reasonable level of productivity—they often beg, cajole, threaten, tease, punish, etc., attempting to get the reluctant student to participate. Depending on how severe this classroom literacy problem is, even the most outstanding teachers begin to experience exasperation and/or frustration with such students.

Some of these students lack a battery of self-regulated learning strategies. And with the knowledge of what the strategies are, how, when, and why to use them; reluctant learners often become much more successful in school. In short, they become much more classroom literate. These cognitive and metacognitive strategies should be introduced to all students in their first school experience and emphasized at each grade level thereafter. To illustrate how to teach students classroom literacy skills, a kindergarten teacher, Sharon Ankerich, developed a successful plan. Other plans addressing the efficient implementation of productive school works habits are provided in Chapter 8, the first section.

CLASSROOM LITERACY IDEAS FOR KINDERGARTEN*

When my students arrive I read them a big book about a special friend Spidey and how he talks to himself about school. First I introduce Spidey (a spider puppet that I made using a black glove. Each of my fingers or the children's fingers becomes one of Spidey's legs when I put on the glove.) I allow each child to handle the

*As described by teacher Sharon Ankerich.

puppet so that they realize for themselves that the spider is not a real spider. I pretend that Spidey wrote the big book and wants to read it to the children. The book is entitled *Spidey Talks to Self*. Spidey "reads" the book and allows the students to practice some helpful self-talk for various situations, such as painting a picture. After the children get the idea of how to talk to themselves to focus attention on their painting, they follow through with self-talk reminders, and finish their work with encouraging and reinforcing self-talk (e.g., "When I finish my painting, I can hang it in the hallway. It will be so pretty hanging there."). We will role-play various school situations in which self-talk might be helpful (e.g., remembering what to take home from school).

The words in the big book are presented below. You may make your own class book using these words or change them any way you need. You may also want to illustrate your book with drawings of Spidey.

Page 1:   Hi! My name is Spidey and I'm in Mrs. Ankerich's Class.

Page 2:   In kindergarten, we learn many wonderful things.

Page 3:   And we "do" school work. We help each other and Mrs. Ankerich helps us too.

Page 4:   One way we can help ourselves is to learn helpful ways to talk to ourselves.

Page 5   For example, if I get to build with the blocks I remind myself to share with others who are building and to put away the blocks when I am finished.

Page 6:   What do you suppose I say? I'll tell you a few things and then you tell me what you would say if you are working a puzzle.

Page 7:   Here's some of my self-talk for "building-blocks" concentration.
    ASK: What will I build today?
    TELL: I want to build a tall building.
    TRY: I'll just put these blocks on top of each other very carefully. I'll do the best I can even if one falls—it's okay.

CHECK:	I'll stand back and see if I have everything the way I want it.
CHEER:	Yay! It's a beautiful building.

Page 8:   Let's hear some of your ideas for self-talk while putting together a puzzle.

ASK: _____

TELL: _____

TRY: _____

CHECK: _____

CHEER: _____

Page 9:   You are a wonderful group of students and I want you to use helpful self-talk.

Page 10:   I'll be back another day to see what helpful things you've been saying to yourself.

In addition to the Spidey big book I use a checklist bulletin board to help foster classroom literacy. On the bulletin board I include four questions:

Did I put my name on my work?

Did I do my best?

Did I clean my area?

Was I a good friend?

The bulletin board has cueing pictures beside the questions to help the non-readers know what each question asks. The students place a check on the work they hand in for each of the four questions. For example, the first check stands for: "Yes, I checked and my name is on my paper." The second check represents: "Yes, I did do the best that I could." The third check stands for: "Yes, I checked and my area is clean." The fourth check represents: "Yes, I was a good friend" (e.g., I did not talk and disturb others; I helped if one of my group members couldn't do the work, etc.). It is the teacher's responsibility to teach what each of these questions means. Children are taught that they do not record a check unless they can provide evidence that they earned their four checks. For example if child A puts a check for question 3 and it is obvious that her area is not clean then the teacher might privately say to Tabitha: "Tabitha I see that your glue, scissors, and paper cuttings are still all around your desk. Please tell me how you earned this third check you gave to yourself. The teacher and child discuss the situation in private and Tabitha erases the third check until she cleans up her area. Then she may put the third check on her paper if this is the first time that Tabitha has not been truthful. If such self-evaluation continues to be inaccurate then I often use my "time-out" plan if I know the child is aware of the dishonesty. If it is a lack of understanding of the system, I conference, demonstrate, use peer helpers until the child understands the self-evaluation and self-recording system.

My time-out is a desk with two cue cards on the top. Please see the illustration on page 152. The cue cards say "My problem is . . . " and "I will . . . ." The students are asked to write or draw a picture of the problem they are having (e.g., hitting a friend, not waiting turns, refusing to share, etc.). I also use a tape recorder at this area so that students can record their own words about their problem. The students are taught how to use the tape recorder. Later in the day, the students and I can listen to the tape together and discuss the student's plan for improvement. This has worked extremely well.

If the teachers in the next grades would build on these beginning skills of self-monitoring, self-recording, and self-evaluation then I believe that we may first, graduate many more students, and second, more of our graduates may be responsible citizens who accept their roles as independent adults. Interdependence (i.e., being a good friend) also may surface as a valued characteristic of an independent, responsible citizen.

SUMMARY

In this chapter, we presented examples of metacognitive strategy research for students in elementary and middle grades in the areas of self-control, mathematics, listening comprehension, reading comprehension, and handwriting. No attempt was made to present an exhaustive review of literature in each of these areas. Only a few examples of studies were provided due to space limitations.

The research evidence indicates that metacognitive experiences have been shown to be instrumental in fostering benefits for students' memory, comprehension, problem solving, and self-control abilities. Education has as one of its major goals to foster these same cognitive abilities. Therefore, metacognitive experiences should be implemented by teachers into virtually every learning activity with students of every age.

Several metacognitive strategies, techniques, suggestions, and approaches were also presented in the latter part of the chapter. These sample plans were written by teachers for their specific groups of students; therefore, modifications, deletions, and extensions are expected before they can be applied to other groups of students. We hope the various classroom metacognitive strategies presented here will stimulate you to develop your own metacognitive interventions.

CHAPTER 8

Applying Metacognitive Strategies for Students' Learning

OVERVIEW

In this chapter, metacognitive strategies for promoting efficient school work habits and teaching in the content areas are outlined. Teacher-developed, teacher-implemented, and teacher-evaluated metacognitive techniques are presented with little or no modification. Too often teachers receive ideas for classroom practice that have not been tested in the confines of a "real classroom." In addition, even though the suggestions in this chapter were derived from classroom teachers, they may not be appropriate for your classroom because each class of students differs. Therefore, adaptations and revisions of the basic ideas presented in this chapter will most likely be necessary in order to meet the needs of your specific group of students. A general preview to school work habits and to content area teaching appears prior to each of these sections; therefore, no additional information is given in the overview.

Self-Questions

1. *Knowledge.* What is one example of an efficient school work habit?

2. *Comprehension.* Explain the differences between the self-talk of more productive versus less productive students as they focus attention, follow through with school tasks, and finish school assignments promptly and accurately.

3. *Application.* Using one of the teacher's plans for introducing helpful self-talk to facilitate school work habits, develop your own metacognitive plan for a specific school assignment.

4. *Analysis.* Detail the three different types of writing as outlined by teacher Amy Haysman and develop accompanying self-talk for one of the types of writing.

5. *Synthesis.* Build a case for adding metacognitive strategy teaching to a subject in school that seems to lend itself to metacognition. Provide a scenario, describe the curriculum, and traditional methodology. Explain how and why the metacognitive strategies should be incorporated as an integral part of your teaching. (If you prefer, you may build a case against the addition of metacognitive strategy teaching).

6. *Evaluation.* List strengths and weaknesses of metacognitive strategies for either the facilitation of efficient school work habits or the teaching of metacognitive strategies within the content areas.

SCHOOL WORK HABITS

Many children eventually drop out of school because they have not learned how to facilitate their own learning (Corno, 1989). Corno and Rohrkemper (1988) discuss the idea that some students just seem to know the skills of functioning well in a class. Knowing the classroom ropes, knowing the student role, knowing the cognitive and metacognitive

	Focus	Follow-Through	Finish
Problem Defining			
Productive Students	What did the teacher say to do first? Where do I start?	How much time do I have to complete spelling? After spelling I'll work on the math page.	Make sure I finished all the assignments. Check it off from the board.
Nonproductive Students	I don't know what to do. I can't do any of this anyway.	I finished one. Time for a break. I hate working, and working all morning.	Finish—that's a joke. I'm supposed to finish five assignments. Be real.
Self-Starting			
Productive Students	Get started on spelling. Better get going.	I need to get back to spelling right now if I want to finish. Stop staring.	Just one more problem. Look up this word first. Then I'll be finished.
Nonproductive Students	This is really stupid stuff. I'm not going to waste my time.	I'm not going to continue this silly stuff. Keep working, she says. Who cares about me?	Try to finish. No! No! No! I got more than half. That's good for me. I'm slow.
Self-Guiding			
Productive Students	Now put the periods in this time. Watch out. This looks tricky.	Now slow down and read this one more time—carefully. Did I skip a sentence just now?	Count the pages—1, 2, 3. Name on every paper?
Nonproductive Students	What is this stuff? Mark has finished five already.	Not another definition! I give up! Where is number three? Forget it.	Andrea will laugh because I didn't finish. Just stop.
Self-Coping			
Productive Students	I'm kind of tired today, but I'll get started anyway. These look long and too hard, but I can figure it out.	I may not be getting every one of these right, but I'm trying.	It's hard to get it all done today, but I'll make it. Hang in there—just two more.
Nonproductive Students	I'm tired. This is going to be too hard. This is too much work.	I'll miss all these anyway. Why work on them? I've had it. I quit.	This is too much work. I won't finish again.
Self-Reinforcing			
Productive Students	I'll get started right away without wasting time. I'm a good worker.	I can stick with this stuff. Even the intercom didn't bother me.	Yay, I finished. looks good.
Nonproductive Students	I'm far behind everyone else. I'll get another F.	I'm the slowest one in class. I hate all this school junk.	Stupid—that's me. I can't ever finish.

side of planning one's own school tasks, focusing attention on assignments, following through on tasks, and finishing tasks accurately and promptly (Manning, 1990b) are referred to by Corno as "classroom literacy." We are referring to these same ideas as productive school work habits. In a series of studies conducted by Manning (1990c), she found that children who were designated by their teachers as productive workers talked to themselves before, during, and after task performance in ways that were qualitatively different from the students who were designated by their teachers as less productive workers during independent school tasks. Independent school tasks are defined as those tasks that teachers assign to students: to begin and complete without prompting and with minimal or no help from the teacher or a peer. The chart on page 154 illustrates the wide discrepancy between the self-talk of students, described by teachers as more productive versus less productive, during independent school work time.

Example One

One effective teaching technique to improve school work habits and to foster classroom literacy that has been developed and tested by Rhonda Brand Horton, classroom art teacher, is to use children's books to help children master the metacognitive skills of self-awareness and self-regulation. Ms. Horton illustrated and wrote a book after interviewing children, with what she termed, "concentration problems." After writing the book she asked children to review the book for her. She revised the book according to their suggestions. When the book was finished, it was read by a number of teachers in a number of classrooms. It became a very popular item in the school. The book is about a student who has concentration problems and how he or she learns to overcome these problems using metacognitive strategies. In a second grade classroom, one student sadly remarked: "I'm the star of that book!" The book and illustrations, just as they were completed by Ms. Horton, are presented on pages 156–161. Ms. Horton reports that this book has helped a number of children realize that they are not the only ones who experience concentration difficulties, that there are ways to help oneself become better at concentration, and that these ways are easy to learn and apply to improve concentration at school.

Example Two

Teacher Cynthia Wilson also uses a Big Book that she wrote and illustrated to help students improve their school work habits. She entitled her book "Vygot Scores School Goals." As you may recall, Vygotsky's (1934/1962, 1978) theory of verbal self-regulation serves as the foundation for the use of self-guiding speech. This book (see pages 162–164) serves as another example of a teacher-developed and teacher-tested book. You may wish to write your own Big Book to address productive school work habits.

Example Three

Second grade teacher Colleen McKibben helps her students remember to problem solve well during mathematics, handwriting, and other school work by placing bears across the top of the desk as shown on page 165. The students are taught the metacognitive thinking process of Ask, Tell, Try, Check, and Cheer. Engaging in these steps helps children to focus attention, follow through, and finish work, as well as perform the mathematics steps per se in a much more efficient manner. An example of this thinking process for solving a mathematics problem is outlined on page 165.

Written and
Illustrated by
RHONDA BRAND
HORTON

I'm my Boa's Buddy.
I'm happy all the time.
But that's because of my Boa.
He helps me walk the line.

I used to have a hard time.
I was never on the ball.
If I was suppose to stand up,
Well, that's just when I would fall.

My mind would not stay focused.
I never was on task.
When all the work was handed in,
Mine would always be last.

Talking, walkers, and the intercom,
Always broke my train of thought.
Completed work, a beautiful "A",
Or even a smile I couldn't have bought.

Let me give you several examples,
So you'll understand.
Then you can see why,
I needed a helping hand.

One day we went to the library,
To hear a story read.
It was a wonderful story,
But other thoughts filled my head.

The librarian started to read,
There's An Alligator Under My Bed,
And then I noticed the pictures,
And my thoughts to other things lead.

I began to think of my room,
And how I'd forgotten to pick up my toys.
Now, Mom would be upset with me,
and I knew when I got home,
I'd definitely hear lots of noise.

I hated it when Mom was mad,
Especially with me.
But sometimes I forget things.
I wish that she could see.

Then suddenly the librarian asked,
If I'd enjoyed the book.
But all that I could give her,
Was a long, blank look.

"Oh, no, I've missed the story."
And it seemed to be so good.
How did he get rid of the alligator?
I wish I'd listened. I know I should.

Now I'll have to check the book out,
And read it for myself.
I hope the words aren't too hard,
and I won't have to ask for help.

I wish I could learn to think better.
I've already goofed once today.
I really blew it in math this morning.
I didn't hear my teacher say,

"You have only 10 more minutes,
To finish your math test.
If I had only concentrated,
I could have done my best.

I did the first three problems,
With the greatest of ease,
But my mind began to drift,
And the rest was not a breeze.

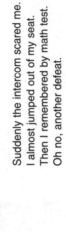

The answer to the third problem,
Was the number 21.
Hey, that's my baseball number.
Baseball is such fun!

Last night we had a game,
And I hit the ball so hard.
My dad was so proud of me,
He went home and made my own
baseball card.

Maybe one day I'll be famous,
And you'll buy my card in gum.
And the money I'll be making,
Will come in in large sums.

Suddenly the intercom scared me.
I almost jumped out of my seat.
Then I remembered by math test.
Oh no, another defeat.

Ten minutes left to finish,
And lots of problems to do.
I'm sure when I get this test back,
I'm going to feel real blue.

I must learn to keep my mind on things,
And not get so behind.
'Cause catching up is impossible.
It's like always being last in line.

And don't let me forget to tell you,
About my lunchroom tale.
I was so hungry that day,
I could have eaten a whale.

I went through the lunch line,
Got my tray and finally sat down.
Yum-m-Chocolate Chip Cookies.
That's my favorite treat in town.

Cookies remind me of Grandma.
She makes them when I go to her house.
We stir and mix and bake,
And eat lots of Chocolate Toll House.

And then we go outside and swing,
On the great big tire.
It hangs from a tree limb,
And I kick hard to go higher.

I remember when Grandma took me,
On a mountain trip.
We picked apples from the orchard,
And drank apple cider.
I wouldn't share a sip.

I remember all those Indians,
Making dolls and stringing beads.
They chanted around the campfire,
And danced to the beat.

All at once I was in a whirlwind,
Of children everywhere,
Headed to the window,
Empty trays aflare.

Oh no, I hadn't eaten
Not even one little bite.
And I am really starving,
My stomach growls are a fright.

I stuffed in my mouth quickly,
A chocolate cookie of course.
But a cookie won't quite cut it,
When you're as hungry as a horse.

My Boa Buddy sits on my desk,
And he never says a word.
But he reminds me all the time to keep working,
But his voice outloud's never heard.

He whispers in my head,
"Keep working, I can do it.
Don't turn my thoughts to baseball,
And in math I'll make a hit.

Watch those pictures in the story.
I don't want to miss the end.
Make my ears listen closely.
Books can be good friends.

And at lunch, don't go on a diet.
My health is important too.
I can count the bites I've eaten,
and chew and chew and chew.

The secret to all this is thinking,
And talking in my head.
Buddy Boa will remind me,
Through all things how to be lead.

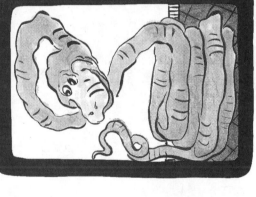

I used to have the same problems,
Just as you say you do.
I seldom finished my math test either,
and I often felt real blue.

I went many a day without eating lunch.
I always daydreamed instead.
My body got so skinny,
You'd think I'd never been fed.

I missed many good stories,
as I stared off into space.
The other boas loved the story,
But my concentration was always too late.

I decided I had to do something.
I was tired of the daydreaming flu.
I made myself a Boa Buddy,
And you can make one too.

These daydreams cause me problems.
I'm always having it tough.
I've got to fix this problem,
Or my life is going to be rough.

All this failure makes me feel awful.
I don't like myself.
And then one day my Boa said,
"I think that I can help!"

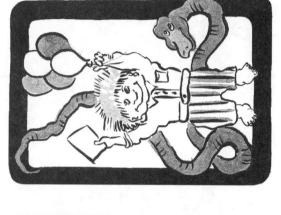

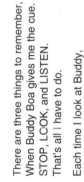

There are three things to remember,
When Buddy Boa gives me the cue.
STOP, LOOK, and LISTEN.
That's all I have to do.

Each time I look at Buddy,
That's a cue to STOP my thoughts.
Am I doing what I ought to?
Or did I just get caught.

I'll LOOK at my work closely,
And get back to concentrating.
I'm going to stay on task this time.
No more procrastinating.

And then I'm going to LISTEN,
To the good things I say in my mind.
I can do it! It won't take long.
I won't get behind.

And since I've learned to STOP, LOOK,
and LISTEN,
I've learned that life gets better.
I've had to pat myself on the back,
'Cause in school, I'm a real go-getter!

Pretty soon I'll find I won't need
Buddy Boa,
But I wouldn't dare give him away.
Buddy Boa loves me,
And with me he wants to stay."

So let's all listen to Boa's advice,
And learn it all by heart.
And soon we'll all discover,
All along we were really smart!

Vygot Scores School Goals

This is Vygot.

When do you think Vygot likes to talk to himself? If you said when he needs to get things done, you're right. Vygot loves to get things done, especially at school. He loves to learn and feels proud when the teacher does not need to remind him of what to do.

Listen! Can you hear him? NO! Neither can I. Vygot talks to himself. Usually, he is the only one who hears what he says. Sometimes Vygot does whisper to himself, so we might be able to hear if we listen very carefully.

Do you remember that sometimes Vygot might whisper the things that he says to himself at school? He is doing that today. Let's see if we can hear him. His teacher is about to give directions.

Look at Vygot. He is ready to listen. This is his goal. How can Vygot make his goal? Let's hear what Vygot whispers to himself. He says "I LISTEN."

Do you know how Vygot reached his goal? He said "I LISTEN" and he talked to himself to help reach his goal. Let's see how Vygot gets a second goal.

After Vygot makes his listen goal, he says to himself "I have another goal. I PLAN." Listen to what Vygot says to himself as he gets ready to work.

Now Vygot has scored two goals. He has listened and planned. Vygot wants to work on a third goal, so he says to himself "I WORK."

Vygot has made three goals so far. He says to himself, "I have listened, planned, and worked. Now all I have left is one goal." Vygot tells himself, "I CHECK."

Vygot has tried so hard at school today. He talked to himself about his work from start to finish. Vygot is proud of himself. No one had to remind him what to do! He told himself. Now Vygot will have time to play. Scoring goals is his favorite thing to do. See if you can be like Vygot. Tell yourself "I CAN SCORE SCHOOL GOALS!"

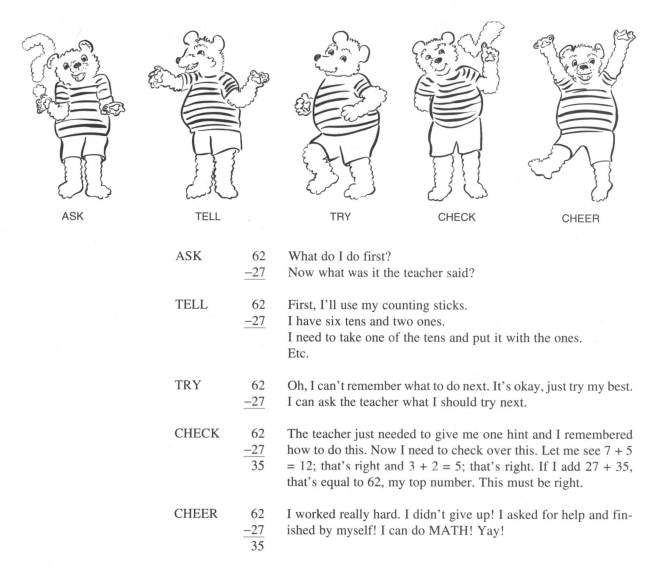

| ASK | TELL | TRY | CHECK | CHEER |

ASK   62   What do I do first?

         −27   Now what was it the teacher said?

TELL   62   First, I'll use my counting sticks.

        −27   I have six tens and two ones.

                 I need to take one of the tens and put it with the ones.

                 Etc.

TRY   62   Oh, I can't remember what to do next. It's okay, just try my best.

       −27   I can ask the teacher what I should try next.

CHECK   62   The teacher just needed to give me one hint and I remembered

         −27   how to do this. Now I need to check over this. Let me see 7 + 5

          35   = 12; that's right and 3 + 2 = 5; that's right. If I add 27 + 35,

                 that's equal to 62, my top number. This must be right.

CHEER   62   I worked really hard. I didn't give up! I asked for help and fin-

         −27   ished by myself! I can do MATH! Yay!

          35

Example Four

Another technique for encouraging productive school work habits is through rapping. Rapping is a rhythmic way to put words into a musical beat. Young and older children seem to enjoy saying the words to a certain rhythm, often accompanied by clapping. Teacher Kelly Goff wrote the following rap. If you would prefer not to use this as a rap, the words create a memorable song or poem. Students might illustrate the words and create a class Big Book.

THINK RAP: EXCELLENT WORK HABITS

Sometimes it seems my mind's in the sky.

     I'm not doing my work. What's the matter? Oh my!

     When that happens I just say to my mind, "Pay attention! Come on! There's knowledge to find!'

     The first thing I do is ASK myself this . . . Am I following directions? Is there something I've missed?

     The next thing I do is TELL myself, "Hey! Put your mind on your work! Yes! That's the way!"Oh! But that's not all! And here's the reason why!

     Always remember to TRY! TRY! TRY!

Guess what? There's more! When I've done my best!

Never forget to CHECK before I rest! Last but not least, there's one more thing to do!

When I'm done with my work, CHEER! Yee hoo!

I have done my best job. It's easy for all to see.

Just ASK, TELL, TRY, CHECK, CHEER, and be the best learner *you* can be!

Some teachers have developed stories that they read to their students to introduce the idea of using more helpful self-talk. The next story was written by teacher Missy McEarchern.

TWIGGY'S HELPFUL SELF-TALK

This is Twiggy, a very forgetful first grader at Tweetsville Elementary. This morning Twiggy forgot most of the classroom rules. He forgot to listen to directions. He forgot to wait his turn to talk. He forgot to be courteous when the teacher was talking. He is having a very, very bad day.

Twiggy knows he's supposed to be doing something, but he can't remember what. He's trying to remember, but he can only think about going outside to play kickball. He doesn't like to feel lost or to get into trouble at school. However, he's not sure how to get back on the right track. Twiggy's feeling pretty bad about himself right now. He tells himself what a stupid bird he is, always getting into trouble, and not finishing his work.

Suddenly Twiggy hears a little worm yelling at him, "Stop!"

TWIGGY: Who are you?

WORM: I'm Hosea, the problem-solving worm and boy do you need me. You've got to change the way you talk to yourself about your life at school.

TWIGGY: Talking to myself, that's crazy!

WORM: Everyone does it but not always out loud. Sometimes you talk to yourself quietly in your head. But those things I've been hearing you say to yourself won't help you at all. Let me tell you how I talk to myself when I have a problem.

First I *ASK* myself: What is the problem? Questions like the following help a whole bunch?

1. What am I supposed to be doing?

2. What did the teacher say?

3. What are our rules?

4. What do I do when I have something to say?

5. What should I start with?

Then I *TELL* myself exactly what I need to do. I decide the right thing to do and how to start. I think about the directions and what I'm supposed to be doing. I tell myself the following kinds of things.

1. I need to concentrate on my work.

2. I follow the rules.

3. I work carefully.

4. Put my name on all my papers.

5. Write neatly so that I can read what I have written.

Then I *TRY* my hardest to follow my plan. I say things to myself such as:

1. I know I can do this.

2. I might have a hard time remembering but at least I'm not daydreaming.

3. I'm concentrating on my work and doing my very best.

4. This is really difficult for me, but I can handle this.

5. I try to do some of the problems even when I can't do every one of them.

Next I *CHECK* what I've done. I say to myself such things as:

1. Did I choose the right action?

2. Have I completed the whole plan?

3. Did I skip any problems?

4. Is there anything else I can do?

5. Is this my best work or can I improve something?

Finally, I *CHEER* for what I've done. I say to myself such things as:

1. I may not have gotten everything right or finished, exactly on time, but I tried my hardest and I'm proud of that!

2. I'm a good student in mathematics.

3. I can get my work done on my own and I don't need anyone else to push me.

4. I'm learning some neat stuff!

5. Great going! Good for me!

> *TWIGGY:*   Wow, maybe your steps will help me. I am certainly going to try your ideas Hosea, and I believe I'll do much better. Now let me make sure I have this.

HOSEA'S METHOD FOR IMPROVING SCHOOL WORK HABITS

1. **ASK** myself questions about the assignment or how to do the assignment. Another name for ASK is PROBLEM DEFINING.

2. *TELL* myself how to proceed with the school task at hand. Another name for TELL is SELF-GUIDING.

3. Tell myself to *TRY* my very best to focus, follow through, and finish my school work even if it is sometimes boring and sometimes too difficult. Another name for TRY is SELF-COPING.

4. Next, I tell myself to *CHECK* over my work to make sure I completed everything I was supposed to and to see if I made any errors. Another name for CHECK is SELF-CORRECTING.

5. Finally, I *CHEER* for myself if I have tried my very best. I note any progress that I have made even if everything is not always 100%. Another name for CHEER is SELF-REINFORCING.

Now that Twiggy knows how to talk to himself at school he's more encouraged about completing his school work. He has some keys for success that may help him to take responsibility for himself and for focusing, following through, and finishing his school work more accurately and promptly. He's proud that he has gained some control over his own school work habits.

Example Five

Another self-instructional method to improve school work habits is the checklist. Instead of the teacher having to repeatedly ask routine questions such as "Did you put your name on your paper?", students are taught to mark their checklist as they ask themselves: "Did I put my name on all of my papers?" A few examples of teacher-developed checklists are presented next. The teachers who use the checklists report healthy independence in their students, and an improvement of self-esteem as a by-product. Often when children learn self-regulated learning strategies such as the ones presented in this chapter, they feel empowered as students and higher self-esteem accompanies these feelings.

HANDWRITING CHECKLIST

Am I sitting correctly?	Yes	No
Is my paper positioned correctly?	Yes	No
Am I holding my pencil correctly?	Yes	No
Are all my letters on the line?	Yes	No
Are all my tall letters touching the top line?	Yes	No
Are all my short letters filling only ½ of the space?	Yes	No
Am I leaving enough space between words?	Yes	No

MORNING CHECKLIST

Did I say good morning to my classmates?	Yes	No
Did I turn in my homework?	Yes	No
Did I get my pencil, paper, and books ready?	Yes	No
Did I put away my coat and bookbag?	Yes	No
Tell myself—I'm going to have a good day today.	Yes	No

AFTERNOON CHECKLIST

Did I turn in all my work today?	Yes	No
Do I have my homework assignment?	Yes	No
Is my desk clean and neat for tomorrow?	Yes	No
Did I say something good about someone today?	Yes	No
Did I say something good about myself today?	Yes	No

LISTENING CHECKLIST

Do I understand these directions?	Yes	No
What am I supposed to do?	Yes	No
Is there anything missing?	Yes	No
Do I know how to begin?	Yes	No
Do I know every step along the way?	Yes	No
What did the teacher say to do when I was finished?	Yes	No

Example Six

Teachers often use cartoon strips to introduce the idea of monitoring your own thinking while engaged in school work. Teacher Donna Ware developed the following comic strips and also the sequence. She began with a model strip (Comic A below) with the self-talk already written. She converts this strip (Comic A) to an overhead transparency to discuss with the whole class. Next, she discusses a transparency of Comic B (below) and gives each student a copy of Comic B. First they work together, using the Comic B transparency, to fill out the captions for each frame. Then each student, or small groups of students, develop a different series of self-talk for their handout (Comic B). This is for guided practice. The third comic strip (Comic C below) is to be used as independent practice to insure that each student understands the concept of guiding one's own school work via self-talk. The third strip (Comic C) may be used as homework, independent seatwork, or as part of an informal assessment on metacognitive processes for learning. The three comic strips A, B, and C are provided below.

Comic Strip A.   Sample comic strip to be used as an overhead transparency to illustrate to children self-talk while listening (Frame 1), while planning work (Frame 2), while working (Frame 3), and while checking over work (Frame 4) (Manning, 1984, 1991).

Comic Strip B.   Sample comic strip to be used as an overhead transparency and an accompanying handout for the students. As a class, students take turns dictating plausible self-talk utterances for each frame. Next, each student or small groups of students write in their own suggestions of a different series of self-talk utterances on the handouts.

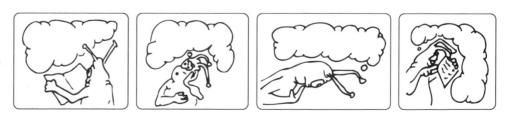

Comic Strip C.   Students are given their own comic strip, such as Comic Strip C above, to develop independently their own self-talk for each frame.

Example Seven

Another method for helping students learn helpful self-talk for productive school work habits is to use peer role models. Jean Marie Rackett teaches first grade and she enlists the help of the fifth graders in her school to model facilitative self-talk for her first graders. She refers to this fifth grade class as her first graders' BUDDY CLASS. The fifth graders write and present skits about helpful self-talk to use at school. The fifth graders also profit because it reinforces their own helpful self-talk and gives them a sense of accomplishment that they are able to help others.

Example Eight

Photographs of students are often used with samples of productive self-talk. These are displayed in classrooms, discussed with the children, and used as reminders when students are not remembering to use their helpful self-talk. A sample of photographs with accompanying self-talk is presented on pages 171–173. In addition to photographs and skits, the students may audiotape themselves using helpful self-talk during independent school work times. Then their audiotapes of helpful self-talk are placed in learning centers or are occasionally played for small groups or the entire class, especially if a great deal of negative self-talk is noted.

In the previous section, the underlying metacognitive processes related to efficient school work habits were addressed. Actual classroom metacognitive strategies, developed and field-tested by teachers were presented. In all cases, the teachers have reported benefits, such as better attitudes about school, more productive school work habits, better grades, and higher levels of student self-esteem. The self-regulated learning strategies were introduced to students by means of children's literature, big books, peer modeling, role play, skits, photographs, comic strips, and checklists. The next section, entitled Content Area Teaching, deals with metacognitive strategies for listening, language, writing, reading, mathematics, and social studies.

CONTENT AREA TEACHING

Metacognitive strategies for teaching and learning a variety of subjects taught in school are presented next. Due to the integration of subject matter in many schools today, the classifications in this chapter (e.g., reading) may also be used as part of a social science or science lesson, for example. Therefore, please keep in mind that these ideas are transportable across the school curriculum and are not limited to the subjects designated as headings.

Listening

One of the primary skills of communication is listening. Listening strategies are not often explicitly taught; and therefore, many students do not develop skills for listening. Monitoring one's own listening is important for every subject taught in school, and for the enhancement of interpersonal skills. Students need to be taught self-monitoring techniques and other metacognitive strategies for improving basic listening skills (Strother, 1987). One of the first steps is to teach students how to be mentally responsible for their listening, such as skills of attending, clarifying, and summarizing. First grade teacher Jean Marie Rackett used stories that emphasized good listening, *modeling* by a fifth grade

"Wait a minute. I need to remember to walk when I'm leaving the classroom."

"Do I understand what the teacher just said? No! Denise is good at math I'll ask her to explain it again."

"Am I showing interest while I'm listening? Yes! Good for me! Everyone else is too!"

171

"When I listen to my friends I look right at them. That helps me be a good listener. Way to go!"

"Am I listening carefully? No. I want to listen carefully so I will know the important bones in my body. I am going to look at Mrs. Lynn while she talks. I want to learn some interesting new things and I have to listen to do that."

"How can I repeat the main points? I'll say it in my head and try to write it down. I'll use my inside voice to repeat what I learned. I'll say what I learned out loud. I'll draw it out."

"Now that I understand I'll type all the steps so I will remember them."

"Do I understand? No. I'll raise my hand and ask a question. I'll keep listening. Yes! I'm doing a great job and I'll keep it up!"

CUE CARDS FOR GOOD LISTENING

"Am I listening carefully?"

Self-Reinforcing	Self-Correcting
"Yes! Good Job!"	"No!"
	"I have to listen carefully; that's what Fuzzy taught me."
	"I'm going to look at the teacher and do a good job!"
	"I have to think about what she is saying."

"Am I looking at the speaker?"

Self-Reinforcing	Self-Correcting
"Yes! I'm doing a great job!"	"No!"
	"I need to look at the speaker while she is talking."
	"I have to look at the speaker so I can learn what he is saying."

"Do I understand?"

Self-Reinforcing	Self-Correcting
"Yes! I'm doing a great job and I'll keep it up."	"No!"
	"I'll raise my hand to ask a question."
	"I'll keep listening."
	"I'll ask a friend to explain it to me."

"How can I summarize what I heard?"

Self-Guiding	Self-Guiding
"I'll say it in my head and try to write it down."	"I'll think about the main points."
"I'll use my inside voice to repeat what I have learned."	"What was really important?"
"I'll say what I learned out loud."	"Just tell the 'big ideas.' "
"I'll draw it out."	"Keep the small details for later."

buddy class, *practicing* by her students during role play, and *cueing* using photographs of students with written cues such as the ones presented on pages 171–174. Shown below is a suggested evaluation of a listening unit of study.

The evaluation of a listening unit (shown below) can be presented orally to students, individually or in small groups. Another option is to request that the students respond to the five statements and questions by answering each one in writing. This assignment can be completed in small groups, pairs, or individually.

EVALUATION OF LISTENING UNIT

1. Describe a good listener. Tell me what a good listener does or doesn't do.

2. If you were playing a new game with your mother and she told you how to play; but you didn't understand her directions, what would you say to yourself? What would you do?

3. If you were playing a game with your friend and she told you how to play; but, you didn't understand the directions would you:

    a. ask your friend a question

    b. try to figure it out yourself

    c. listen more carefully and hope you understand

    d. look at your friend while she is talking

    e. wait for your friend to explain better

4. Tell me a way that you can summarize what someone has said.

5. What would you say to yourself if your teacher was teaching you a new game and you needed to listen to understand the directions?

Whole Language

Teacher Dorothy Rice incorporated cognitive and metacognitive strategies into a whole language approach that she used in her classroom. She tells her own story:

> As I think about my whole language classroom, I believe that metacognition enhances my plan very nicely. The underlying concept of whole language is to encourage students to work more independently on topics that are of a higher interest level to them. With metacognitive processes the student is also encouraged to learn to work more independently through verbal self-instruction. By combining these two concepts students should be able to master a higher level of achievement while enjoying what they are learning.
>
> Reading workshop is a vital part of my classroom. Most days, reading workshop begins with a mini-lesson over some necessary reading skill. I use mini-lessons that help my students understand how they can use self-regulation during reading workshop to make their reading more meaningful.
>
> Writing workshop is the other main component of my whole language classroom. I also believe that metacognitive strategies blend in with this part through the use of cue cards to guide self-questioning. Because there is so much going on during writing workshop, it is extremely important for students to be self-regulated so that quality work can be produced.

Since metacognition is a new concept I introduce it to my students using direct instruction during a mini-lesson. The lesson will begin like many lessons in my classroom, with my sharing a book. Some of the books I like to use include: *The Little Red Caboose*, by Marian Potter, *The Little Engine That Could*, by Watty Piper, *Lon Po Po*, by Ed Young, or *The Frog Prince . . . Continued*, by Jon Scieszka. In all of these books the character(s) have a problem to solve. After reading the book I lead the students through a discussion of how the characters solved the problem. The big question and major focus is to discover what the character says to self to help with the problem. We brainstorm a list of possible self-talk utterances.

At this point the students are introduced to the Ask, Tell, Try, Check, and Cheer Series using verbal self-instruction for problem solving. I will assume the identity of the character from the book. By doing this I can model each of the five steps: Ask, Tell, Try, Check, and Cheer. After I model each step by talking aloud to myself to illustrate these steps I show the students the posters that we use as visual reminders of the steps. These are illustrated below.

| ASK | TELL | TRY | CHECK | CHEER |

What am I supposed to do?   How can I do it?   Am I following my plan?   How did I do?   Am I proud of my work?

At this point in the lesson the students are divided into groups and given a book to read with that group. Each group is asked to generate a list of questions or statements for each of the five steps (i.e., Ask, Tell, Try, Check, and Cheer) that match the situation for the character in their book. When each group has completed the task, they are asked to share their ideas with the large group. The large group will pick the statements they like the best and generalize them to be written on the posters. The poster will be laminated before the questions are added, so that they can be changed and revised as needed during the year. This provides group ownership which is very important in whole language instruction.

It should be noted that only the first part of this mini-lesson may be accomplished on the first day. It might, and probably will, take several days to work all the way through this idea. It should also be noted that the process might need to be completely repeated several times using different books until the students gain an understanding of basic verbal self-regulation. Hopefully, after completing this direct instruction phase the students will be able to ask themselves pertinent questions as they are reading during reading workshop. This should help increase comprehension skills.

Writing Workshop

Teacher Dorothy Rice continues by describing how she has incorporated metacognition into writing workshop. Again, she writes in first person:

> The way I conduct writing workshop in my classroom requires that the students possess a certain amount of independent work skills. They go through several steps in the writing process which needs to be directed by metacognitive awareness and regulation. Since many of my students choose locations other than their desks to write, cue cards on desks would not be appropriate. Instead, I use a self-guiding checklist in the front of their writing folders. This checklist is designed by me to begin the year, and later revised and changed by the students as we discover together cues that would mean more to the students as they write. An example of the self-guiding checklist is included next.

WRITING FOLDER CUE SHEET

1. I add at least <u>one</u> new <u>topic</u> to my list.	2. I put the <u>date</u> on my paper.
3. I spend my time writing.	4. I use a friend or a dictionary to help me spell.
5. I circle words I'm not sure of.	6. I put <u>all</u> my writing in my folder.
7. I leave my work area clean.	8. I put my writing folder in the basket.

Another teacher, Amy Haysman includes metacognitive strategies to help middle school students improve their writing. For her sixth grade language arts class she created a set of posters with the theme: "What Do Writers Say to Themselves?" These are illustrated on page 178.

WRITING FOLDER CUE SHEET
(to be used later when students make their own)

What do writers say to themselves?

I only chose topics that I care about.

If I don't like my piece, I don't have to continue writing it.

I enjoy using my creativity by writing.

I share my writing with others if I wish.

Amy Haysman also developed a poster entitled "What To Say to Myself Before Each Step of the Writing Process."

What to say to myself before each step of the writing process ...

Brainstorm
Do I want to begin a new piece, return to an old piece, or finish a piece in progress?

Writer 1
Do I have plenty of writing materials?

Revise
Do I have a colored pen to use while revising?

Edit
Do I have a grammar book and a dictionary close by?

Proofread
Am I in a quiet and comfortable place?

Final Copy
Do I have my piece exactly how I want it?

Conference
What do I want to accomplish by conferencing or sharing?

Share
Are my eyes, ears, and concentration focused on the reader?

In addition to the large posters, Amy Haysman designed a small pocket that holds cue cards to help conquer writer's block. She posts this on a wall in her classroom. Students have access to these cards whenever they are blocked and can't (or won't) think of a writing topic?

Cue Cards to Help Conquer Writer's Block

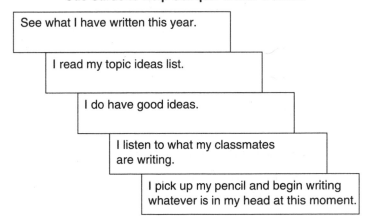

See what I have written this year.

I read my topic ideas list.

I do have good ideas.

I listen to what my classmates are writing.

I pick up my pencil and begin writing whatever is in my head at this moment.

A very substantive component of Amy Haysman's self-monitoring materials includes a checklist for each step of the writing process in three areas of writing. The areas include fictional story, personal narrative, and poetry. After teaching a lesson on each of the three areas of writing, the corresponding cognitive monitoring checklist for each of the areas is posted in the room for easy access. In addition, students have their own copy of the checklist to be kept in their writing folders. The three checklists for (1) fictional story, (2) personal narrative, and (3) poetry are presented next.

WRITING WORKSHOP CHECKLISTS

FICTIONAL STORY: The writer's intent is to tell a fictional story in order to entertain an audience.

Brainstorming Checklist

- Who is my favorite author and what type of stories does he/she write?

- What type of story do I want to write?

- What do I want the theme of my story to be?

Writing Draft 1 Checklist

- Using my knowledge of the elements of a story, I write a fictional story.

- I write a fitting title for my story that will capture a reader's interest.

Revising Checklist

- Does my story have a strong lead that will catch the reader's interest?

- Have I used the same narrator throughout my story?

- Can I form a clear picture of each character in my head?

- Is my setting clear throughout the story?

- Is my dialogue natural and appropriate for each character?

- Does my story flow smoothly from incident to incident?

- Is the climax the most exciting part of my story?

- Is my story's ending clear and believable?

- Did I use new and interesting vocabulary?

Editing Checklist

- Is each sentence a complete thought?

- Did I begin each sentence with a capital letter?

- Did I end each sentence with a punctuation mark?

- Did I spell each word correctly?

- Is my piece's internal punctuation correct?

Proofreading Checklist

- Have I said what I want to say?

- Am I pleased with my work?

- Do I need to revise or edit any further?

- Where am I going to take this piece from here?

Sharing, Conferencing Checklist

- What do I want to accomplish by sharing this piece?

- What are the results of my conference?

For Listeners Checklist

- What did I really like about this piece?

- What can I suggest to the writer that would help improve this piece?

Final Copy Checklist

- I legibly rewrite my revised and edited piece.

- Is my piece written in paragraphs with margins?

- Is my piece dated?

- Did I reread my piece in my head?

PERSONAL NARRATIVE: The writer's intent is to share personal experiences from his/her life.

Brainstorming Checklist

- What are some memories that stick out in my mind?

- What is the — most embarrassing — most confusing — funniest — most devastating — most joyful moment of my life?

Writing Draft 1 Checklist

- On paper, I list all the specific moments that came to mind while brainstorming.

- After my list is complete, I narrow it down by crossing out choices until I'm left with only one choice.

- I write everything I can remember about my experience.

- I may need to ask others involved to fill any memory gaps I may have.

Revising Checklist

- Have I written my memory of my experience in logical order?

- Did I leave out any important information?

- Do I need to take out any repetitive or unnecessary sentences?

- Have I used words that will cause the reader to feel as if he/she is part of the experience?

Editing Checklist

- Is each sentence a complete thought?

- Did I begin each sentence with a capital letter?

- Did I end each sentence with a punctuation mark?

- Did I spell each word correctly?

- Is my piece's internal punctuation correct?

Proofreading Checklist

- Have I said what I wanted to say?

- Am I pleased with my work?

- Do I need to revise or edit any further?

- Where am I going to take this piece from here?

Sharing, Conferencing Checklist

- What do I want to accomplish by sharing this piece?

- What are the results of my conference?

For Listeners Checklist

- What did I really like about this piece?

- What can I suggest to the writer that would help improve this piece?

Final Copy Checklist
- I legibly rewrite my revised and edited piccc.

- Is my piece written in paragraphs with margins?

- Is my piece dated?

- Did I reread my piece in my head?

POETRY: The writer's intent is to express, in poetic form, feelings, ideas, or experiences to which others can relate.

Brainstorming Checklist
- What words create an image that portrays the feelings and ideas I want expressed in my poem?

- What type of poem do I want to write?

Writing Draft 1 Checklist
- On paper, I list the image words that came to mind while brainstorming.

- Using my list of images, and my knowledge of the elements of poetry, I write a poem that clearly, creatively expresses my ideas, thoughts, and feelings.

Revising Checklist
- Does my poem have a clear theme?

- Do my words create vivid images?

- Have I used figurative language?

- Is the rhythm of my poem consistent with the poem's theme?

Editing Checklist
- Have I punctuated the poem in the most effective way?

- Have I made use of blank space?

- Have I spelled the words correctly or used poetic license?

Proofreading Checklist
- Have I expressed what I want to express?

- Am I pleased with my work?

- Do I need to revise or edit any further?

- Where am I going with this piece from here?

Sharing, Conferencing Checklist
- What do I want to accomplish by sharing this poem?

- What are the results of my conference?

For Listeners Checklist
- What did I really like about this poem?

- What can I suggest to the writer that would help improve this poem?

Final Copy Checklist
- I legibly rewrite my revised and edited poem.

- Is my poem dated?

- Did I reread the poem aloud or in my head to listen to the sound and rhythm of the words?

Reading

Another helpful teaching aid is the Self-Instructional (SI) Reading Wheel that was developed by teacher Krista Aaron for her gifted class.

In Chapters 6 and 7 we discussed reciprocal teaching and provided an example of how this method can be implemented in a classroom. Visual reminders are extremely important to suggest to students the componential segments of reciprocal teaching. Teacher Jo Ann Moore placed reading reminders on pennants (page 184). She reports that they have been very helpful to remind the students and herself to employ these strategies of prediction, clarification, question-generating, and summarization. Of course each of these four processes must be modeled by the teacher and peers, practiced, explained, and cued. Techniques for accomplishing this were presented previously in Chapters 6 and 7.

Mathematics Word Problems

Teacher Pamela Moosmann uses cognitive monitoring skills to help students solve mathematics word problems. Teachers, parents, and students report that word problems cause a great deal of difficulty for students. One of the reasons is because students lack problem-solving process skills. Using four light bulbs (page 184) as visual stimuli students are taught to (1) identify the problem, (2) plan the solution, (3) solve the problem, and (4) check the solution for accuracy.

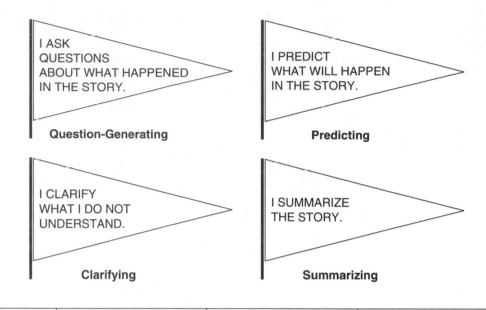

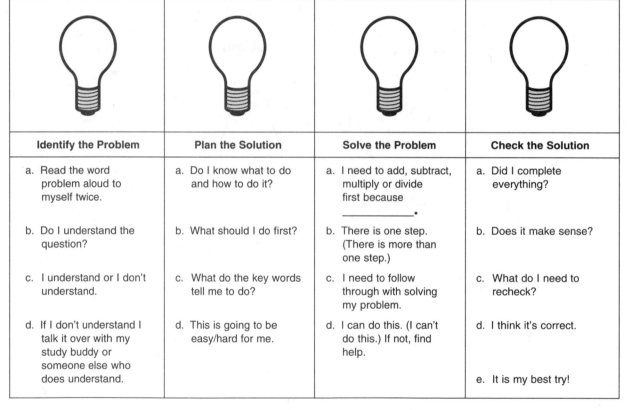

Identify the Problem	Plan the Solution	Solve the Problem	Check the Solution
a. Read the word problem aloud to myself twice.	a. Do I know what to do and how to do it?	a. I need to add, subtract, multiply or divide first because _____.	a. Did I complete everything?
b. Do I understand the question?	b. What should I do first?	b. There is one step. (There is more than one step.)	b. Does it make sense?
c. I understand or I don't understand.	c. What do the key words tell me to do?	c. I need to follow through with solving my problem.	c. What do I need to recheck?
d. If I don't understand I talk it over with my study buddy or someone else who does understand.	d. This is going to be easy/hard for me.	d. I can do this. (I can't do this.) If not, find help.	d. I think it's correct.
			e. It is my best try!

The previous section of this chapter dealt with using metacognitive strategies in content area teaching. Metacognitive strategies included the following: peer modeling, role play, cueing using photographs with accompanying written self-verbalizations, self-questioning, pictoral cues, teacher made posters, reading wheel with self-questions, visual reminders to use the reciprocal teaching processes, scaffolded instruction, and formal evaluations. Content area examples were presented to outline prototypic ways to implement these metacognitive strategies. However, as was emphasized previously, these strategies are not particular to a certain subject area and may be adapted for use across the curriculum.

SUMMARY

Two main sections appear in this chapter: metacognitive strategies for (1) promoting efficient school work habits and (2) teaching in the content areas. Suggestions were provided by classroom teachers. It was noted that these ideas were built around the needs of a specific group of students and are therefore limited in generalizability, unless your population of students is very similar to the classroom teachers' students. Nevertheless, these metacognitive strategies were implemented in an ecologically-valid context since some of the parameters surrounding classroom teaching are common to most classrooms (e.g., interruptions during the day). In addition, the strategies may serve as a general conceptual springboard from which you may develop your own metacognitive teaching procedures, specific to your own group of students. Some of the strategies presented in this chapter are as follows: modeling, role play, cueing, self-questioning, checklists, and the use of children's literature. Manning's classroom model (1991) of cognitive self-instruction (CSI) was followed by a majority of the teachers: teacher and peer modeling, student practice, and teacher and student cueing. In addition, Meichenbaum's types of internal dialogue (1977) (e.g., problem-defining, attention focusing, self-guiding, self-correcting, self-coping, and self-reinforcing) also served as a basis for many of the strategies. Often, the teachers employed the ASK, TELL, TRY, CHECK, and CHEER self-talk series developed by Manning (Manning, White, & Daugherty, 1994) as a way to explicitly and appropriately teach a metacognitive problem-solving series via verbal self-guidance for learners in a regular classroom setting.

CHAPTER 9

Applying Metacognitive Strategies for Students' Personal Growth

OVERVIEW

In this chapter, three main sections: (1) Problem solving, decision making, and goal setting; (2) Learning to use healthy self-talk; and (3) Addressing social issues, serve as the organizers for thinking about metacognition in the affective domain. In the first section dealing with problem solving, decision making, and goal setting; metacognitive strategics include teacher-developed informed training lessons that explicitly address the metacognitive language for decision making, student role-play, posters, dramatic play written and acted out using middle school students, S.O.S. (Solving it Ourselves) stations with accompanying worksheets, Action Plan worksheet, and the goal story interview. These strategies can be applied in many other contexts, and are not limited to the ones presented in this chapter. In the second section, learning how to use healthy self-talk, strategies include modeling, practice sheets for changing unhelpful self-talk to helpful self-talk, self-talk journals, using helpful self-talk affirmations for anger control, and children's literature to promote helpful self-talk. The final section, addressing social issues, includes such strategies as appropriate classroom rules and procedures, adding self-talk to existing classroom management plans, posters, bulletin board displays, class and individual cue cards, club membership, time-out guidelines incorporating self-talk to promote a plan of improvement, weekly conduct report sheet, cue cards addressing test anxiety, and a class play integrating self-talk awareness and regulation to help children deal with divorce.

Teachers provided the ideas for each of the strategies presented in this chapter. They developed the ideas, tried them with their students, and evaluated their effectiveness. These metacognitive strategies have the potential to improve students' problem solving, decision making, and goal setting performance, as well as improve their self-esteem, stress levels, health, behaviors, and interpersonal skills when self-talk progresses from unhelpful to more helpful self-guidance. In addition students' positive adjustment to social maladies such as exaggerated competition, test anxiety, and divorce are possible outcomes of implementing the educational philosophy espoused by the teachers in this chapter.

Self-Questions

1. *Knowledge.* Name one way to foster helpful self-talk for students.

2. *Comprehension.* Explain the reason for incorporating self-talk strategies with the usual classroom management ideas.

3. *Application.* Use the five steps for helping students learn healthy self-talk as the basis for a lesson plan in your teaching and/or learning area.

4. *Analysis.* Discuss the pros and cons of the Decision Making Self-Questions. Develop a list of at least five specific classroom purposes for these self-questions.

5. *Synthesis.* Write an action research proposal for studying the use of metacognitive awareness and self-regulated learning strategies for dealing with important social issues (e.g., AIDS education, drug awareness).

6. *Evaluation.* Support or refute the use of healthy self-talk to improve behavior, feelings, attitudes, stress levels, and/or interpersonal skills.

PROBLEM SOLVING, DECISION MAKING, AND GOAL SETTING

One of the important goals of classroom instruction is to engender sound decision making skills, excellent problem solving, and realistic goal setting. Especially due to life-saving decisions related to AIDS, drugs, and alcohol abuse it is critical for the youngsters of today to have unwavering decision making power. Vickie Davis, a middle school teacher developed and tested lesson plans for using facilitative self-talk to help middle school students set goals and make decisions. Also included are decision making self-questions.

LESSON PLANS FOR DECISION MAKING AND GOAL SETTING/ USING METACOGNITION

GOAL: Students will understand how to use self-talk to help them set goals and make decisions.

Session 1: The students are introduced to the term goal setting and how it relates to decision making. Students are asked to set a short term goal that can be accomplished during the current six-week period. Have them set their goal by using the following self-talk model.

Question 1: What is something I would like to accomplish this six weeks? (Example: Make 8th grade basketball team.)

Question 2: What are 3 steps I can take to help me accomplish my goal? (Example: Practice my skills, eat healthy food, get right amount of sleep.)

Question 3: What is a way I can know if I am accomplishing my goal? (Example: Keep diary of practice, diet, sleep.)

Session 2: Have students make a list of any decision they can remember making in the recent past. Have the students look at this list and ask themselves "Which of these decisions did I make unconsciously or automatically, and which ones did I make consciously (i.e., use mental deliberation)? Have students write down some of the questions they may have asked themselves when trying to make the conscious decisions.

Session 3: Introduce terms related to goal setting and decision making: short term goal, long term goal, decision, value. Introduce students to 5 types of decision makers: compliant, impulsive, fatalistic, systematic, delayed. Give examples of self-talk used by each of these types of decision makers.

Compliant: I don't want anyone mad with me so I'll just go along with their decision.

Impulsive: This is what I feel like doing, so I'm going to do it.

Fatalistic: I know whatever I decide will be wrong, so I'll just choose the easiest one.

Systematic: I need to write down all my choices and then decide which will really be best for me.

Delayed: I don't feel like deciding now. I'll wait until tomorrow.

Have students give their own examples of when they have personally used these types and give examples of self-talk used in each instance.

Session 4:   Teacher introduces decision making model and self-talk questions used with this model.

Step 1:   Know your values. Self-question—What are the values that are most important to me in this decision?

Step 2:   Know goals. Self-question—What are my main goals or goal in making this decision?

Step 3:   Know choices. Self-question—What are all the possible choices I have when making this decision?

Step 4:   Seek information. Self-question—Where can I get the information I need to make this decision?

Step 5:   Know advantages and disadvantages of each choice. Self-question—What are the advantages and disadvantages of each of my possibilities?

Step 6:   Narrow alternatives, make choice. Self-question—Looking at the choices I have, which one best meets my needs at this time?

Step 7:   Assess decision. Self-question—Are things working out the way I want them to? Do I need to change my decision to another alternative?

Session 5:   Have students implement decision making model using teacher example involving different areas of students' lives. (Example: social, family, education).

Example 1:   You have two major projects due on the same day. Each project will require about equal amounts of time to do correctly. In one subject you have a solid A, but retention of that grade would depend on this project. In the other class you have a C, but this project's grade will raise or lower your average. Which will you spend the most time on?

Example 2:   You know for a fact that your best friend's boyfriend/girlfriend is planning on breaking up with him/her. You are also friends with the boyfriend/girlfriend and he/she has asked you not to tell your best friend.

Example 3:   Your parents are going out for a late evening. Your older brother has invited several friends over for a small party which is against parental rules. If your parents find out, you will also be in trouble for not having told them. If you tell, you will destroy any chance of getting along with your brother.

Example 4:   Your sixteenth birthday is approaching. Your parents have told you they will buy you a used car, but you will have to furnish money for gas and insurance costs which will necessitate a part-time job. The college you are planning on attending has very rigid admission requirements. You are afraid a part-time job will interfere with your studies.

Session 6:   Have students work individually to write their own decision examples. Have them share their examples in small groups and work through the Decision Model Self-Questions together.

The following list of questions can be used in a variety of ways. Teachers will be able to generate ideas that are not presented here. However, several suggestions are (1) to use these self-questions as a bulletin board or other room display, (2) to separate the self-questions, and give one question each to small groups of students, and (3) ask each group to develop a decision making scenario germane to their lives and then generate a list of possible answers for their self-question.

DECISION MAKING SELF-QUESTIONS

Question 1:   What are the values that are most important in this decision?

Question 2:   What goal am I trying to accomplish with this decision?

Question 3:   What are all the possible choices that I have?

Question 4:   Where can I get the information I need to make this decision?

Question 5:   What are the advantages and disadvantages of each of my possibilities?

Question 6:   Looking at the choices, which one best meets my needs at this time?

Question 7:   Are things working out the way I want them to? Do I need to change my decision to another alternative?

Another elementary classroom teacher, Jane E. Roehm used metacognition to address conflict resolution between, among, and within students. Ms. Roehm tells about her own experience.

CONFLICT RESOLUTION

In search for solutions, children often come to me to solve their problems, whether it be a problem they are having with someone else or a problem they are having themselves. In an attempt to assist individual students in solving their conflicts, I try to ask them questions that will result in the students finding their own resolutions. When children are fighting among themselves, I try to act as a mediator by facilitating communication between the children which will hopefully result in a meaningful resolution. This process, though probably more effective than traditional authoritative methods of conflict resolution, can be extremely time consuming.

I believe that the development of conflict resolution skills is important and necessary. I feel that children can be taught these skills so as to utilize them in the school setting as well as outside the learning environment. I have developed a program that teaches students a strategy involving them in their own problem solving without an external party.

In my classroom there is an area specified as the S.O.S. corner. This stands for "solving it ourselves." If children are having a problem with a classmate they go to the S.O.S. corner and complete the form "Solving it with Someone Else." Please refer to this form below. The framework of the questions on the form is based on Meichenbaum's categories (1977): problem defining, attention focusing, self-guiding, self-coping, and self-reinforcing. Upon completion of the form they read over their responses and decide if the problem can be solved by themselves, or if they need to involve the other person. If they approach the other person, they share with them their responses to the questions as well as their plan towards a solution. At this point, the problem may be resolved or it may not be. If the problem remains unsolved, then the other person involved completes a form and shares his/her responses with the other person. Hopefully, with the communication of their concerns and needs through "I" messages, they can begin to negotiate towards meeting those needs, keeping in mind, that this involves give and take by both parties.

Name _____ Date _____

Solving it with Someone Else

Define

1. What is the problem I am having?

_____
_____
_____
_____

Focus

2. Who does my problem involve?

_____
_____
_____
_____

Guide

3. I need to talk to them in a positive and productive manner. What "I" message can I give them?

_____
_____
_____

Cope

4. It may be difficult, but I know I can work things out. I just need to.

_____
_____
_____

Reinforce

5. Way to go! I solved my problem. This is how things worked out:

_____
_____
_____

Name _____ Date _____

Solving it with Myself

1. What is the problem I am having?

Define

_____

_____

_____

_____

2. My problem involves only me.

Focus

_____

_____

_____

_____

3. I need to get back on track. What "I" message can I give myself?

Guide

_____

_____

_____

4. It may be difficult, but I know I can work things out. I just need to.

Cope

_____

_____

_____

5. Way to go! I solved my problem. This is how things worked out:

Reinforce

_____

_____

_____

If children are having a problem that involves only themselves, they can go to the S.O.S. corner in an attempt to come up with a solution. These problems may be: concentrating on their work; talking a lot; shouting out answers or not listening to directions, just to name a few. Children complete the form, "solving it with myself." Please refer to this form above. In problem-defining, children are asked to write the problem that they are experiencing. Attention-focusing involves identifying who all is involved in the problem. Next, in an attempt to get themselves back on track, children write a self-guiding statement that consists of an "I" message. This puts the responsibility of problem resolution on the child—"What can I do to solve this problem?", at which point, they may choose to implement one of the many ideas that we have brainstormed as a class (cue cards or checklists). A self-coping statement recognizes the difficulty children might have in solving the problem by allowing them to write their frustration followed by an encouraging, " . . . but I can do it!", statement. Finally, self-reinforcement recognizes and rewards children for working hard to accomplish a resolution. This final reinforcing statement assumes that the problem will not go unsolved, and that they are responsible for its resolution.

As a classroom teacher, I strongly believe that children are capable of developing the skills needed to facilitate their own conflict resolution. However, to effectively accomplish this, they must be taught explicitly the skills needed as well as be provided with the time to practice. I would like to see conflict resolution become a part of the regular curriculum, and made available to all students.

Problem Solving: Action Plan Worksheet

Teacher Beth Peterson developed a worksheet for students to use to develop their own action plans when students are solving their own problems. This worksheet may also be given to students during time-out to help them focus on solving the problem, rather than feeling that they are being punished. Time-out should be nonpunitive time for students and teachers to deliberate on ways to improve behavior, thinking, and/or feelings. The Action Plan Worksheet is provided on page 193.

Goal Setting: Goal Story Interview

At times all of us have had goals that we are not able to obtain for one reason or another. Unfortunately in education we often do not prepare students or ourselves to deal with goals that are thwarted or abandoned by us. The goal story interview technique is an attempt to help students prepare for the achievement of goals and the blocking of our goals via self-talk skills of coping and reinforcing. The goal story interview was first introduced by Goldman (1982) and modified by Manning (1991) to include a self-talk component. The goal-setting process is outlined here and continues on page 194.

MY GOAL STORY INTERVIEW

1. What is one thing that I really want and why do I want it?

   _____

   _____

2. What is my plan of action to get it? Write the plan on the lines below.

   _____

   _____

   _____

   _____

   _____

3. Now an obstacle blocks my efforts to get what I want. Rats! What is the obstacle?

   _____

   _____

Name _____   Date _____

ACTION PLAN

What is my problem?

My problem is:

What can I do?

My plan is:

Am I using my plan?

I am:

4. How can I alter my plan so I can overcome the obstacle and realize my dreams? How can I use my self-talk skills of reinforcing to obtain my goal?

_____

_____

_____

_____

_____

_____

_____

5. If I cannot overcome the obstacle, how can I use my self-talk skills of coping to make me feel better?

_____

_____

_____

_____

_____

_____

_____

The next section will provide classroom suggestions for learning to use healthy self-talk. Children do not automatically learn facilitative ways to verbally guide their own thinking and behaving. Some students will possess a better repertoire of focusing, guiding, coping, and reinforcing self-talk than others. This is most likely due to the former group of students growing up in environments where the adults and older peers modeled these more healthy types of self-talk. In addition, these verbal role models scaffolded the learning of their children/peers using patience, encouragement, and detailed focusing, guiding, and coping social speech. As these children internalized the language surrounding them, they developed their own healthy repertoire of self-guiding speech. Unfortunately too many children live in homes where verbal interaction is minimal and when it does occur, the linguistic interaction is characterized by impatience, discouragement, pessimism, and put-downs. Such children are in desperate need of high quality verbal exchanges; whereby, their cognitive and affective learning is guided with acceptance, patience, and explicit, clear explanations. This skill is critical to learning and to positive intrapersonal and interpersonal skills.

LEARNING TO USE HEALTHY SELF-TALK

Just as adults use helpful self-talk to impact favorably on stress levels, interpersonal skills, feelings, attitudes, behaviors, and health (refer to Chapters 1–3), children can be taught and can learn to use helpful self-talk to keep anger under control, to overcome fears, to make friends, and to live a healthy life (Isaacs & Ritchey, 1989). Self-talk for more cognitively-oriented learning (Chapter 8) is also encouraged.

Self-talk for the affective domain is a means for directing ourselves to relate positively to ourselves and to others. Many of our feelings and attitudes are conditioned by the things we say to ourselves whether or not we even realize that we are talking to ourselves. Findings have shown that self-talk can be altered in adults and children to enhance lives and help solve annoying problems.

Childhood is an ideal time to teach self-talk techniques. This is due to the fact that many life-long patterns of coping skills are established early and are more resistant to change as we age. Before the age of three or four, it is best to teach helpful, coping self-talk through adult and older sibling models. Modeling of facilitative self-talk is a key throughout the teaching and learning of metacognition. As the child exhibits awareness of speech-to-self, then steps for improving the quality of self-talk may be implemented.

Several activities that help students learn facilitative self-talk are provided below. Please refer to exercises 1, 2, and 3. These are excellent activities for pairs of students or small groups of students, no more than three or four. For exercise number 1, as a team they rewrite the unhelpful self-talk into helpful versions. In so doing, their metacognitive awareness is heightened and they begin to notice their unhelpful self-talk. In addition, self-regulation skills of metacognition are more probable, because the students have engaged in the thinking process, with peers, of changing this unhelpful self-talk to helpful self-talk. Exercise numbers 2 and 3 illustrate two ideas for self-talk journal pages that may be copied for students or used as a model, from which you may wish to modify and develop your own self-talk journal pages.

EXERCISE 1

Name: _____   "☺ I can change my unhelpful talk!"

CHANGING UNHELPFUL SELF-TALK

Each of the following statements was made by a student. Each is an UNHELPFUL statement; it does not help the student to solve the problem. Re-write each statement as a HELPFUL one.

1. Rats! I missed another multiplication problem. I never get them right.

   _____
   _____

2. Nobody likes me. I'll never get any friends at this school.

   _____
   _____

3. Science is stupid. I won't ever make a good grade in this dumb subject.

   _____
   _____

4. This work problem is too hard. I just never get these!

   _____
   _____

5. I'll never get this project completed. I don't have enough time.

   _____
   _____

6. I can't understand how to find that adjective in this sentence. I'll never learn this.

_____

_____

7. The people around me always talk. They never let me finish my work. It's their fault I always get in trouble.

_____

_____

8. I was terrible in kickball today. I think I'm the worst player in the school and I hate that.

_____

_____

9. This test is dumb.

_____

_____

10. I can't do this.

_____

_____

11. Why study? I always fail science tests.

_____

_____

12. When it comes to sports, I'm a spaz.

_____

_____

13. I'll never catch up. I quit.

_____

_____

14. People don't listen to me so why should I join the group.

_____

_____

15. I write so slow I'll never finish this dumb report.

_____

_____

16. My parents never let me do anything. They think I'm still a little kid.

_____

_____

17. I would like mathematics if I had a better teacher.

_____

_____

EXERCISE 2

SELF-TALK JOURNAL

Directions: During the day complete the chart below. As you use self-talk write down exactly what you are saying. Be sure to include the situation that caused you to use the self-talk.

Date: _____   Situation: _____

Self-Talk Response

_____

_____

_____

_____

Date: _____   Situation: _____

Self-Talk Response

_____

_____

_____

_____

Date: _____   Situation: _____

Self-Talk Response

_____

_____

_____

_____

EXERCISE 3

SELF TALK JOURNAL

Option B:

Directions: Describe five situations that cause self-talk. For each situation give both positive and negative examples of what you say.

1. Situation: _____

    Positive: Negative:

    _____   _____
    _____   _____
    _____   _____

2. Situation: _____

    Positive: Negative:

    _____   _____
    _____   _____
    _____   _____

3. Situation: _____

    Positive: Negative:

    _____   _____
    _____   _____
    _____   _____

4. Situation: _____

    Positive: Negative:

    _____   _____
    _____   _____
    _____   _____

5. Situation: _____

    Positive: Negative:

    _____   _____
    _____   _____
    _____   _____

Helpful Self-Talk for Anger Control

As students begin formal schooling, even at the preschool level, teachers usually attempt to help them find positive ways to deal with angry feelings. One way to accomplish this is to help students develop an inner voice that will calm them and help them think of alternatives to physical aggression or yelling. One plausible explanation that explains why children continue to have problems with anger and aggression after the preschool years, is due to inadequacies in helpful self-talk and a resulting positive inner voice. Studies consistently indicate that aggressive, angry children are also the most unpopular students with their peers.

Children's Stories to Introduce Helpful Self-Talk

One method for learning helpful self-talk is through children's stories, focusing on a new way to talk to yourself to cope with frustration. Teachers may use stories in any manner they normally use children's literature: to introduce a new concept, teach a concept, and/or reinforce a concept. The story (pages 200–202) is entitled "Chelsea Learns to Talk to Self." The teacher is Debbie Wood and she developed this story for her kindergarten students to introduce the idea of talking to yourself in a kind and helpful manner.

ADDRESSING SOCIAL ISSUES

Metacognitive Ways to Encourage Adherence to Class Rules and Procedures

In most classrooms today teachers display the classroom rules. Over the past 10 years as we have supervised student teachers and visited in numerous classrooms, we developed a habit of reading and evaluating these posted rules. These displays range from downright hostile (e.g., Keep your mouth shut!) to very positive (e.g., Be a good friend!). Some are too general for children to really understand what is being requested. For example, many children, especially young children, have not defined what it means to be a good friend. On pages 203–204 are listed some examples of exemplary sets of rules. Note that they meet the following criteria for "good rules":

1. Written in first person

2. Written in present tense

3. Specific as to expectations

4. Express unconditional regard

5. Express positive and high expectations

6. Number and content of rules match appropriately with the age and developmental level of the students.

    a. 3–5 year olds = two to three rules

    b. 6–10 year olds = three to five rules

    c. 11–15 year olds = five to ten rules

The next set of rules (page 203) seems to meet all of the criteria mentioned above. They were written by Krista Aaron for 12-year-old, gifted students. They can be modified to meet other teachers' needs.

CHELSEA LEARNS TO TALK TO SELF
By Debbie Wood

Hi! I'm Dolly Dingo and this is my big, black dog, Chelsea. I just reminded Chelsea that tomorrow is her first day of kindergarten. Chelsea is scared—she keeps begging me to let her stay home.

When I asked Chelsea why she didn't want to go to school, she said, "I am too big! I won't follow the rules—I don't even know what rules are. No one will like me—I'll do everything wrong!" When I heard that, I told Chelsea, "Well, if you keep talking to yourself that way, you probably will have a terrible time in kindergarten!"

I explained to Chelsea that all the unhelpful self-talk she is using is what is making her feel so scared and bad inside. I told her she needed a new script. That means she needs to change all the bad, unhelpful things she is saying to herself into good, helpful things. I promised her that this would make her feel better and could help her to behave.

I raise my hand and wait to be called on.

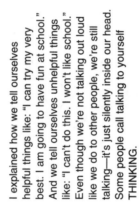

I explained how we tell ourselves helpful things like: "I can try my very best. I am going to have fun at school." And we tell ourselves unhelpful things like: "I can't do this. I won't like school." Even though we're not talking out loud like we do to other people, we're still talking—it's just silently inside our head. Some people call talking to yourself THINKING.

I listen and follow directions.

Chelsea didn't know what in the world I meant by talking to herself. She said she never talked to herself, but I told her everyone does.

Chelsea practiced saying good, helpful things to herself. She said, "I can try my very best and I will make lots of friends." And you know what?

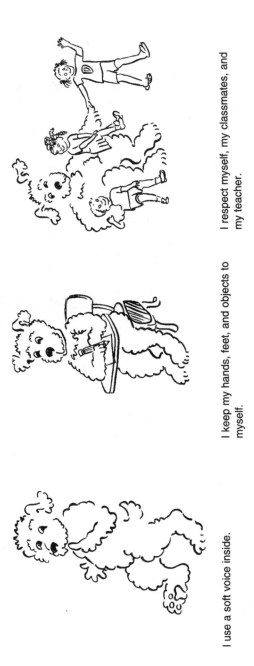

I use a soft voice inside.

I keep my hands, feet, and objects to myself.

I respect myself, my classmates, and my teacher.

Chelsea felt better right away. She said lots of good things to herself that first day of school. And you know what? She had a great day! She had an easy time following the rules and she made lots of new friends. Good ol' Chelsea.

P.S. Chelsea wants *you* to learn to talk to *yourself* in good ways. She says it will help you to follow your rules and make new friends. Remember, if it gets hard—look at Chelsea—it helped her.

MS. AARON'S CLASS RULES

I am eager to learn.

I pay attention, follow directions, and am a good listener.

I complete all of my assignments and make up missed work within a week.

I read 30 minutes a day.

I cheerfully do my work without complaining or eye-rolling.

This is my room. I take care of the materials in here.

I respect my classmates, my teacher, and myself.

This is a GOOD day.

Most rules that we have read in classrooms seem to focus on individual self-control and self-regulation of behavior (e.g., Wait my turn.). This promotion of independence is a worthwhile goal for education; however, we should not forget to encourage healthy interdependence habits as well. Skills of independence may be prerequisite to skills of interdependence. To explicate, children may have to exhibit sufficient self-regulation before they are able to work with others, using high levels of interdependence. We all know that we work alone sometimes and with others at times. Quality of life requires both skills of self-regulation and interdependence. One kindergarten teacher believes that a focus on interdependence should begin early and should become a heavy emphasis throughout school. She believes, as we do, that looking out for each other, supporting one another, and putting others first a great deal of the time have not received a fair share of attention. In fact we too often encourage competition: every "man" for himself, and being better than someone else. This kindergarten teacher's rules are as follows:

SUGGESTIONS FOR LIVING TOGETHER IN THIS CLASSROOM

I help my friends by:

1. being quiet while they are trying to work.

2. sharing my materials.

3. teaching them when I know how to do something that they don't.

Mrs. Bennett's rules are simple, but powerful. She is directly fostering interdependence and the value of cooperation. If her line of thinking were continued throughout school, we feel strongly that there would most likely be less violence in our schools today.

Teacher Nancy Monohan calls her reminders *Boosters*. She emphasizes the responsibility of students to say these "boosters" to themselves. Note that after each reminder she explains what self-talk to use and when to use it. (See Fluff's Script). In this way she has correctly incorporated informed training techniques (see Chapter 5) with the explanation of her classroom rules and procedures.

FLUFF'S PLAN

There once was a bunny named Fluffy
Whose days at school were quite rough
"Sit down!" "Be Quiet!" "Listen up!" he'd hear
But his efforts were never enough!

So then Fluffy decided to try
a plan to help him "fly!
"Fly through his day in a positive way
without ever having to cry!

He wrote his plan down here for you
so that you might realize too
that you, can help make a day that
is great by the things you say and do!

FLUFF'S SCRIPT

Hi! I'm Fluff! I am going to tell you about my special "boosters" that help me to have a great day at school. A "booster" is something that I say to myself quietly that helps me to remember how to act at school. I say them to myself at different times during the day to check and make sure I am working hard and following directions. Here is my first "booster."

1. *I work quietly and until I am finished.* I say this to myself when I am working to make sure I'm not bothering my friends and so I can be proud of myself when I finish all of my work. My second "booster" is:

2. *I keep my hands, feet, and objects to myself.* I say this to myself when I feel like I need to touch or hit someone, or when I see others fighting. It helps keep me out of trouble. My third "booster" is:

3. *I listen carefully.* I ask myself if I am listening carefully during lessons and when my teacher is giving directions to make sure I understand what she is saying. If I don't I can ask a question. The next "booster" is:

4. *I raise my hand and get a signal to speak.* I say this to myself when I have something to share out loud so I don't talk out and interrupt my teacher or a friend. I also remember to do this when my teacher asks questions so my friends have time to think about the answer. The fifth "booster" is:

5. *I walk quietly and calmly in the halls.* This is what I say to myself when I am walking in the halls so I don't disturb others who are in their classrooms trying to work. They may be taking a test. The last "booster" is:

6. *I use good manners at all times.* I say this to myself when I am in the restroom or at lunch to make sure that I am being polite. (There will be discussion with the children after each "booster" is presented.)

There they are! My six "boosters." Saying them to myself during the day is a great way to stay on track and do a good job at school. I brought you these posters to keep on the wall in your room to help you remember my six "boosters." Say them to yourself over and over during the day and if you do a good job working and following directions you will get to be in my special club, *Bunny's Booster Club*! All you have to do is say my "boosters" to yourself and have a great day!

As students are taught the rules through teacher explanation, modeling, peer demonstration, practice, and feedback (Evertson et al., 1989), then they are also taught self-monitoring skills along with this instruction. Ideas for doing this were presented in Chapter 5.

A number of teachers use the idea of a red light to help children see in a more concrete way the consequences of not following the classroom rules and procedures. A description of how this works is below:

**BEHAVIOR MANAGEMENT SYSTEMS (INCLUDING SELF-TALK) FOR
ELEMENTARY STUDENTS**

Students begin the day with their name arrow on green light.

If students must be reminded more than twice to get themselves "in control" and to remember the rules, then they must move their arrow from green light to yellow light.

If students must be reminded again after their name arrow is on yellow light then they must put their arrow on red light and go to the time-out chair. Students write their own plan of improvement. They may return to the group once they have written and committed themselves to their own plan.

At the end of each week the teacher sends home a sheet noting students' behavior for each day during the week.

Addition of Self-Talk

At the beginning of the year when the teacher teaches the children the behavior management system, she will also have the children learn appropriate self-talk for each "light" through role play.

If the situation calls for a different self-talk sentence (not included in those sentences already practiced by the class), then the teacher will help the students develop a more related, appropriate statement.

Green Light

When students see their name arrow on green light, they can tell themselves positive statements, such as the ones listed below:

Examples for "green light"

I am in control of myself.

I respect others space.

I can control my voice.

I know how to use class materials.

Yellow Light

When students must put their name arrow on yellow light, they say to self "yellow light" sentences or another sentence that may be more appropriate for a particular situation. These statements (sentences) focus on the child's control of a particular misbehavior and helps to avoid placement on "red light" and in time-out.

Examples for "yellow light"

I need to slow down.

I need to work quietly in my area.

I need to be respectful of others.

I am going to ignore those who distract me.

Red Light

When students must put their name arrow on red light, they go to the "time-out" chair and say to self "red light" sentences or another sentence that may be more appropriate for a particular situation. These statements (sentences) focus on increasing the students' positive feelings about themselves and on encouraging them to regroup and return to the group with a fresh resolve to behave in a controlled manner.

Examples for "red light"

I can control myself: others are trying to learn.

I will start over again.

I will have a good rest of the day.

Worksheet

Teacher Elinor Hale developed a worksheet for students to complete while in time-out. This worksheet helps students take responsibility for their classroom behavior. The student who is regrouping in a time-out station is using the time-out in a productive manner: making an improvement plan. Ms. Hale combined a baseball theme into her overall management system.

Working My Way To A HOMERUN!

1. What is my problem?

   _____
   _____
   _____

2. This is my plan for changing my behavior:

   _____
   _____
   _____

3. How can I do it? Be sure to include my improved self-talk.

   _____
   _____
   _____

4. Am I using my plan?

   _____

5. How did I do?

   _____
   _____
   _____

I, (the teacher), promise to help, (student's name), work out his/her plan for behavior change, to the best of my abilities.

_____ teacher's signature

I, (the student), promise to try my best to work out my plan and change what I recognize as negative behavior.

_____ student's signature

_____
Date

Teacher Beth Peterson created a Weekly Conduct Report Sheet that is a self-evaluative assessment. Students in grades three through seven may find this a helpful tool to learn self-management skills.

Name _____

WEEKLY CONDUCT REPORT SHEET
Please sign and return at the beginning of each week.

When three or more checks are earned for any one descriptor across the six weeks period, that area will be credited on the student's report card. A checkmark indicates that the student believes that he or she successfully accomplished that descriptor for that week.

	1	2	3	4	5	6
I used self-control.						
I worked independently.						
I had necessary school materials						
I returned materials sent home.						
I had a positive attitude about my school work.						
I controlled my talking.						
I used good manners in the cafeteria.						
I played and worked well in a group.						
I listened and followed directions.						
I finished my work on time.						
I used my materials and time wisely.						
I talked to myself in helpful ways.						
Signatures: Student _____ Teacher _____ Parent _____						

Test Anxiety

A middle school teacher Myrtle Cook was concerned about the high anxiety of her students prior to and during tests. She discussed her concern with the students and they role-played helpful self-talk before and during tests. The students who had excellent self-talk coping skills were paired with their more anxious peers. The better "copers" talked about how they prepared for tests and mentally readied themselves to handle the testing situations. The class helped Ms. Cook develop a set of cue cards that reflected their cognitive and metacognitive strategies.

Divorce

The last strategy in the "Social Issues" section of Chapter 9 is a play written and directed by Cynthia Darsch, third grade teacher. Mrs. Darsch is concerned about the growing number of children from dysfunctional families. She quickly adds that not all children of divorce and single-parent homes are troubled. This is often due to how the parents and others prepare and nurture their children through family discord, such as a divorce. Mrs. Darsch wanted an educational strategy for directly confronting the confusion and anger of children when their families experience troublesome times. She chose the issue of divorce since approximately one out of two children in her class are from divorced homes. She interviewed the children about their thoughts on divorce. From their responses, she, with the help of her students wrote the following play. They incorporated the idea of self-talk for coping with divorce.

METACOGNITION FOR DEALING WITH DIVORCE

Scene 1:

NARRATOR:	This play is titled Coping Self-Talk for Dealing with Divorce. As the scene opens up, we find Taylor on the playground at school.
NOTE:	1st boy and 2nd boy represent Taylor's unhelpful self-talk. They wear cards tied with yarn that say "Unhelpful Self-Talk" to remind those watching the play that they are not "real characters", but exist only in the mind of Taylor.
	(Taylor sits with head down, knees drawn up to chin; 2 boys (Taylor's self-talk) enter talking, pause, and then approach Taylor.)
1ST BOY: (UNHELPFUL SELF-TALK, UST)	"Let's see who we can pick on today? I know, let's pick on Taylor. His parents are getting a divorce!"
2ND BOY: (UST)	"Hey look! There he is sitting all alone on the seesaw. Come on let's go!"
	(They circle around Taylor, 1st boy with back to Taylor, arms crossed, over his shoulder.)
1ST BOY: (UST)	"It's all your fault, you know. If you acted better, your parents wouldn't be getting a divorce."
2ND BOY: (UST)	(laughingly) "Yea! that's why your Mom and Dad are always fighting; cause you're always in trouble at school."
1ST BOY: (UST)	"Yea, they probably don't even love you anymore."
	(Jill enters with a ball in hand)
JILL:	(from doorway) "Hey, Taylor come and play kickball with us! We need you on our team."
2ND BOY: (UST)	Naw, he doesn't feel like playing or doing anything!"
TAYLOR:	"I don't feel like it."
JILL:	(approaches Taylor) "Come on Taylor! You are a great kicker! You always kick home-runs!"
1ST BOY: (UST)	"Yea (laughing) except at home!"
JILL:	"What's the matter, Taylor?" (sits down beside Taylor)
2ND BOY: (UST)	"He's a loser! That's what!"
TAYLOR:	"I'm just a loser! I'm always getting into trouble and now Dad say he's going away."
JILL:	"Where's he going?"
TAYLOR:	"My parents are getting a divorce and my Dad's not going to live with us anymore."
	(Teacher enters)
MRS. D:	"Jill, Taylor, why aren't you playing kickball with the others?"
JILL:	"I'm trying to get Taylor to play with us, Mrs. Darsch; but he's sad today. He doesn't feel like doing anything!"
1ST BOY: (UST)	"Yea, cause he's not good at anything!"
2ND BOY: (UST)	"That's right (slaps Taylor on the shoulder, smiles at 1st boy)

MRS. D: "Jill, would you run over and see how the kickball game is coming? I want to talk to Taylor for a minute."

JILL: "Sure, Mrs. Darsch, see you later, Taylor."

(Jill exits, Mrs. D. sits down beside Taylor)

MRS. D: "What's upsetting you, Taylor? I've noticed you've been very sad lately and you've been having a hard time getting your work done at school. What's bothering you?"

1ST BOY: (UST)   "He just can't concentrate!"

TAYLOR: "I just can't concentrate, Mrs. D (tearfully). My mom and dad fight all the time and last night my dad yelled bad words at my mom and said he wants a divorce."

2ND BOY: (UST)   "It's because he's so bad." (points at Taylor)

TAYLOR: "I think they are getting a divorce because I'm so bad."

Mrs. D: (moves closer, arm around Taylor) "Oh no, Taylor! It's not your fault! When parents get a divorce, it's because they can't get along. You aren't to blame. I know you are probably scared because you don't know what's going to happen or you probably want to try and fix things, but your mom and dad are the ones that have to fix things."

TAYLOR: "I can't think about anything else. I don't care about planning or doing my schoolwork. (2 boys nod and smile, cross arms with satisfaction). I just think about my parents fighting all the time. And then I start saying all these bad things about myself like: I'm such a loser!"

MRS. D: "Oh, Taylor, you aren't a loser! Let's think of some things you are good at. (2 boys have worried looks, act like trying to speak). You've just been remembering all the bad and you've forgotten the good in your life."

1ST BOY: (UST)   "He's not good at anything." (rub hands together gleefully)

TAYLOR: "I'm not good at anything."

MRS. D: "If you tell yourself that; you won't be! Now you need to say something nice to yourself. Think of something good to say about yourself and your parents' divorce."

(Taylor rolls eyes toward ceiling)

TAYLOR: "Well the next time I think it's my fault I could tell myself it's not."

(2 boys plug ears with fingers and screw up faces (ohhhh)

MRS. D: "Great Taylor! You could also tell yourself that even though you are scared about the divorce; it will get easier to accept and it won't be so scary after a while."

TAYLOR: "Right! (excitedly) and I'm still important and my mom and dad still love me!"

MRS. D: "Yes they do! And I do too! Remember Taylor, you aren't alone. Other kids in our class have gone through divorce, also; so don't think you are the only one."

1ST BOY: (UST)   "Oh, don't tell him that!" (hands on face)

2ND BOY: (UST)   "Yea! He might believe it!"

TAYLOR: "Sometimes I feel like I'm the only one that hurts."

MRS. D: "Well, you're not! Lots of kids have felt just like you: sad, hurt, and scared. Just remember your parents still love you and they aren't trying to hurt you.

Now, when we go inside we'll get some note cards and write down some of these helpful things to say when you start to feel sad and down about your parents' divorce."

TAYLOR: "Okay."

(Teacher and Taylor exit; 2 boys unhelpful self-talk follow)

2ND BOY: (UST) "Oh bother! We'll have to work extra hard now to get him to use our unhelpful self-talk."

1ST BOY: (UST) "Yea, just when we thought we were making real progress."

Scene 2
(Jill enters with bus stop sign and "The Next Day" sign) (Taylor enters with backpack and goes and stands by the bus stop sign) (The 2 unhelpful self-talk boys are following him)

2ND BOY: (UST) "Well, this is going to be a rotten day."

1ST BOY: (UST) "Yea! You probably won't get your work done again today because all you can think about is your parents' divorce."

(Taylor reaches in his pocket and pulls out cue cards; reads silently, looks around, and says loudly)

TAYLOR: "I'm important and my mom and dad love me."

1ST BOY: (UST) "Yea! (laughingly) Then why are they getting a divorce?"

(looking at another cue card)

TAYLOR: "It's not my fault they are getting a divorce!"

TAYLOR: (yells at 2 unhelpful self-talk boys) "I'm important and my mom and dad still love me!"

2ND BOY: (UST) (huffy) "Well, he's getting bossy!"

1ST BOY: (UST) "Yea! Let's go pester someone else. He's no fun anymore!" (hand slash through air)

(2 unhelpful self-talk boys exit)

(Taylor goes toward exit, normal voice, then a whisper)

TAYLOR: "It's not my fault. I'm important and my mom and dad still love me."

SUMMARY

This chapter encompasses issues related to metacognition for the affective domain. Metacognitive strategies are included for problem solving, decision making, and goal setting; learning healthy self-talk; and addressing social issues. Each strategy was developed, implemented, and evaluated by classroom teachers for students of early elementary, elementary, and middle grades. The strategies are adaptable in that they easily can be modified for another grade level and another curricula topic. The strategies generally are represented by teacher and peer modeling, student practicing, and teacher and student cueing: an educational approach developed from the classroom research on metacognition conducted by Manning (1988, 1991).

Conclusions

The underlying philosophy of this book is that teachers teach what they know and have experienced themselves. Before we can hope for widespread use of metacognitive teaching and learning strategies, teachers must experience first-hand the benefits of metacognition. Teachers' personal lives must brush against metacognitive awareness and regulation of their feelings, attitudes, beliefs, and interpersonal relationships. This very personal interaction with the benefits of one's own cognitive monitoring and self-regulation; assuming a mental stance of personal responsibility for one's own thinking and feelings, attitudes and beliefs, is the decision crux, gravitating a teacher toward or away from metacognitive teaching and learning strategies in the classroom. These personal experiences of metacognition are not optional; instead they are central. Teachers void of them may attend workshops on metacognition, read numerous books on metacognition; but, it is still very doubtful that they will teach students a process that they have not experienced personally. This is our rationale for beginning this book with Teachers' Personal Use of Metacognition, Part I, Chapters 1–3.

After teachers assume a posture of awareness and regulation of their thinking for their own intrapersonal and interpersonal lives; then, the professional use of metacognition is a natural sequel. Teachers use mental deliberation and overseeing of their own thinking as they plan, organize, revise, develop, implement, and evaluate classroom learning experiences for their students. Part II is comprised of information targeted toward the professional side of teachers' lives: Teachers' Professional Use of Metacognition, Chapters 4–6.

The circle seems incomplete without providing stimuli for applying metacognitive strategies to advance the emotional, social, physical, and cognitive worlds of children and youth. Part III includes research support for classroom practice of metacognitive strategies. There is a consistent body of literature that reinforces the benefits of mental awareness and regulation of thinking and behavior. But in spite of this impressive body of research, recommending the inclusion of metacognition or self-regulated learning strategies in our schools today, it should be emphasized again that teachers will teach what they know, have experienced, and believe is important in the lives of their students. This brings us full circle, revisiting Part I and Part II of this book: the Teachers' Personal and Professional Use of Metacognition. This prerequisite underlines the nature of teacher education as it needs to be: the teacher as an active participant in his/her own learning and development. Part III assumes the thorough reading and completion of the exercises in Part I and Part II. Part III is an account of related research and a collection of prototypic examples entitled Metacognitive Strategies for Student Learning, Chapters 7–9. These strategies were developed, tried, and evaluated by teachers in preschool to eighth grade. They are not recipes or prescriptions; they are case accounts of the beneficial use of metacognition for the students in these particular classrooms. There is no recommendation that the readers of this book should use these ideas with their students. As we all know and appreciate, each group of students is different. Therefore, modification will most likely be necessary if teachers are interested in trying some of these self-regulated strategies with their own students.

Our original intent of this book, as stated in the Introduction, was to report what happens when the complexity and unpredictability of the classroom meet metacognitive practice and research. It is our hope that by beginning with the teacher as a person, moving through the teacher as a professional, and making extensive use of teacher-valid suggestions for classroom practice; that we have in some small way explicated the dynamic and multidimensional aspects of mental awareness and self-regulation of teachers and learners of all ages.

References

Anastopoulos, A. D., & Krehbiel, G. C. (1985, April). *The development of private speech: A review of empirical evidence addressing Vygotsky's theoretical views*. Paper presented at the biennial meeting of the Society for Research in Child Development, Toronto, Ontario.

Anderson, J. (1981). *Thinking, changing, and rearranging: Improving self-esteem in young people*. Eugene, OR: Timberline Press.

Armor, D., Conry-Osequera, P., Cox, M., King, N., McDonnell, L., Pascal, A., Pauly, E. & Zellman, G. (1976). *Analyses of the School Preferred Reading Program in selected Los Angeles minority schools*. (Report No. R–2007-LAUSD). Santa Monica, CA: Rand Corporation. (ERIC Document Reproduction Service No. ED 130243)

Ashcraft, M. H. (1989). *Human memory and cognition*. Glenville, IL: Scott, Foresman.

Ashton, P. (1984). Teacher efficacy: A motivational paradigm for effective teacher education. *Journal of Teacher Education, 35*, 28–32.

Ashton, P. T., & Webb, R. B. (1986). *Making a difference: Teachers' sense of efficacy and student achievement*. New York: Longman.

Aspy, D. N., & Buhler, J. H. The effect of teachers' inferred self-concept upon student achievement. *Journal of Educational Research, 47*, 386–389.

Aspy, D. N., & Roebuck, N. R. (1982). Affective education: Sound investment. *Educational Leadership, 39*, 489–493.

Baker, L., & Brown, A. L. (1981). Metacognition and the reading process. In D. Pearson (Ed.), *A handbook of reading research*. New York: Plenum Press.

Baltes, P., & Schaie, W. (1976). On the plasticity of intelligence in adulthood and old age. *American Psychologist, 31*, 720–725.

Bandura, A. (1969). *Principles of behavior modification*. New York: Holt, Rinehart and Winston.

Bandura, A. (1984). Behavior theory and the models of man. *American Psychologist, 29*, 859–869.

Bandura, A. (1977). Self-efficacy: Toward a unifying theory of behavior change. *Psychological Review, 84*, 191–215.

Bandura, A. (1980). The self and mechanisms of agency. In J. Suls (Ed.), *Psychological perspectives on the self* (vol.1). Hillsdale, NJ: Erlbaum.

Bandura, A. (1981). Self-referent thought: A developmental analysis of self-efficacy. In J. H. Flavell, & L. D. Ross (Eds.), *Social cognitive developments: Frontiers and possible futures*. New York: Cambridge University Press.

Bandura, A. (1982). Self-efficacy mechanism in human agency. *American Psychologist, 37* (2), 122–147.

Bandura, A. (1986). *Social foundations of thought and action: A social cognitive theory*. Englewood Cliffs, NJ: Prentice-Hall.

Bandura, A. (1989). Human agency in social cognitive theory. *American Psychologist, 44*, 1175–1184.

Bandura, A., Grusec, J. E., & Menlove, F. L. (1967). Some social determinants of self-monitoring reinforcement systems. *Journal of Personality and Social Psychology, 5*, 449–455.

Bandura, A., & Kupers, C. J. (1964). The transmission of patterns of self-reinforcement through modeling. *Journal of Abnormal and Social Psychology, 69*, 1–9.

Barfield, V., & Burlingame, M. (1974). The pupil control ideology of teachers in selected schools. *Journal of Experimental Education, 42*, 6–11.

Bartlett, F. C. (1932). *Remembering*. London: Cambridge University Press.

Bash, M., & Camp, B. (1975). *Think aloud program: Group manual*. Unpublished manuscript. University of Colorado Medical School.

Beck, A. T. (1976). *Cognitive therapy and emotional disorders*. New York: International Universities Press.

Berk, L. E. (1985). Why children talk to themselves. *Young Children, 40*, 46–52.

Berk, L. E. (1986a). Relationship of elementary school children's private speech to behavioral accompaniment to task, attention, and task performance. *Developmental Psychology, 22*, 671–680.

Berk, L. E. (1986b). Private speech: Learning out loud. *Psychology Today, 20*(5), 34–42.

Berk, L. E., & Garvin, R. A. (1984). Development of private speech among low-income Appalachian children. *Developmental Psychology, 20*, 271–286.

Berman, P., McLaughlin, M. W., Bass, G., Pauly, E., & Zellman, G. (1977). *Federal programs supporting educational change vol. VII: Factors affecting implementation and continuation*. Santa Monica, CA: Rand Corporation. (ERIC Document Reproduction Service No. ED 433)

Bernard, M. E. (1984). *Rational-emotive therapy with children and adolescents: Theory, treatment strategies, preventative methods*. New York: Wiley

Berne, E. (1964). *Games people play: The psychology of human relations*. New York: Grove Press.

Bivens, J. A., & Berk, L. E. (1990). A longitudinal study of the development of elementary school children's private speech. *Merrill-Palmer Quarterly, 36*, 443–463.

Blackham, G., & Silberman, A. (1979). *Modification of a child and adolescent behavior* (3rd ed.). Belmont, CA: Wadsworth.

Blandford, B. J., & Lloyd, J. W. (1987). Effects of a self-in-

213

structional procedure on handwriting. *Journal of Learning Disabilities, 20*(6), 342–346.

Borkowski, G., Day, J. D., Saenz, D., Dietmeyer, D., Estrada, T. M., & Groteluschen, A. (1992). Expanding the boundaries of cognitive interventions. In B.Y.L. Wong (Ed.). *Contemporary intervention research in learning disabilities—An international perspective* (pp. 1–21). New York: Springer-Verlag.

Borkowski, J. G., Johnston, M. B., & Reid, M. K. (1987). Metacognition, motivation, and the transfer of control processes. In S. J. Ceci (Ed.), *Handbook of cognitive, social, and neuropsychological aspects of learning disabilities.* Hillsdale, NJ: Erlbaum.

Bousfield, W. A. (1953). The occurrence of clustering in the recall of randomly arranged associates. *Journal of General Psychology, 49*, 229–240.

Broden, M., Hall, R. V., & Mitts, B. (1971). The effect of self-recording on the classroom behavior of two eighth-grade students. *Journal of Applied Behavior Analysis, 4*, 191–199.

Brophy, J. E. (1983). Conceptualizing student motivation to learn. *Educational Psychologist, 18*, 200–215.

Brophy, J. E. (1986). Teacher influences on student achievement. *American Psychologist, 41*, 1069–1077.

Brophy, J. E., & Good, T. (1974). *Teacher-student relationships: Causes and consequences.* New York: Holt, Rinehart, and Winston.

Brookover, W., Beady, C., Flood, P., Schweitzer, J., & Wisenbaker, J. (1979). *School social systems and student achievement: Schools can make a difference.* New York: Praeger.

Brown, A. L. (1987). Metacognition, executive control, self-regulation, and other more mysterious mechanisms. In F. E. Weinert, & R. H. Kluwe (Eds.), *Metacognition, motivation, and understanding.* Hillsdale, NJ: Erlbaum.

Brown, A., Bransford, J., Ferrara, R., & Campione, J. (1983). Learning, remembering, and understanding. In Paul H. Mussen (Ed.), *Handbook of Child Psychology, 3.* New York: John Wiley and Sons.

Brown, A. L., Campione, J. C., & Day, J. D. (1981). Learning to learn: On training students to learn from texts. *Educational Researcher, 10*(2), 14–21.

Brown, A. L., & Deloach, J. S. (1978). Skills, plans, and self-regulation. In R.S. Siegler (Ed.), *Children's thinking: What develops?* Hilsdale, NJ: Erlbaum.

Brown, A. L., & Ferrara, R. A. (1985). Diagnosing zones of proximal development. In J. V. Wertsch (Ed.), *Culture, communication, and cognition: Vygotskian perspectives.* New York: Cambridge University Press.

Bruner, J. (1985). Vygotsky: A historical and conceptual perspective. In J. Wertsch (Ed.), *Culture, communication, and cognition: Vygotskian perspectives.* New York: Cambridge University Press.

Burger, A. L., Blackmon, L. S., Holmes, M., & Zetlin, A. (1978). Use of active sorting and retrieval strategies as a facilitator of recall, clustering, and sorting by EMR and nonretarded children. *American Journal of Mental Deficiency, 83*, 253–261.

Burns, D. D., (1980). *Feeling good: The new mood therapy.* New York: William Morrow and Company, Inc.

Buscaglia, L. (1978). *Personhood: The art of being fully human.* Thorofare, NJ: C.B. Slack.

Buscaglia, L. (1982). *Living, loving and learning.* New York: Ballantine Books.

Buscaglia, L. (1984). *Loving each other.* New York: Holt, Reinhart, and Winston.

Butler, P. E. (1981). *Talking to yourself: Learning the language of self-support.* San Francisco: Harper and Row.

Butler, P. E. (1992). *Talking to yourself: Learning the language of self-affirmation.* San Francisco: Harper and Row.

Camp, B. W. (1977). Verbal mediation in young aggressive boys. *Journal of Abnormal Psychology, 86*, 145–153.

Camp, B. W., & Bash, M. A. S. (1981). *Think Aloud: Increasing social and cognitive skills: A problem-solving program for children* (Primary level). Champaign, IL: Research Press.

Camp, B. W., & Bash, M. A. S. (1985). *Think Aloud: Increasing social and cognitive skills: A problem-solving program for children* (Classroom Program, Grades 1–2). Champaign, IL: Research Press.

Camp, B. W., Blom, G. E., Hebert, E., & Doorninck, W. J. (1977). "Think Aloud": A program for developing self-control in young aggressive boys. *Journal of Abnormal Psychology, 3*(2), 157–196.

Campbell, A., Converse, P. E., Rodgers, W. L. (1976). *The quality of American life.* New York: Russell Sage.

Canfield, J., & Wells, H. C. (1976). *100 ways to enhance self-concept in the classroom: A handbook for teachers and parents.* New Jersey: Prentice Hall.

Cazden, C. B., Cox, M., Dickinson, D., Steinberg, Z., & Stone, C. (1979). "You all gonna hafta listen": Peer teaching in a primary classroom. In W. A. Collins (Eds.), *The Minnesota Symposia on Child Psychology* (Vol. 12). Hillsdale, NJ: Erlbaum.

Chomsky, N. (1959). A review of *Verbal Behavior* by B.F. Skinner. *Language, 35*, 26–58.

Clark, C. M., & Lampert, M. (1986). The study of teachers' thinking: Implications for teacher education. *Journal of Teacher Education, 37*(5), 27–31.

Clark, C. M., & Peterson, P. L. (1986). Teacher's thought process. In M. Wittrock (Ed.), *Handbook of research on teaching* (3rd ed.). New York: Macmillan.

Clark, C. M., & Yinger, R. J. (1979). Teacher's thinking. In P. L. Peterson & H. J. Walberg (Eds.), *Research on teaching.* Berkeley, CA: McCutchen.

Coleman, J. S., Campbell, E. Q., Hobson, C. J., McPortland, J., Mood, A. M., Weinfield, F. D., and York, R. L. (1966). *Equality of educational opportunity.* Office of Education, U.S. Department of Health, Education, and Welfare. Washington, D.C.: U.S. Government Printing Office.

Cooper, H. M., & Good, T. (1983). *Pygmalian grows up: Studies in the expectation communication process.* New York: Longman.

Corno, L. (1987). Teaching and self-regulated learning. In D.C. Berliner & B.V. Rosenshine (Eds.), *Talks to teachers.* New York: Random House.

Corno, L. (1989). What it means to be literate about classrooms. In D. Bloome (Ed.), *Classrooms and literacy* (pp. 29–52). Norwood, NJ: Ablex.

Corno, L., Collins, K., & Capper, J. (1982, March). *Where there's a way there's a will: Self-regulating the low-achievement student.* Paper presented at the annual meeting of the American Educational Research Association, New York.

Corno, L. & Mandinach, E. B. (1983). The role of cognitive

engagement in classroom learning and motivation. *Educational Psychologist, 18*, 88–108.

Corno, L. & Rohrkemper, M. M. (1985). The intrinsic motivation to learn in classrooms. In C. Ames and R. Ames (Eds.), *Research on motivation in education: The classroom milieu.* Orlando, FL: Academic Press.

Corsini, D. A., Pick, A. D. & Flavell, J. H. (1968). Production deficiency of non-verbal mediators in young children. *Child Development, 39*, 53–58.

Cousins, N. (1981). *Anatomy of an illness as perceived by the patient: Reflection on healing and regeneration.* New York: Bantam.

Craighead, W. F. (1982). A brief clinical history of cognitive-behavior therapy with children. *School Psychology Review, 11*, 5–13.

Dagley, P. L. (1988). *The utility of cognitive self-instruction in altering teacher expectations and locus of control orientations.* Unpublished doctoral dissertation. University of Georgia, Athens.

Davydov, V. V., & Radzikhovskii, L. A. (1985). Vygotsky's theory and the activity-oriented approach in psychology. In J. Wertsch (Ed.), *Culture, communication, and cognition: Vygotskian perspectives* (pp. 35–65). New York: Cambridge University Press.

Day, J. D., French, L. A., & Hall, L. K. (1985). Social influences on cognitive development. In D. L. Forrest-Pressley, G. E. MacKinnon, & T. Gary Waller (Eds.), *Metacognition, cognition, and human performance* (pp. 33–56). New York: Academic Press, Inc.

Denham, C., & Michael, J. (1981). Teacher sense of efficacy: An important factor in school improvement. *The Elementary School Journal, 86*, 173–184.

Denny, D. R. (1975). The effects of exemplary and cognitive models and self rehearsal on children's interrogative strategies. *Journal of Experimental Child Psychology, 19*, 476–488.

Dewey, J. (1904). The relation of theory to practice in education. In C. A. McMurry (Ed.), *Third Yearbook, Part I: National Society for the Scientific Study of Education* (pp. 9–30). Chicago: University of Chicago Press.

Diaz, R. M. (1986). Issues in the empirical study of private speech: A response to Frawley and Lantolf's commentary. *Developmental Psychology, 22*, 709–711.

Diaz, R. M. (1992). Methodological concerns in the study of private speech. In R. Diaz & L. Berk (Eds.), *Private speech: From social interaction to self-regulation* (pp. 55–81). Hillsdale, NJ: Lawrence Erlbaum.

Dryden, W., & DiQuiseppe, R. (1990). *A primer on rational-emotive therapy.* Champaign, IL: Research Press.

Dusek, J. (Ed.). (1985). *Teacher expectations.* Hillsdale, NJ: Erlbaum.

Dusek, J. B., & Joseph, G. (1983). The bases of teacher expectancies: A metanalysis. *Journal of Educational Psychology, 75*, 327–346.

Dyer, W. (1978). *Pulling your own strings.* New York: Thomas Y. Crowell Co.

Dyer, W. (1980). *The sky's the limit.* New York: Simon and Schuster.

Edson, B. A. (1986, February). *Communicating intrapersonally about stress: The dynamics on self.* Paper presented at the annual meeting of the Western Speech Communication Association, Tuscon, AZ.

Eisner, E. W. (1967). Educational objectives: Help or hindrance. *School Review. 75*, 250–266.

Ekanayake, N. (1986). *The effects of cognitive self-instruction on preservice teachers' locus of control.* Unpublished doctoral dissertation, University of Georgia, Athens.

Elashoff, J. D., & Snow, R. E. (1971). *Pygmalian reconsidered.* Worthington, OH: Charles A. Jones.

Elliott-Faust, D. J., & Pressley, M. (1986). How to teach comparison processing to increase children's short-and long-term listening comprehension monitoring. *Journal of Educational Psychology, 78*(1), 27–33.

Ellis, A. (1962). *Reason and emotion in psychotherapy.* New York: Lyle Stuart.

Ellis, A. (1969). A weekend of rational encounter. In R.J. Corsini (Ed.), *Current Psychotherapies.* Itasca, Illinois: Peacock.

Ellis, A. (1973). Rational-emotive therapy. In R. Corsini (Ed.), *Current psycho-therapies.* Itasca, IL: F. E. Peacock Publishers.

Ellis, A. (1975). *How to live with a neurotic.* New York: Crown.

Ellis, A. (1976). The biological basis of irrationality. *Journal of Individual Psychology, 32*, 145–168.

Ellis, A. (1977a). *Reason and emotion in psychotherapy* . Secaucus, NJ: Citadel Press.

Ellis, A. (1977b). *How to live with—and without—anger.* New York: Reader's Digest Press.

Ellis, A., & Harper, R. A. (1975). *A new guide to rational living.* Englewood Clifts, NJ: Prentice-Hall.

Ernst, K. (1973). *Games students play, and what to do about them.* Melbrae, CA: Celestial Arts.

Evertson, C. M., Emmer, E. T., Clements, B. S., Sanford, J. P., & Worsham, M. E. (1989). *Classroom management for elementary teachers.* NJ: Prentice Hall.

Fish, M. C., & Pervan, R. (1985). Self-instruction training: A potential tool for school psychologists. *Psychology in the Schools, 22*, 83–91.

Fischer, K. W., & Bullock, D. (1984). Cognitive development in school-aged children: Conclusions and new directions. In W. A. Collins (Ed.), *Development during middle childhood: The years from six to twelve* (pp. 70–146). Washington, DC: National Academic Press.

Flavell, J. H. (1976). Metacognitive aspects of problem solving. In L. Resnick (Ed.), *The nature of intelligence.* Hillsdale, NJ: Erlbaum.

Flavell, J. H. (1979). Metacognition and cognitive monitoring. *American Psychologist, 34*, 906–911.

Flavell, J. H. (1987). Speculations about the nature and development of metacognition. In F. E. Weinert and R. H. Kluwe (Eds), *Metacognition, motivation, and understanding.* Hillsdale, NJ: Erlbaum.

Flavell, J. H., Beach, D. H., & Chinsky, J. M. (1966). Spontaneous verbal rehearsal in memory tasks as a function of age. *Child Development, 37*, 283–299.

Flavell, J. H., Friedrichs, A. G., & Hoyt, J. D. (1970). Developmental stages in memorization processes. *Cognitive Psychology, 1*, 324–340.

Floden, A. R., & Klinzing, S. H. (1990). What can research on teacher thinking contribute to teacher preparation? A second opinion. *Educational Researcher, 19*(5), 15–20.

Forman, S. C. (1982). Stress management for teachers: A cognitive behavior program. *Journal of School Psychology, 20*, 180–187.

Forrest-Pressley, D. L., & Waller, T. G. (1984). *Cognition, metacognition, and reading.* New York: Springer-Verlag.

Frauenglass, M. H., & Diaz, R. M. (1985). Self-regulatory functions of children's private speech: A critical analysis of recent challenges to Vygotsky's theory. *Developmental Psychology, 21,* 357–364.

Fredricks, A. (1974, March). *Labeling of students by prospective teachers.* Paper presented at the annual meeting of the American Educational Research Association, Chicago.

Freed, A. M. (1971). *TA for kids (and grown-ups too).* Sacramento, CA: Jalmar Press.

Freed, A. M. (1973). *TA for teens (and other important people).* Sacramento, CA: Jalmer Press.

Friday, N. (1977). *My mother, myself.* New York: Delacorte Press.

Furrow, D. (1992). Developmental trends in the differentiation of social and private speech. In R. Diaz & L. Berk (Eds.), *Private speech: From social interaction to self-regulation* (pp. 143–158). Hillsdale, NJ: Erlbaum.

Gallimore, R., Dalton, S., & Tharpe, R. G. (1986). Self-regulation and interactive teaching: The effects of teaching conditions on teachers' cognitive activity. *The Elementary School Journal, 86*(5), 613–631.

Gallwey, W. T. (1974). *The inner game of tennis.* New York: Random House.

Gallwey, W. T. (1976). *Inner tennis: Playing of the game.* New York: Random House.

Gardner, W., & Rogoff, B. (1982). The role of instruction in memory development: Some methodological choices. *The Quarterly Newsletter of the Laboratory of Comparative Human Cognition, 4,* 6–12.

Gibson, S., & Dembo, M. H. (1984). Teacher efficacy: A construct validation. *Journal of Educational Psychology, 76,* 569–582.

Glasser, W. (1984). *Take effective control of your life.* New York: Harper and Row.

Goldman, S. (1982). Knowledge systems for realistic goals. *Discourse Processes, 5,* 279–303.

Good, T. (1986). Recent classroom research: Implications for teacher education. In D. Smith (Ed.), *Essential knowledge for beginning educators.* Washington, DC: American Association of Colleges for Teacher Education.

Good, T. (1987). Two decades of research on teacher expectations: Findings and future directions. *Journal of Teacher Education,* 32–44.

Good, T. L., & Brophy, J. R. (1984). *Looking in classrooms.* New York: Harper and Row.

Goodlad, J. I. (1984). *A place called school: Prospects for the future.* New York: McGraw-Hill.

Goodlad, J.I. (1990). *Teachers for our nation's schools.* San Francisco: Jossey-Bass Publishers.

Gordon, J. (1974). *T.E.T.: Teacher effectiveness training.* New York: David McKay.

Gordon, D. A. (1977). Children's belief in internal-external control and self-esteem as related to academic achievement. *Journal of Personality Assessment, 41,* 383–386.

Gordon, T. (1984). *TET: Teacher effectiveness training.* New York: David McKay.

Guskey, T. R. (1988). Teacher efficacy, self-concept, and attitudes toward the implementation of instructional innovation. *Teaching and Teacher Education, 4,* 63–69.

Hallahan, D., Lloyd, J. W., & Stoller, L. (1982). *Improving attention with self-monitoring: A manual for teachers.* Unpublished manuscript, University of Virginia Learning Disabilities Research Institute.

Haller, E. P., Child, D.A., and Walberg, H.G. (1988). Can comprehension be taught? A quantitative synthesis of "metacognitive" studies. *Educational Researcher, 17* (9), 5–8.

Harris, K. R. (1982). Cognitive behavior modification: Application with exceptional students. *Focus on Exceptional Children, 15,* 1–16.

Harris, K. R. (1986). The effects of cognitive behavior modification on private speech and task performance during problem solving among learning disabled and normally achieving children. *Journal of Abnormal Child Psychology, 14,* 63–77.

Harris, T. A. (1969). *I'm OK—you're OK: A practical guide to transactional analysis.* New York: Harper & Row.

Hazareesingh, N. A., & Bielawski, L. L. (1989, March). *Modifying student teachers' perceptions of control during lesson planning using cognitive self-instruction.* Paper presented at the annual meeting of the American Educational Research Association, San Francisco, CA.

Helmstetter, S. (1986). *What to say when you talk to yourself.* New York: Simon and Schuster.

Helmstetter, S. (1987). *The self-talk solution.* New York: Simon and Schuster.

Helmstetter, S. (1991). *You can excel in times of change.* New York: Simon and Schuster.

Hess, R. D., & Shipman, V. C. (1965). Early experience and the socialization of cognitive modes in children. *Child Development, 36,* 377–388.

Hess, R. D., & Shipman, V. C. (1967). Cognitive elements in maternal behavior. In J. P. Hill (Ed.), *Minnesota symposia on child psychology* (Vol. 1, pp. 68–72). Minneapolis: University of Minnesota Press.

Hill, R. (1978). Internality: The educational imperative. *Journal of Humanistic Psychology, 18,* 43–57.

Homme, L. E. (1965). Perspectives in psychology: Control of coverants, the operants of the mind. *Psychological Record, 15,* 501–511.

Hood, L., McDermott, R., & Cole, M. (1980). "Let's try to make it a good day": Some not so simple ways. *Discourse Processes, 3,* 155–168.

Hoover-Dempsey, K. V., Bassler, O. C., & Brissie, J. S. (1987). Parent involvement: Contribution of teacher efficacy, school socioeconomic status, and other school characteristics. *American Educational Research Journal, 24,* 417–435.

Hormuth, S. E. (1986). The sampling of experiences *in situ. Journal of Personality, 54*(1), 262–293.

Hoy, W. K. & Woolfolk, A. E. (1990). Socialization of student teachers. *American Educational Research Journal, 27,* 279–300.

Hughes, J. N. (1985). Parents as cotherapists in think aloud. *Psychology in the Schools, 22,* 436–443.

Jackson, P. W. (1968). *Life in classrooms.* New York: Holt, Rinehart, and Winston.

Jensen, A. R. (1971). The role of verbal mediation in mental development. *Journal of Genetic Psychology, 118,* 39–70.

Johnson, B. W., & Kanoy, K. W. (1980). Focus of control and self-concept in achieving and underachieving bright elementary students. *Psychology in the Schools, 17,* 395–399.

Keeny, T. J., Cannizzo, S. R., & Flavell, J. H. (1967). Spontaneous and induced verbal rehearsal in a recall task. *Child Development, 38*, 953–966.

Kohlberg, L., Yaeger, J., & Hjertholm, E. (1968). Private speech: Four studies and a review of theories. *Child Development, 3*, 691–736.

Kounin, J. S. (1970). *Discipline and group management in classrooms*. New York: Holt, Rinehart and Winston.

Kracht, C. R., & Casey, I. P. (1968). Attitudes, anxieties and student teaching performance. *Peabody Journal of Education, 45*, 214–217.

Kremer, L. & Kurtz, C. (1983). Locus of control, perceptions, and attributions of student teachers in educational situations. *College Student Journal, 17*, 245–251.

Kuhl, J. (1984). Volitional aspects of achievement motivation and learned helplessness: Toward a comprehensive theory of action control. In B. A. Maher (Ed.), *Progress in experimental personality research* (Vol. 13, pp. 99–171). New York: Academic Press.

Kuhl, J. & Beckmann, J. (1985). Historical perspectives in the study of action control. In J. Kuhl, & J. Beckman, (Eds.), *Action control: From cognition to behavior*. W. Berlin: Springer-Verlag.

Kurtz, B. E. & Borkowski, J. G. (1984). Children's metacognition: Exploring relations among knowledge, process, and motivational variables. *Journal of Experimental Child Psychology, 37*, 335–354.

Lampert, M. (1984). Teaching about thinking and thinking about teaching. *Journal of Curriculum Studies, 16* (1), 1–18.

Landry, R. G. (1974). *Achievement and self-concept: A curvilinear relationship*. Paper presented at the annual meeting of the American Educational Research Association, Chicago.

Lee, B. (1985). Intellectual origins of Vygotsky's semiotic analysis. In J. Wertsch (Ed.), *Culture, communication, and cognition: Vygotskian perspectives* (pp. 66–93). New York: Cambridge University Press.

Leon, J. A., & Pepe, H. J. (1983). Self-instructional training: Cognitive behavior modification for remediating arithmetic deficits. *Exceptional Children, 50*(1), 54–61.

Lewin, K. (1926). Untersuchungen zur Handlungs-und Affekt-psychologie. II. Vorsatz, Wille und Bedurfnis. *Pscychologische Forschung, 7*, 330–385.

Lloyd, J. (1980). Academic instruction and cognitive behavior modification: The need for attack strategy training. *Exceptional Education Quarterly, 8*, 53–63.

Long, N. J. (1984). Teaching self-control and prosocial behavior by using therapeutic signs and sayings in classrooms for emotionally disturbed people. *The Pointer, 28*(4), 36–39.

Lovitt, T., & Curtiss, K. (1968). Effects of manipulating an antecedent event on mathematics response rate. *Journal of Applied Behavior Analysis, 1*, 329–333.

Luria, A. R. (1959). The directive function of speech in development and dissolution. *Word, 16*, 341–352.

Luria, A. R. (1961). *The role of speech in the regulation of normal and abnormal behavior*. New York: Basic Books.

MacDonald, J. B. (1965). Myths about instruction. *Educational Leadership, 22*, 571–576, 609–617.

Maltz, M. (1960). *Psycho-cybernetics*. New York: Simon and Schuster.

Manning, B. H. (1984a). A self-communication structure for nlearning mathematics. *School Science and Mathematics, 84*(1), 43–51.

Manning, B. H. (1984b). Problem-solving instruction and oral comprehension aid for reading disabled third graders. *Journal of Learning Disabilities, 17*, 457–461.

Manning, B. H. (1988). Application of cognitive behavior modification: First and third graders self-management of classroom behaviors. *American Educational Research Journal, 25* (2), 193–212.

Manning, B. H. (1990a). Self-talk and learning. *Teaching K–8*, April, 56–58.

Manning, B. H. (1990b). Cognitive self-instruction for an off-task fourth grader during independent academic tasks: A case study. *Contemporary Educational Psychology, 15*, 36–46.

Manning, B. H. (1991). *Cognitive self-instruction for classroom processes*. Albany, NY: State University of New York Press.

Manning, B. H., & Payne, B. D. (1989a). A cognitive self-direction model for teacher education. *Journal of Teacher Education, 40*(3), 27–32.

Manning, B. H., & Payne, B. D. (1989b). Verbal introspection: A contrast between preservice and inservice teachers. *Teacher Education Quarterly, 16*(3), 73–84.

Manning, B. H., & Payne, B. D. (1992). A correlational study of preservice teachers' reported self-talk reactions to teaching dilemmas. *Teacher Education Quarterly, 19*(2), 85–95.

Manning, B. H., & Payne, B. D. (1993). A Vygotskian-based theory of teacher cognition: Toward the acquisition of mental reflection and self-regulation. *Teaching and Teacher Education: An International Journal of Research and Studies*.

Manning, B. H., & White, C. S. (1990). Task relevant private speech as a function of age and sociability. *Psychology in the Schools, 27*, 62–68.

Manning, B. H., White, C. S., & Daugherty, M. (1994). Young children's private speech as a precursor to metacognitive strategy use for task execution. *Discourse Processes: A Multidisciplinary Journal, 17*(2), 191–212.

Markman, E. M. (1977). Realizing that you don't understand: A preliminary investigation. *Child Development, 46*, 986–992.

Markman, E. M. (1979). Realizing that you don't understand: Elementary school children's awareness of inconsistencies. *Child Development, 50*, 643–655.

Marsh, H. W., & Shavelson, R. (1985). Self-concept: Its multifaceted, hierarchical structure. *Educational Psychologist, 20*, 107–123.

Marshall, J. C., & Morton, J. (1978). On the mechanics of EMMA. In A. Sinclair, R.J. Jarvella, & W. J. M. Levett (Eds.), *The child's conception of language*. Berlin: Springer.

Marzano, R. J. (1987). Staff development for teaching thinking. *Journal of Staff Development, 8*(3), 6–11.

Maslow, A. H. (1970). *Motivation and personality* (2nd ed.). New York: Harper and Row.

Maultsby, M. C. (1975). *Help yourself to happiness through rational self-counseling*. New York: Institute for Rational Living, Inc.

McCombs, B. L. (1986). The role of the self-system in self-regulated learning. *Contemporary Educational Psychology, 11*, 314–332.

McCombs, B. L. (1988). Motivational skills training: Combining metacognitive, cognitive, and affective learning strategies. In C.E. Weinstein, E.T. Goetz, & P.A. Alexander (Eds.), *Learning and study strategies: Issues in assessment, instruction, and evaluation.* New York: Academic Press.

McCombs, B. L. (1989). Self-regulated learning and academic achievement: A phenomenological view. In B. Zimmerman & D. Schunk (Eds.), *Self-regulated learning and academic achievement: Theory, research and practice* (pp. 51–82). New York: Springer-Verlag.

McMahan, I. D. (1973). Relationships between causal attributions and expectancy of success. *Journal of Personality and Social Psychology. 28*, 108–114.

McNair, K. (1978). Capturing inflight decisions: Thoughts while teaching. *Educational Research Quarterly, 3*(4), 26–42.

Meichenbaum, D. (1975a). Enhancing creativity by modifying what subjects say to themselves. *American Educational Research Journal, 12*, 129–145.

Meichenbaum, D. (1976). Cognitive factors as determinants of learning disabilities: A cognitive functional approach. In R. M. Knights & D. J. Baker (Eds.), *The neuropsychology of learning disorders: Theoretical approaches.* Baltimore, MD: University Park Press.

Meichenbaum, D. (1977). *Cognitive behavior modification: An integrative approach.* New York: Plenum Press.

Meichenbaum, D. (1985). Teaching thinking: A cognitive behavioral perspective. In J.W. Segal, S. F. Chipman, & R. Glaser (Eds.), *Thinking and learning skills: vol. 2. Research and open questions* (pp.407–426). Hillsdale, NJ: Erlbaum.

Meichenbaum, D., & Asarnow, J. (1979). Cognitive-behavioral modification and metacognitive development: Implications for the classroom. In P. C. Kendall and S. D. Hollon (Eds.), *Cognitive behavioral interventions: Theory, research, and procedures.* New York: Academic Press.

Meichenbaum, D., & Goodman, J. (1971). Training impulsive children to talk to themselves: A means of developing self-control. *Journal of Abnormal Psychology, 77*, 115–126.

Midgley, C., Feldlaufer, H., & Eccles, J. S. (1989). Change in teacher efficacy and student self-and task-related beliefs in mathematics during the transition to junior high school. *Journal of Educational Psychology, 81*, 247–258.

Miller, G. A., Galanter, E., & Pribram, K. H. (1960). *Plans and the structure of behavior.* New York: Holt.

Miller, I., & Norman, W. (1979). Learned helplessness in humans: A review and attribution-theory model. *Psychological Bulletin, 86*, 93–118.

Miller, P. A. (1983). *Theories of developmental psychology.* San Francisco, CA: W. H. Freeman.

Mischel, W. (1968). *Personality and its assessment.* New York: Wiley.

Mizelle, N. (1993). *Middle grade students' motivational processes and use of strategies with expository text.* Unpublished doctoral dissertation, University of Georgia, Athens.

Morris, M. (1993). *Sociolinguistic experiences in the home and school: A case study of spontaneous utterances.* Unpublished doctoral dissertation, University of Georgia, Athens.

Moss, E. (1990). Social interaction and metacognitive development in gifted preschoolers. *Gifted Child Quarterly, 34*(1), 16–20.

Murray, H., & Staebler, B. K. (1974). Teacher's locus of control and student achievement gains. *Journal of School Psychology, 12*, 3005–3009.

Myers, A. W., Cohen, R., & Schlester, R. (1989). A cognitive behavioral approach to education: Adopting a broad-based perspective. In J. N. Hughes & R. J. Hall (Eds.), *Cognitive behavioral psychology in the schools: A comprehensive handbook* (pp. 62–84). New York: Guilford.

Neely, A. M. (1986). Planning and problem solving in teacher education. *Journal of Teacher Education, 37*(3), 29–33.

Nicholls, J. G. (1984). Achievement motivation: Conceptions of ability, subjective experience, task choice, and performance. *Psychological Review, 91*, 328–346.

Noad, B. M. (1979). Influences of self-concept and educational attitudes on elementary student performance. *Educational Research Quarterly, 4* (1), 68–79.

Novak, J. D., & Gowan, D. B. (1984). *Learning how to learn.* Cambridge, England: Cambridge University Press.

Nowicki, S., & Strickland, B. (1973). A locus of control scale for children. *Journal of Consulting and Clinical Psychology, 40*, 148–154.

Nowicki, S., & Walker, C. (1973). Achievement in relation to locus of control: Identification of a new source of variance. *The Journal of Genetic Psychology, 123*, 63–67.

Oldfather, P. (1989). *Teachers' ways of knowing: Paradigms for teacher education.* The Claremont Graduate School, Claremont, CA.

Olszewski, P., & Fuson, K. (1982). Verbally expressed fantasy play of preschoolers as a function of toy structure. *Developmental Psychology, 18*, 57–61.

Palincsar, A. S. (1986). Metacognitive strategy instruction. *Exceptional Children, 53*(2), 118–124.

Palincsar, A. S. (1987). Reciprocal teaching: Can student discussion boost comprehension? *Instructor, 96*(5), 56–58, 60.

Palincsar, A. S. (1991, September). Reciprocal teaching. In K. Hambrick (Ed.), *Making connections II: Four educational perspectives* (pp. 10–13). Symposium Proceedings of the Appalachia Educational Laboratory.

Palincsar, A. S., & Brown, A. L. (1984). Reciprocal teaching of comprehension-fostering and comprehension-monitoring activities. *Cognition and Instruction, 1*, 117–175.

Palkes, H., Stewart, M., & Freedman, J. (1972). Improvement in maze performance of hyperactive boys as a function of verbal-training procedures. *Journal of Special Education, 5*, 337–342.

Palkes, H., Stewart, M., & Kahana, B. (1968). Porteus maze performance after training in self-directed verbal commands. *Child Development, 39*, 817–826.

Palmer, D., & Goetz, E. (1983). *Students' perceptions of study strategy attributes as a mediator of strategy use.* Paper presented at the meeting of the American Educational Research Association, Montreal, Canada.

Paris, S. G. (1988). Models and metaphors of learning strategies. In C. E. Weinstein, E.T. Goetz, & P. A. Alexander (Eds.), *Learning and study strategies: Issues in assessment, instruction, and evaluation* (pp. 299–321). San Diego: Academic Press.

Paris, S. G., & Byrnes, J. P. (1989). The constructivist approach to self-regulation and learning in the classroom.

In B. Zimmerman & D. Schunk (Eds.), *Self-regulated learning and academic achievement: Theory, research, and practice* (pp. 169–200). New York: Springer-Verlag.

Patriarca, L. A., & Kraght, D. M. (1986). Teacher expectations and student achievement: The ghost of Christmas future. *Curriculum Review, May/June,* 48–50.

Payne, B. D., & Manning, B. H. (1988). The effect of cognitive self-instructional strategies on preservice teachers' locus of control. *Contemporary Educational Psychology, 13,* 140–145.

Payne, B. D., & Manning, B. H. (1990). The effect of cognitive self-instructions on preservice teachers' anxiety about teaching. *Contemporary Educational Psychology, 15,* 261–267.

Payne, B. D., & Manning, B. H. (1991). Cognitive self-direction methodological model. *Teacher Education Quarterly, 18*(1), 49–54.

Payne, B. D., & Manning, B. H. (1992). Basal reader instruction: Effects of comprehension monitoring training on reading comprehension strategy use and attitudes. *Reading Research and Instruction, 32*(1), 29–38.

Pearlin, L. I., & Radbaugh, C. (1976). Economic strains and the coping function of alcohol. *American Journal of Sociology, 82,* 652–663.

Peterson, P. L., & Clark, C. M. (1978). Teacher planning, teacher behavior, and student achievement. *American Educational Research Journal, 15*(3), 417–432.

Peterson, P. L., Marx, R. W., & Clark, C. M. (1978). Teacher planning, teacher behavior, and student achievement. *American Educational Research Journal, 15*(3), 417–432.

Petrusich, M. M. (1966). Separation anxiety as a factor in the student teaching experience. *Peabody Journal of Education, 44,* 353–356.

Piaget, J. (1926). *The language and thought of the child.* New York: Harcourt Brace.

Piaget, J. (1952). *The origins of intelligence in children.* New York: International Universities Press.

Pintrich, P. R., & DeGroot, E. V. (1990). Motivational and self-regulated learning components of classroom academic performance. *Journal of Educational Psychology, 82* (1), 33–40.

Popham, J. W., & Baker, E. L. (1970). *Systematic instruction.* New York: Prentice Hall.

Purkey, W. W. (1970). *Self-concept and school achievement.* Englewood Clifts, NJ: Prentice-Hall, Inc.

Raitt, A. (1988). Weight control: A rational-emotive approach. In W. Dryden & P. Trower (Eds.), *Development in rational-emotive therapy* (pp. 197–209). Philadelphia: Open University Press.

Reeve, R. A., & Brown, A. L. (1985). Metacognition reconsidered: Implications for intervention research. *Journal of Abnormal Child Psychology, 13,* 343–356.

Rest, S. (1976). Schedules of reinforcement: An attributional analysis. In J. H. Harvey, W. J. Ickes, & R. F. Kidd (Eds.), *New directions in attribution research* (Vol. 1). Hillsdale, NJ: Erlbaum.

Riley, J. F. (1981). Creative problem solving and cognitive monitoring as instructional variables for teacher training in classroom problem solving. *Dissertation Abstracts International* (University Microfilms, No. 81-07, 943).

Ringel, B. A., & Springer, C. (1980). On knowing how well one is remembering: The persistence of strategy use during transfer. *Journal of Experimental Child Psychology, 29,* 322–333.

Roberts, R. N. (1979). Private speech in academic problem solving: A naturalistic perspective. In G. Zivin (Ed.), *The development of self-regulation through private speech* (pp. 265–294). New York: John Wiley and Sons.

Robin, A. L., Armel, S., & O'Leary, K. D. (1975). The effects of self-instruction on writing deficiencies. *Behavior Therapy, 6,* 178–187.

Rogers, B. C. (1983). Metacognition: Implications for training teachers of the gifted. *Roeper Review, 6,* 20–21.

Rogoff, B. (1990). *Apprenticeship in thinking: Cognitive development in social context.* New York: Oxford University Press.

Rohrkemper, M. & Corno, L. (1988). Success and failure on classroom tasks: Adaptive learning and classroom teaching. *The Elementary School Journal, 88,* 297–312.

Rose, J. S., & Medway, F. J. (1981). Teacher locus of control, teacher behavior, and student behavior as determinants of student achievement. *Journal of Educational Research, 74,* 375–381.

Rosenthal, R. (1974). *On the social psychology of the self-fulfilling prophecy: Further evidence for Pygmalian effects and their mediating mechanisms.* New York: MSS Modular Publications.

Rosenthal, R., & Jacobsen, L. (1968). *Pygmalian in the classroom.* New York: Holt, Rinehart, and Winston.

Rotter, J. B. (1966). Generalized expectancies for internal versus external control of reinforcement. *Psychological Monographs, 80* (1, Whole No. 609).

Rubin, K. H. (1979). The impact of the natural setting on private speech. In G. Zivin (Ed.), *The development of self-regulation through private speech* (pp. 265–294). New York: John Wiley and Sons.

Sadowski, C. J., & Woodward, H. R. (1983). Teacher locus of control and classroom climate: A cross-lagged correlational study. *Psychology in the Schools, 20,* 506–509.

Sadowski, C. J., Blackwell, M., & Willard, J. L. (1985). Locus of control and student teacher performance. *Education, 105,* 391–393.

Sarason, J. G., & Stoops, R. (1978). Test anxiety and the passage of time. *Journal of Consulting and Clinical Psychology, 46,* 102–109.

Schmitt, M. C., & Baumann, J. F. (1986). How to incorporate comprehension monitoring strategies into basal reader instruction. *The Reading Teacher, 35*(10), 28–31.

Schunk, D. H. (1986). Verbalization and children's self-regulated learning. *Contemporary Educational Psychology, 11,* 347–369.

Schunk, D. H. (1988, April). *Perceived self-efficacy and related social cognitive processes as predictors of student academic achievement performance.* Paper presented at the annual meeting of the American Educational Research Association, New Orleans.

Schunk, D. H. (1989). Social cognitive theory and self-regulated learning. In B. Zimmerman & D. Schunk (Eds.), *Self-regulated learning and academic achievement: Theory, research, and practice* (pp. 83–110). New York: Springer-Verlag.

Schunk, D. H., & Rice, J. M. (1984). Strategy self-verbalization during remedial listening comprehension instruction. *Journal of Experimental Education, 53,* 49–54.

Segal, J. W., Chipman, S. F., & Glaser, R. (1985). *Thinking and learning skills (vol. 1). Relating instruction to research.* Hillsdale, NJ: Erlbaum.

Seligman, M. E. P. (1975). *Helplessness: On depression, development, and death.* San Francisco: Freeman.

Shapiro, E. S. (1984). Self-monitoring procedures. In T. H. Ollendick & M. Hersen (Eds.), *Child behavior assessment: Principles and procedures* (pp. 148–165). New York: Pergamon.

Shavelson, R. J., & Stern, P. (1981). Research on teachers' pedagogical thoughts, judgments, decisions, and behaviors. *Review of Educational Research, 52*(4), 455–498.

Shrauger, J., & Rosenberg, S. (1970). Sclf-esteem and the effects of success and failure feedbacks on performance. *Journal of Personality, 33*, 404–414.

Siegel, B. S. (1986). *Love, medicine and miracles.* New York: Harper and Row.

Siegel, B. S. (1989). *Peace, love and healing.* New York: Harper and Row.

Skinner, B. F. (1953). *Science and human behavior.* New York: Macmillan.

Sonnenschein, S., Baker, L., & Cerro, L. (1992). Mothers' views on teaching their preschoolers in everyday situations. *Early Education Development, 3*, 5–25.

Spencer-Hall, D. (1981). Looking behind the teacher's back. *Elementary School Journal, 81*, 281–289.

Spring, H. T. (1985). Teacher decision-making: A metacognitive approach. *The Reading Teacher, 39*, 290–295.

Sprinthall, N. A., & Thies-Sprinthall, L. (1983a). The need for theoretical frameworks in educating teachers: A cognitive-developmental perspective. In K. Howey and W. Gardner (Eds.), *The education of teachers* (pp. 74–97). NY: Longman.

Sprinthall, N. A., & Thies-Sprinthall, L. (1983b). The teacher as an adult learner: A cognitive developmental view. In G. Griffin (Ed.), *Staff development, 82nd Yearbook of the National Society for the Study of Education, Part II* (pp. 13–35). Chicago: University of Chicago Press.

Sternberg, R. J. (Ed.), (1982). *Handbook of human intelligence.* Cambridge, England: Cambridge University Press.

Strother, D. B. (1987). On listening. *Phi Delta Kappan, 16*, 624–631.

Swinn, R. M., & Geiger, J. (1965). Stress and the stability of self and other attitudes. *Journal of General Psychology, 73*, 177–180.

Szykula, S. A., & Hector, M. A. (1978). Teacher instructional behavior change through self-control. *Psychology in the Schools, 15*(1), 87–94.

Taba, H. (1962). *Curriculum development, theory, and practice.* New York: Harcourt, Brace, and World.

Tharp, R. G., & Gallimore, R. (1988). *Rousing minds to life.* New York: Cambridge University Press.

Tharp, R. D., Gallimore, R., & Calkins, R. P. (1984). On the relationship between self-control and control by others. *Advances in Psicologia Clinical Latinoamericano, 3*, 45–58.

Torrance, E. P., & Myers, R. E. (1970). *Creative learning and teaching.* New York: Harper and Row.

Trentham, L., Silvern, S., & Brogden, R. (1985). Teacher efficacy and teacher competency ratings. *Psychology in the Schools, 22*, 343–352.

Trimbur, J. (1987). Beyond cognition: The voices in inner speech. *Rhetoric Review, 5*(2), 211–220.

Tyler, R. W. (1950). *Basic principles of curriculum and instruction.* Chicago: University of Chicago Press.

Usher, R., and Hanke, J. (1971). The "third force" in psychology and college teacher effectiveness research at the University of Northern Colorado. *Colorado Journal of Educational Research, 10* (2), 3–10.

Velton, E. (1988). Withdrawal from heroin and methadone with RET: Theory and practice. In W. Dryden & P. Trower (Eds.), *Developments in rational-emotive therapy* (pp. 210–225). Philadelphia: Open University Press.

Venezky, R. L. (1991). The development of literacy in the industrialized nations of the west. In R. Barr, M. L. Kamel, P. Mosenthal, & P. D. Pearson (Eds.), *Handbook of reading research* vol. II (pp. 46–67). New York: Longman.

Vygotsky, L. S. (1934/1962). *Thought and language.* Cambridge, MA: MIT Press.

Vygotsky, L. S. (1978). *Mind in society: The development of higher psychological processes.* Cambridge, MA: Harvard University Press.

Vygotsky, L. S. (1987). Thinking and speech. In *The collected works of L. S. Vygotsky: Vol. 1, Problems of general psychology.* New York: Plenum Press.

Warren, R., Deffenbacher, J., & Brading, P. (1976). Rational-emotive therapy and reduction of test anxiety in elementary school students. *Rational Living, 11*, 26–29.

Watson, R. I. (1963). *The great psychologies.* New York: Lippincott.

Watson, D. R., & Tharp, R. G. (1988). *Self-directed behavior* (5th ed.). Monterey, CA: Brooks/Cole.

Weaver, R. L., Cotrell, H. W., & Churchman, E. C. (1988). Destructive dialogue: Negative self-talk and positive imaging. *College Student Journal,* Fall, 230–240.

Weiner, B. (1979). A theory of motivation for some classroom experiences. *Journal of Educational Psychology, 71*, 3–25.

Weiner, B. (1980). The role of affect in rational (attributional) approaches to human motivation. *Educational Researcher, 9*, 4–11.

Weiner, B., Nirenburg, R. & Goldstein, M. (1976). Social learning (locus of control) versus attributional (causal stability) interpretations of expectancy of success. *Journal of Personality and Social Psychology, 44*, 52–68.

Weinert, F. E., & Kluwe, R. H. (1987). *Metacognition, motivation, and understanding.* Hillsdale, NJ: Lawrence Erlbaum.

Weinstein, C. E., & Mayer, R. E. (1986). The teaching of learning strategies. In M. C. Wittrock (Ed.), *Handbook of research on teaching* (pp. 315–327). New York: Macmillan.

Wellman, H. M. (1983). Metamemory revisited. In M. Chi (Ed.), *What is memory development the development of? A look after a decade* (pp. 31–51). Basel: Karger.

Wertsch, J. V. (1978). Adult-child interaction and the roots of metacognition. *Quarterly Newsletter of the Institute for Comparative Human Development, 1*, 15–18.

Wertsch, J. V. (1979). From socialization to higher psychological processes: A clarification of and application of Vygotsky's theory. *Human Development, 22*, 1–22.

Wertsch, J. V. (1985). *Vygotsky and the social formation of the mind.* Cambridge, MA: Harvard University Press.

Wertsch, J. V., McNamee, G., Budwig, N., & McLane, J. (1980). The adult-child dyad as a problem-solving system. *Child Development, 51*, 1215–1221.

Wertsch, J. V., & Rogoff, B. (1984). Editor's notes. In B. Rogoff & J. V. Wertsch (Eds.), *Children's learning in the "zone of proximal development"* (pp. 1–6). San Francisco: Jossey-Bass.

White, E. B. (1941). *A subtreasury of American humor.* New York: Coward-McCann, Inc.

White, S. H. (1970). The learning theory tradition for child psychology. In P.H. Mussen (Ed.), *Carmichael's manual of child psychology* (vol.1). New York: Wiley.

Williams, R., & Cole, S. (1968). Self-concept and school adjustment. *Personnel and Guidance Journal, 1,* 478–481.

Wolfgang, C. H., & Glickman, C. D. (1986). *Solving discipline problems: Strategies for classroom teachers.* Boston: Allyn and Bacon, Inc.

Wood, D. J., Bruner, J. S., & Ross, G. (1976). The role of tutoring in problem solving. *Journal of Child Psychology and Psychiatry, 17*(2), 89–100.

Woolfolk, A. E. (1993). *Educational psychology* (5th ed.). Needham Heights, MA: Allyn and Bacon.

Wylie, R. (1968). The present status of self-theory. In E. Borgotta & W. Lambert (Eds.), *Handbook of personality theory and research* (pp. 728–787). Chicago: Rand McNally.

Young, H. S. (1984a). Practising RET with Bible-belt christians. *British Journal of Cognitive Psychotherapy, 2* (2), 60–76.

Young, H. S. (1984b). Practising RET with lower-class clients. *British Journal of Cognitive Psychotherapy, 2,* 33–59.

Zahorik, J. A. (1975). Teachers' planning models. *Educational Leadership, 33,* 134–139.

Zentall, S. S., & Kruczek, T. (1988). The attraction of color for active attention problem children. *Exceptional Children, 12*(4), 193–212.

Zimmerman, B. J. (1990). Self-regulated learning and academic achievement: An overview. *Educational Psychologist, 21,* 3–18.

Zimmerman, B. J., & Schunk, D. H. (Eds.). (1989). *Self-regulated learning and academic achievement: Theory, research, and practice.* New York: Springer-Verlag.

Zivin, G. (1979). *The development of self-regulation through private speech.* New York: John Wiley & Sons.

Zumwalt, K. K. (1988). Are we improving or undermining teaching? In L. Tanner (Ed.). *Critical issues in curriculum: Eighty-seventh yearbook of the National Society for the Study of Education,* Part I (pp. 148–174). Chicago: The University of Chicago Press.

Author Index

A

Anastopoulos, A. D., 73
Anderson, J., 47, 53
Armel, S., 137, 139
Armor, D., 15
Asarnow, J., 17
Ashton, P., 13, 15
Aspy, D. N., 34, 40

B

Baker, E. L., 93
Baker, L., 108, 109
Bandura, A., 13, 14, 15, 112, 113
Barfield, V., 15, 41
Bash, M., 131, 135, 143
Bass, G., 15
Bassler, O. C., 15
Baumann, J. F., 148
Beach, D. H., 1
Beck, A. T., 112, 113
Beckmann, J., 17
Berk, L. E., 73, 74
Berman, P., 15
Bernard, M. E., 4
Berne, E., 7
Blackmon, L. S., 105, 112
Blackwell, M., 41
Blandford, B. J., 137
Blom, G. E., 135
Bommarito, B., 138
Borkowski, J. G., 13, 17
Brading, P., 114
Bransford, J., 105
Brissie, J. S., 15
Brogden, R., 15
Brookover, W., 45
Brophy, J. E., 31, 87, 112, 113
Brown, A. L., 2, 17, 79, 104, 105, 109, 111, 133, 136, 141

Bruner, J. S., 79, 105, 111
Budwig, N., 108
Buhler, H. J., 34
Burger, A. L., 105
Burlingame, M., 15, 41
Burns, D. D., 48
Buscaglia, L., 27, 28
Butler, P. E., 1, 6, 19, 20, 21, 34, 47, 48, 49, 88
Byrnes, J. P., 82

C

Camp, B., 130, 135, 143
Campbell, A., 41
Campione, J. C., 104, 105, 136
Capper, J., 136
Canfield, J., 29, 65
Cannizzo, S. R., 2
Casey, I. P., 93
Cazden, C. B., 109
Cerro, L., 108, 109
Chinsky, J. M., 1
Child, D. A., 2
Churchman, E. C., 39
Clark, C. M., 59, 93, 94, 98
Clements, B. S., 204
Cohen, R., 113
Cole, M., 109
Cole, S., 34
Coleman, J. S., 41
Collins, K., 136
Conry-Osequera, P., 15
Converse, P. E., 41
Cooper, H. M., 31
Corno, L., 16, 17, 58, 83, 84, 136, 149, 154, 155
Corsini, D. A., 1
Cotrell, H. W., 39
Cousins, N., 27
Cox, M., 15, 109

Craighead, W. F., 113
Curtiss, K., 114, 137

D

Dagley, P. L., 121
Daugherty, M., 74, 185
Davydov, V. V., 80
Day, J. D., 17, 104, 136
Deffenbacher, J., 114
DeGroot, E. V., 16
Dembo, M. H., 13, 15
Denham, C., 14, 15
Denny, D. R., 17
Dewey, J., 27
Dickinson, D., 109
Dietmeyer, D., 17
DiQuiseppe, R., 6
Dryden, W., 6
Dusek, J. B., 30, 31
Dyer, W., 37, 38

E

Eccles, J. S., 15
Edson, B. A., 47, 52
Eisner, E. W., 94
Ekanayake, N., 93
Elashoff, J. D., 31
Elliott-Faust, D. J., 138
Ellis, A., 3, 4, 5, 6, 34, 47, 88, 92, 112, 113
Emmer, E. T., 99, 204
Epanchein, L., 99
Ernst, K., 7
Estrada, T. M., 17
Evertson, C. M., 99, 204

F

Feldlaufer, H., 15
Ferrara, R. A., 79, 105
Flavell, J. H., 1, 2, 74, 89
Forrest-Pressley, D. L., 2
Freed, A. M., 7
Freedman, J., 134
French, L. A., 104
Friday, N., 7
Friedrichs, A. G., 2, 30

G

Gallwey, W. T., 36
Gardner, W., 108
Garvin, R. A., 73

Geiger, J., 34
Gibson, S., 13, 15
Glasser, W., 47
Goetz, E., 13
Glickman, C. D., 99
Goldman, S., 192
Goldstein, M., 12, 67
Good, T. L., 30, 31, 87
Goodlad, J. I., 7, 84
Goodman, J., 91, 114, 115, 126, 127, 133, 134, 135, 136, 137, 139
Gordon, D. A., 41
Gordon, T., 42, 55
Gottfredson, D., 59
Gowan, D. B., 17
Groteluschen, A., 17
Guskey, T. R., 15

H

Hall, L. K., 104
Hallahan, D., 131
Haller, E. P., 2
Hanke, J., 34
Harper, R. A., 4, 5
Harris, K. R., 112, 113
Harris, T. A., 7, 11
Hazareesingh, N. A., 94
Hebert, F., 135
Helmstetter, S., 5, 18, 19, 34, 48, 49, 56, 57, 88, 92
Hess, R. D., 108
Hill, R., 41
Hobson, C. J., 41
Holmes, M., 105
Homme, L. E., 112
Hood, L., 109
Hoover-Dempsey, K. V., 15
Hoy, W. K., 15
Hoyt, J. D., 2
Hughes, J. N., 135
Hunter, M., 94

J

Jackson, P. W., 59, 94
Jacobsen, L., 31
James, W., 38
Johnson, B. W., 41
Joseph, G., 30

K

Kahana, B., 130, 131, 134
Kanoy, K. W., 41

Keeny, T. J., 2
King, N., 15
Kluwe, R. H., 89
Kounin, J. S., 59, 60, 61
Kracht, C. R., 93
Kraght, D. M., 30, 93
Krehbiel, G. C., 73
Kremer, L., 41
Kruczek, T., 132
Kuhl, J., 17, 82
Kupers, C. J., 41
Kurtz, B. E., 13
Kurtz, C., 41

L

LaFave, S., 61
Lampert, M., 96, 98, 100
Landry, R. G., 34
Leon, J. A., 137, 138
Lloyd, J., 114
Lloyd, J. W., 131, 137
Long, N. J., 131
Lovitt, T. C., 114, 137
Luria, A. R., 113, 114, 134

M

MacDonald, J. B., 94
Maltz, M., 35, 36
Mandinach, E. B., 17
Manning, B. H., 2, 13, 16, 17, 67, 69, 74,
    84, 88, 89, 92, 114, 115, 123, 127, 136,
    138, 155, 185, 192, 210
Markman, E. M., 121
Marx, R. W., 94
Maslow, A. H., 45
Maultsby, M. C.,52
McCombs, B. L., 13, 82, 83, 84
McDermott, R., 109
McDonnell, L., 15
McLane, J., 108
McLaughlin, M. W., 15
McMahan, I. D., 12
McNamee, G., 108
McPortland, J., 41
Medway, F. J., 41, 92
Meichenbaum, D., 2, 13, 17, 47, 55, 90,
    91, 92, 102, 112, 113, 114, 115, 116,
    126, 127, 132, 133, 134, 135, 136, 137,
    139, 190
Michael, J., 14, 15
Midgley, C., 15
Miller, I., 12

Mood, A. M., 41
Morris, M., 109
Moss, E., 108
Murray, H., 41
Myers, A. W., 113
Myers, R. E., 122

N

Neely, A. M., 93
Nicholls, J. B., 13
Nirenburg, G., 12
Noad, B. M., 34
Norman, W., 12
Novak, J. D., 17
Nowicki, S., 41

O

O'Leary, K. D., 137, 139

P

Palincsar, A. S., 17, 109, 111, 112, 133,
    141
Palkes, H., 130, 131, 134
Palmer, D., 13
Paris, S. G., 82
Park, G., 92
Pascal, A., 15
Patriarca, L. A., 30
Pauly, E., 15
Payne, B. D., 88, 89, 92, 114
Pearlin, L. I., 41
Pepe, H. J., 137
Peterson, P. L., 59, 94
Petrusich, M. M., 93
Piaget, J., 77, 103
Pick, A. D., 1
Pintrich, P. R., 16
Popham, J. W., 93
Pressley, M., 138
Purkey, W. W., 34

R

Radbaugh, C., 41
Radzikhovskii, L. A., 80
Raitt, A., 4
Rest, S., 12
Rice, J. M., 137
Ringel, B. A., 105
Robin, A. L., 137, 139
Roebuck, N. R., 40

Rogers, B. C., 41
Rogoff, B., 80, 105, 108
Rohrkemper, M., 16, 17, 58, 83, 84, 154
Rose, J. S., 41, 92
Rosenberg, S., 34
Rosenthal, R., 31
Ross, G., 105
Rotter, J. B., 40, 65, 92
Rushton, A., 93

S

Sadowski, C. J., 41
Saenz, D., 17
Sanford, J. P., 204
Sarason, J. G., 13
Schlester, R., 113
Schmitt, M. C., , 148
Schunk, D. H., 16, 17, 72, 81, 82, 83, 136, 137
Seligman, M. E. P., 17
Shavelson, R. J., 96
Shipman, V. C., 108
Shrauger, J., 34
Siegel, B. S., 36
Silberman, A., 112
Silvern, S., 15
Skinner, B. F., 112
Slaby, T., 92
Snow, R. E., 31
Sonnenschein, S., 108, 109
Spencer-Hall, D., 30
Springer, C., 105
Staebler, B. K., 41
Steinberg, Z., 109
Stern, P., 96
Sternberg, R. J., 17
Stewart, M., 130, 131, 134
Stoddard, M., 99
Stoller, L., 131
Stone, C., 77, 109
Stoops, R., 13
Strother, D. B., 170
Swinn, R. M., 34

T

Taba, H., 93
Torrance, E. P., 122
Townsend, K., 99
Trentham, L., 15

Trimbur, J., 137
Tyler, R. W., 93

U

Usher, R., 34

V

VanDoormick, C., 135
Velton, E., 4
Vygotsky, L. S., 7, 18, 72, 73, 74, 75, 76, 77, 78, 79, 80, 81, 82, 83, 85, 89, 90, 103, 105, 108, 113, 114, 134, 155

W

Walberg, H. G., 2
Walker, C., 41
Waller, T. G., 2
Warren, R., 114
Weaver, R. L., 39
Webb, R. B., 15
Weiner, B., 12, 13
Weinfield, F. D., 41
Wells, H. C., 29
Wertsch, J. V., 77, 79, 80, 108, 109
White, C. S., 74, 185
Willard, J. L., 41
Williams, R., 34
Wolfgang, C. H., 99
Wood, D. J., 105
Woodward, H. R., 41
Woolfolk, A. E., 15, 16, 33, 113
Worsham, M. E., 204

Y

Yinger, R. J., 93
York, R. L., 41
Young, H. S., 4

Z

Zahorik, J. A., 93
Zellman, G., 15
Zentall, S. S., 132
Zetlin, A., 105
Zimmerman, B. J., 16, 72, 81, 83
Zivin, G., 89

Subject Index

A

A-B-C Framework (Dyer), 376
Action Plan Worksheet, 192–193, 206
Attribution theory, 12–13

B

Behavior management, 199–207

C

Classroom literacy, 149–152
  in kindergarten, 149
Classroom management, 99–101,
  199–207
Classroom procedures, 199–205
Classroom rules, 199–205
Classroom strategies, 133–152
  in language arts, 140–141
  in mathematics, 141
  in reading comprehension, 141
  and student use, 139–152
Cognition:
  definition, 2
  examples, 2
Cognitive behavior modification
  and cognitive psychology, 113
  origins, 112–113
  self-instruction, 114
  and Soviet psychologics,
    113–114
  techniques, 114–115
Cognitive self-direction:
  and classroom management, 99–101
  curriculum and methodological model,
    87–101
  exercise, 101
  and interactive instruction, 96–99
  and research, 92–93
  and teacher planning, 93–96

Cognitive self-instruction:
  definition, 115
  exercise, 119
  Manning classroom approach, 116–132
    cueing, 127–132
    modeling, 116–119
    practicing, 120–127
Conflict resolution, 189–192
  exercises, 190–191

D

Decision making, 187–189
Discipline, 99–101, 199–207
Divorce, 208–210

F

Futurizing, 37–38

G

Goal-Setting, 192–194
  and goal story interview, 192, 194

H

Handwriting and metacognition, 139

I

I-messages, 42–44, 52
  exercise, 43–44
Informed training, 104
Interactive instruction, 96–99

L

Listening, 170, 174–175
  comprehension and metacognition,
    137–138
Locus of control, 41, 42

M

Mathematics and metacognition, 137, 141, 183
Mediation, 80
Metacognition:
    for classroom management, 99–101, 199–207
    classroom strategies, 133–152
    vs. cognition, 2
    for conflict resolution, 189–192
    for dealing with divorce, 208–210
    for decision making, 187–189
    definition, 2
        examples, 2
    and emotional reactions, 47
    for goal setting, 192–194
    for healthy self-talk, 194–199
    and interactive instruction, 96–99
    and interfunctioning, 24
    and intrafunctioning, 24
    and metamemory, 10
    for problem solving, 189–192
    for professional development, 86–87
    research for academic uses:
        handwriting, 139
        listening comprehension, 137–138
        mathematics, 136–137
        reading comprehension, 138
    and self-acceptance, 27–39
    and self-awareness, 25–26
    and self-control, 134–136
    and self-responsibility, 40–44
    and social issues, 199–121
    strategies for students:
        for classroom literacy, 149–152
        for language arts, 140–141
        for mathematics, 141
        for reading comprehension, 141–149
    and teacher planning, 93–96
    for test anxiety, 207
    theories, 1
Metacognitive teaching strategies:
    for listening, 170, 174–175
    for mathematics, 183–184
    for reading, 183
    for school work habits, 154–170
    for social studies, 184–185
    for whole language, 175–176
    for writing workshop, 177–182
Motivation, 16

N

Negative thinking, 46

O

Other-regulation models, 80–81, 103
    cognitive behavior modification, 112–115
    cognitive self-instruction, 115–132
    informed training, 104
    proleptic/dyadic instruction, 105–109
    reciprocal teaching, 109–112
    supported instruction, 104

P

Personal growth, 23–44, 186–210
    and decision making, 187–189
    and goal setting, 192–194
    and self-talk, 194–199
    and problem solving, 189–192
    and social issues, 199–210
    of students, 186–210
Private speech, 73–75
    classification, 75
    definition, 73
    exercises, 73–74
Problem solving, 189–192
    action plan worksheet, 192
    for conflict resolution, 189–192
Proleptic/dyadic instruction, 105–109
    definition, 105
    exercises, 106–107
    four levels, 108
    functions, 106

R

Rational-emotive therapy/thinking, 2–6, 34–35, 113
    application to education, 6
    examples, 53–54
    exercises, 35
    irrational beliefs, 4
    rational beliefs, 52
Reading comprehension, 138, 141–149, 183
Reciprocal teaching method, 143–147
    definition, 109, 111
    example, 110
    in large groups, 143
    in small groups, 144
    tips for teachers, 111–112

Scaffolding, 111
School work habits, 154–170
Self-acceptance, 27–40
    exercise, 39
    low expectation, 32–33
    rational thinking, 34–35
    and self-image, 35–37
    and teacher expectations, 30–33
Self-awareness, 25–26
    exercises, 25, 26
Self-control and metacognition, 134–136,
    140
Self-efficacy, 13–14
Self-fulfilling prophecy, 31
Self-image, 35–37
    visualization, 36
Self-instruction definition, 114
Self-regulated learning:
    and concept of mediation, 80
    definition, 16–17
    theories of, 81–82
    and theory of verbal self-regulation,
        72–80
    Vygotskian view of, 82–84
        causal model, 83
        and zone of proximal development,
            79–80
Self-regulated teaching, 84–85
Self-responsibility, 40–42
    exercise, 40
    locus of control, 41
Self-talk:
    for children's stories, 199, 200–202,
        203–204
    and classroom management, 199–207
    components, 19
    confusers, 21–22
    for dealing with divorce, 208–210
    drivers, 19–20
    exercises, 48–49, 195–198
    examples, 49–51
    and healthy use, 194–199
    for journals, 197–198
    levels, 18
    permitters, 20–21
    stoppers, 20–21
    and test anxiety, 207
Social issues, 199–210
    behavior management, 199–207
    class procedures, 199–205
    class rules, 199–205
    conduct report sheet, 207
    dealing with divorce, 208–210

exercise, 206
    test anxiety, 207
Social studies, 184–185
Sociolinguistic experiences, exercise, 76

T

Teachers:
    and anger, 55–56
    and anxiety, 56–58
        exercises, 57
    efficacy:
        construct of, 14–16
        theory, 13–14
    expectations, 30–33
    and frustration, 58–61
    planning, 93–96
    stress:
        definition, 47
        guide for coping, 61–71
Test anxiety, 207
Theory of verbal self-regulation, 72–80
    concept of mediation, 80
    goal-directed speech, 78–79
        planful speech, 73–75
        sociolinguistic experiences, 76
        stages, 76–78
        thought/speech convergence, 75–76
        zone of proximal development,
            79–80
Time-out, 192–193, 206
Transactional analysis, 6–11
    adult, 8
    child, 8
    examples, 9–11
    life positions, 11
    parent, 7
    structural analysis, 8

V

Visualization, 36
    exercise, 37

W

Whole language, 175–176
Writing workshop, 177–182

Z

Zone of proximal development, 79–80,
    104